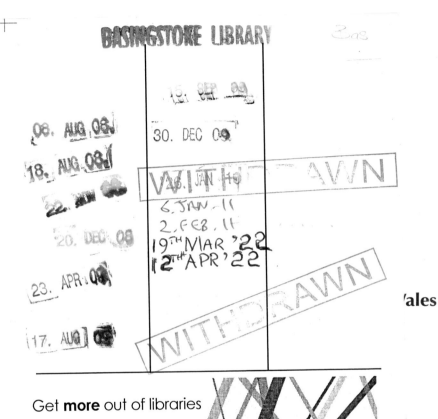

About the Author

Paddy Dillon is a prolific outdoor writer with almost 40 books to his name, as well as contributions to another 25 books, covering walking routes and walking areas around Britain and Europe. He writes for a number of outdoor magazines and other publications, as well as producing materials for tourism groups and other organisations. He lives on the fringe of the Lake District, and has walked, and written about walking, in every county in England, Scotland, Ireland and Wales. He has walked all the national trails in Britain twice and produced detailed guidebooks to some of them. He has led guided walking holidays overseas and has walked in many parts of Europe, as well as Nepal, Tibet and the Rocky Mountains of Canada and the USA.

While walking his routes, Paddy inputs his notes directly into a palmtop computer every few steps. His descriptions are therefore precise, having been written at the very point at which the reader uses them. He takes all his own photographs, and often draws his own maps to illustrate routes. He has appeared on television, and is a member of the Outdoor Writers and Photographers Guild.

THE NATIONAL TRAILS

The 19 National Trails of England, Scotland and Wales

by

Paddy Dillon

CICERONE

2 POLICE SQUARE, MILNTHORPE, CUMBRIA LA7 7PY
www.cicerone.co.uk

CONTENTS

Long Distance Routes

*Rock stacks at the mouth of Ceibwr Bay,
with Cemaes Head in the distance
(Pembrokeshire Coast Path)*

*Looking along the rocky coastline
after leaving Boscastle Harbour
(Day 11 of the South West Coast Path)*

First edition 2007
ISBN-13: 978-1-85284-504-9

A catalogue record for this book is available from the British Library

Photos and maps by the author
Design and book layout by Clare Crooke
Colour images scanned by Next Print Ltd
Printed in Singapore by KHL Limited

Advice to Readers

Readers are advised that while every effort is taken by the author to ensure the accuracy of this guide-book, changes can occur which may affect the contents. It is advisable to check locally on transport, accommodation, shops, etc, but even rights of way can be altered.

The publisher would welcome notes of any such changes.

Map Key

~	route		land
·····~···	route		AONB
○	town		national park
▲	peak		sea

Front cover: (main picture) Castle Rock rises high above the sea as the South West Coast Path leads into the Valley of the Rocks
(inset top) Bossington Hill, above Porlock Bay on the South West Coast Path
(inset middle) An old marker stone on the Cleveland Way
(inset bottom) A whitewashed lighthouse overlooks Loch Lochy near Gairlochy (Great Glen Way)

The National Trails

N

0   50   100
km

Great
Glen Way

Speyside
Way

SCOTLAND

West
Highland
Way

Dundee

Glasgow   Edinburgh
Southern
Upland Way

Hadrian's
Wall Path

Newcastle

(projected)

Cleveland
Way

Pennine
Way

Yorkshire
Wolds Way

Liverpool

Leeds

Pennine
Bridleway

Glyndŵr's
Way

ENGLAND

Peddars Way &
Norfolk Coast Path

WALES

Offa's
Dyke Path

Cotswold
Way

Pembrokeshire
Coast Path

Thames Path

Ridgeway

Cardiff

Thames Path

Bristol

Ridgeway

North Downs
Way

South Downs
Way

South West
Coast Path

A rocky cove before the coast path turns round Black Head to reach Coverack (Day 23 of the South West Coast Path)

FOREWORD

I can't think of anyone better qualified to write about our national trails than Paddy Dillon. He's been afflicted by wanderlust for more years than even he cares to admit to, having a compelling and delectable addiction to wandering the lonely byways that lace our wild areas at home and abroad. But Paddy has never been content to simply seek out and enjoy for himself the rich experiences that wild places bestow on us, for he suffers from an imperative to record what he sees along the way, so that others may follow in his footsteps and gain from his accumulated knowledge.

Paddy is generous in his sharing of knowledge. Arguably the UK's most prolific guidebook writer, accumulating experience, information and hard facts as he walks, he records the details of his routes on a day-by-day basis, on the route itself, via a tiny hand-held computer. I make this point not to applaud the functionality of electronic devices but to illustrate Paddy's commitment to the task in hand. One of the joys of hiking long-distance trails, for me and many like me, is to escape from such contrivances, to connect with the land without the aid of man-made inventions, to return to a simpler, more nomadic way of life that releases us from the pressures and tensions of 21st-century living. I've experimented with Paddy's technique of writing on the hoof and I've found that it takes more commitment and energy than I'm prepared to give. The point I make is that Paddy Dillon works very hard indeed to collate the up-to-date information that is necessary to compile a guide for others to follow, and that is why his guidebooks can be followed, and enjoyed, with confidence.

I recall meeting Paddy on the GR20 in Corsica, that wonderful mountain-clinging route that has been described as the toughest waymarked trail in the world. We were slavishly following the route along the tight and narrow crests of mountain ridges, in and out of deep rocky cauldrons and over steep, vertiginous crags. Paddy, on the other hand, had been nipping off-route here and there collecting information for a forthcoming guidebook – checking out village accommodation and restaurants, asking what *bergeries* sold cheese or milk, seeking out alternative routes for those less keen to tackle the steep sections, talking to local folk, prodding them for information and all the time collating the facts in his little mobile computer. It quickly became very clear that while we were on holiday, Paddy was working very hard indeed, and it's such hard graft that makes Paddy Dillon's guidebooks amongst the best.

Paddy is familiar with all the national trails of England and Wales and the official long distance footpaths of Scotland. He's spent a lifetime wandering the routes, and he would be among the first to suggest that they constitute a magnificent, if underused, resource. My hope is that the publication of this fine book, overlaid with Paddy's enthusiasm, might spawn a new generation of long-distance backpacker, a newer breed of hiker who will enjoy and care for this wonderfully varied collection of routes so that our children and grandchildren may enjoy them as we have done.

Cameron McNeish, 2007
Editor, TGO Magazine

The abrupt rocky western edge of the Cleveland Hills overlooks the lowland plains (Day 3 of the Cleveland Way)

INTRODUCTION

The broad waters of Langdon Beck are followed past isolated whitewashed farms (Day 10 of the Pennine Way)

I never consciously set out to walk all the national trails in Britain. Events just turned out that way, and not just once, either, but twice! I'm not complaining, though, as I enjoy long-distance walking immensely and I can't think of a better way to explore the country. Travelling by train or car, the scenery flashes past and there is no real sense of connection with it. Travelling on foot is a completely different matter. The landscape is real and readily to hand, and can be viewed at leisure, and touched, smelled, heard and appreciated both in all its vastness, and in its most secret recesses. There is a sense of change as you pass through the landscape, but there is also the opportunity to stop and appreciate anything along the way simply for its own merit. On the world stage Britain is a tiny country, but those who explore it on foot, day after day, discover a land so vast in its variety that in my opinion it can put whole continents in the shade.

The national trails (known in Scotland as long distance routes, but mainly referred to in this guide as 'national trails' for simplicity) wriggle their way through some of Britain's finest landscapes, making them readily accessible and allowing walkers to explore these areas with relative ease. Of course walkers must put in all the actual footwork, but they travel in the knowledge that the way ahead is open and well blazed, leading them from one splendid vista to another, while taking in heritage features that bring Britain's long and complex history to life. Charming lowlands give way to bleak uplands, but with careful planning you will end the day in the lap of comfort, with food, drink and a bed for the night.

The trail network is rooted in the British people's long-standing respect for public access to the countryside, and the national trails stretch the length and breadth of Britain, from the 'garden of England' to the 'larder of Scotland'. They are inextricably intertwined with British history and legend, and you can follow in the footsteps of ancestors who walked some of these trails over 5000 years ago. A few routes start or finish in cities, or pass through them, but most of the time they wander from one small town and village to another, making the most of open spaces. Some trails pass through quite wild and remote countryside, but none of them are beyond the capabilities of reasonably fit and organised walkers. If you can enjoy a full day's walk and finish in good shape, then you could probably manage another walk the following day without any problem. Even the longest trails are really nothing more than a series of one-day walks.

Walkers approach the national trails in different ways. Some walk at a leisurely pace and return time and time again to complete a long trail over a series of weekends or holidays. Others feel the need to challenge themselves, racing at record speeds from start to finish. Some plan well in advance, while others seize the day and take pot luck over the availability of accommodation. Some carry immense loads and camp in the wilds, while others have their bags carried ahead and stay in luxurious lodgings. The only 'rule', it seems, is to cover the distance – the rest is entirely up to you – and with over 5000km (3100 miles) of national trails available, including loops and variants, there is certainly no shortage of distance.

Wanted: A Long Green Trail

You could say it all started on 22 June 1935. An article by the ramblers' champion Tom Stephenson appeared in the *Daily Herald*, entitled 'WANTED: A LONG GREEN TRAIL'. 'Why should we not press for something akin to the Appalachian Trail?' he asked. 'A Pennine Way from the Peak to the Cheviots.' He imagined that the route would be 'a faint line on the Ordnance Maps which the feet of grateful pilgrims would, with the passing years, engrave on the face of the land.' Well, the engraving has gone rather deep in places (you could even claim the route was carved in stone), but that is a testimony to the popularity of long-distance walking in Britain.

Making Trails

It took thirty years of lobbying and hard work to steer the Pennine Way to its official opening in 1965, but the ground was already being prepared for more long-distance trails. The Cleveland Way was declared open in 1969, while in Wales the Pembrokeshire Coast Path was opened in 1970. Running between England and Wales, Offa's Dyke Path was opened in 1971. Throughout the 1970s, more trails were blazed across the south of England. In 1980 the West Highland Way was the first long distance route to be designated in Scotland. Work continues to this day, with improvements to all the trails, and a long extension north for the Pennine Bridleway. Some trails link end to end, or cross over each other, or are within easy reach of each other, so there are plenty of opportunities for dedicated long-distance walkers to keep trekking through the countryside.

Trail Themes

Britain's national trails have strong themes, usually based on landscape features or historical events. The South West Coast Path and Pembrokeshire Coast Path are splendid, rich and varied coastal trails, but other trails also include good stretches of coast, such as the Cleveland Way and Norfolk Coast Path. The longest riverside trail is the Thames Path, while other routes within easy reach of London traverse the North Downs and South Downs, twin chalk escarpments that feature wonderfully extensive views, despite being of no great height. The Ridgeway and Peddars Way are two remnants of a Bronze Age coast-to-coast trail that traversed the south of England.

Some trails are strongly linked with a particular person, such as Hadrian's Wall Path or Offa's Dyke Path, following ancient frontiers that helped to define the countries that make up Britain. Glyndŵr's Way wanders through the little-known countryside of mid-Wales chasing the ghost of a mighty warrior. The North Downs Way is based on the former pilgrim's way that led to the shrine of St Thomas à Becket, while much further north, in

Low Force comprises a series of small waterfalls near Bowlees in Teesdale (Day 10 of the Pennine Way)

Scotland, walkers on the West Highland Way follow a military road engineered by General Caulfeild. None of these people realised that they were laying the foundations of a trail network, but today's walkers call them to mind as they trek through the countryside.

Many national trails simply strive to scale high hills and traverse lonely moorlands, relishing the sense of open space and fresh air. The Pennine Way was the first to do this, and the Cleveland Way and Offa's Dyke Path enjoy high and wild landscapes as much as the Southern Upland Way does. Other trails cross much lower hills, such as the Yorkshire Wolds Way, Speyside Way or Great Glen Way. New trails are being added to the network, such as the recently designated Cotswold Way and the evolving Pennine Bridleway. There have been calls for the popular 'unofficial' Coast to Coast Walk to be honoured with national trail status. Walkers are assured that the national trails

An Offa's Dyke Path waymark post on the descent to the village of Bodfari (Day 10, Offa's Dyke Path)

offer the chance to explore some of the most scenic and interesting natural and historic landscapes in Britain, in the certain knowledge that access and signposting are maintained in good order throughout.

Waymarking

The national trails are state funded and, on the whole, very well maintained. Right from the start, with the creation of the Pennine Way, a standard waymark symbol was adopted for use on all the trails developed in England and Wales. An acorn symbol is used exclusively on national trails, so that where complex junctions of paths and tracks occur, the 'acorn' will quickly reveal the way forward. In Scotland a thistle waymark symbol is used, and the same principle applies at any complex junctions. Signposts often carry the name of the trail that is being followed, while simple waymark posts may simply bear the appropriate trail symbol and a directional arrow.

Despite being well marked, these trails still require the use of a map and basic navigational skills. Routes are easily lost in fields and woods, or on moorlands in poor visibility, while signposts and marker posts can be damaged or destroyed. When a trail enters a town or city, it is not always obvious how you should pass through the streets to return to the countryside. A decent map, and the ability to read it, will ensure that you stay on the route. Look on the signposts and waymarks as simply a means of confirming that you are still on course.

Path Associations

A few of the national trails have thriving 'path associations'. The Pennine Way Association is naturally one of the oldest, as is the Offa's Dyke Association. The South West Coast Path Association arguably has the toughest job, since they lobby in support of the longest of all Britain's national trails. The path associations are largely made up of people who have walked the route and are therefore in the best possible position to promote it. With a thriving membership, they are able to report problems and get them attended to quickly, working closely with the relevant authorities in each area. They keep an eye on local services, and produce invaluable accommodation guides, often based on the personal recommendation of members and other walkers.

Ideally, every national trail should have a path association, but in fact only a handful do. However, every trail has a 'path manager', employed to deal with the many issues relating to a particular trail, and these managers are in direct contact with the authorities that have the funding and manpower to attend to these issues.

Maps

Detailed Ordnance Survey maps cover every national trail in Britain, and a list of these is included in this guidebook with each trail description. Walkers who want a lot of detail should use the Explorer series, which at a scale of 1:25,000 shows virtually every wall, fence and building along the way. Others will be happy to use the Landranger series, at a scale of 1:50,000, which is adequate on well-signposted routes, even though less detail is shown. For full details see www.ordnancesurvey.co.uk.

Harveys, an independent map maker, produces strip maps at a scale of 1:40,000 covering many of the national trails. The advantage of these maps is that they are waterproof, show dedicated information for each trail, and drastically cut down the bulk of mapping required. For full details see www.harveymaps.co.uk.

Guidebooks

Each of the national trails has an 'official' guidebook. Originally, each new trail was provided with a guidebook produced by Her Majesty's Stationery Office. In more recent years, in England and Wales,

Heavy seas pound the natural rock arch of the Green Bridge on the Castlemartin Ranges (Day 10 of the Pembrokeshire Coast Path)

Aurum Press has published the 'official' guide-books, including Ordnance Survey mapping at a scale of 1:25,000 – see www.aurumpress.co.uk. In Scotland the Mercat Press covers some trails, having bought the Scottish outdoor titles published by HMSO – see www.mercatpress.com. Almost every national trail has a guidebook published by Cicerone, and these generally include Ordnance Survey mapping at a scale of 1:50,000 – see www.cicerone.co.uk.

Throughout this book, guides containing OS maps or similar mapping are listed, though some trails have simpler guides too. Most trail guide-books offer detailed commentaries on the routes as well as notes about the landscape, its history, her-itage and wildlife. Guides often have different angles and walkers should ideally browse through all of them to find out which best meet their needs.

Long-distance Laughs

No matter which trail you walk, or how much you suffer, you'll always find someone suffering more than you. There must be something about long-dis-tance walking that compels some people to keep trekking when they'd be better advised to quit. A certain grim stoicism seems to sustain them when the going gets tough, and this has led to the publi-cation of a small sub-genre of long-distance walk-ing books with a distinct humour all of their own. Those who are struggling, or feel they may struggle once they start, or those who wonder if anyone has ever suffered as badly as they are suffering, should realise that they are not alone and read one or all of the following:

- *One Man and his Bog*, by Barry Pilton, Corgi
- *Pennine Walkies*, by Mark Wallington, Arrow
- *500 Mile Walkies*, by Mark Wallington, Arrow.

Websites

The main online resource for all the national trails in England and Wales is www.nationaltrail.co.uk. This site gives links to the 'official' sites for each national trail, where abundant up-to-date informa-tion can be discovered. Most of the sites include accommodation details and plenty of other practi-cal notes that are useful for anyone planning a trek. The odd one out is the Pembrokeshire Coast Path, whose 'official' site is part of the Pembrokeshire Coast National Park website, and this trail also lacks a dedicated accommodation list. In Scotland each of the 'official' trail websites gives links to the others, but there is no overall website dealing with the Scottish long distance routes. Throughout this guide the 'official' websites are noted for each trail, and in a few cases another authoritative site is also listed. Walkers who search the web for information will of course be able to find plenty of other resources, including 'blog'-type accounts written and illustrated by walkers who have trekked the trails. (See also Appendix 1, Useful Contacts.)

Accommodation

When the Pennine Way was opened in 1965 it was generally assumed that the majority of walkers would carry full packs and camp at intervals along the trail. Many did, but there was also good provi-sion of youth hostels along the way, and the Youth Hostels Association once offered a service allow-ing walkers to book all their bed-nights in one fell swoop. Things have changed over the years, and while there are still plenty who camp, the provi-sion of hostels has been drastically reduced. Many now choose to stay in bed-and-breakfast accom-modation, and some are quite happy to pay some-one else to make all the arrangements for them, booking their long-distance walk through commer-cial trekking companies.

Some national trails are eminently suitable for backpacking and camping, but others have very few campsites. Some trails have far more youth hostels than others, but Glyndŵr's Way has none at all. Anyone planning to stay indoors every night will have to mix and match several types of accom-modation. Almost every national trail has a dedi-cated accommodation list, and a wise walker will be sure to obtain one of these at an early stage. Some locations may offer plenty of lodgings, but may also be very popular and likely to completely

The bracken slopes of Hergest Ridge rise above the village of Gladestry (Day 4 of the Offa's Dyke Path)

run out of space in high summer. Other crucial stops may have nothing more than a single, small bed and breakfast, and if you can't get your name on a bed, then your entire trip might fall apart because of it. The Southern Upland Way has some very long distances between services, and walkers will either have to cover that distance, camp in between, or spend a night at a bothy to get a roof over their heads. Careful planning will ensure that you have a bed each night.

I'm sure there are many who would love to walk a national trail, but find themselves overwhelmed by the minutiae of planning. For these people, all is not lost, since many trails are covered by commercial trekking companies who will, at a price, make all the arrangements. Usually, these are 'self-guided' treks, where walkers take care of their own navigation along the trail, with all their meals and accommodation booked and waiting for

them. Some companies ensure that luggage is transported from place to place, so that walkers can travel light, carrying nothing more than a day-sack. If this appeals, then by all means make further enquiries, but the extra services come at a price, and not every trail is covered. In a very few instances, it may be possible to join a guided party along a national trail, but this is very rare.

Food and Drink

The national trails run through such rich and varied countryside that it is unsurprising to find services along the way can also be very varied. When a trail passes through a city or town, it is safe to assume that there will be abundant offers of food and drink, so there is no need to carry excess weight. While many villages will have a shop or two, and perhaps a pub and restaurant, many others will have absolutely nothing to offer the passing wayfarer,

Gritstone outcrops jut from the bleak moors around Gorple and Widdop (Day 6 of the Pennine Bridleway)

and you need to know in advance what you are likely to find. There is little point carrying huge loads of food past lots of convenient shops, but it is much worse to have no food at all, and no chance of buying any.

Rural services are in decline in some places, and increasing in others. Most, but not all, of the latest national trail accommodation guides also include up-to-date notes about the provision of services along each trail, and it seems likely that in future more and more information will be made available in advance. Bear in mind that some shops and pubs in rural areas open and close at odd hours, and even a thriving town might observe a rigorous half-day closing. It is a good idea to make sure you always have a little extra food in your pack, just to cover emergencies. (I once walked into a village and headed for a shop that I knew from previous visits, only to find it had closed its doors for the last time just two days earlier!)

Tourist Information Centres

Walking into a tourist information centre to ask for detailed route directions will generally cause raised eyebrows – use your map and guidebook for all that! However, TICs are the best places to head if you need any kind of hard, local, up-to-date information. If you are travelling and taking pot luck on the availability of accommodation, then most TICs will be able to help you find a bed, and some will be able to book ahead on your behalf for the next two or three nights. The expertise of TIC staff can save you a huge amount of time and frustration walking from door to door, or making expensive rounds of phone calls. If you need information about local attractions and public transport, they can help, and they usually keep detailed notes of opening times for museums and heritage centres, along with admission prices. Many TICs are good sources of local maps and guides, if you find yourself in an area that you may want to return to and explore more thoroughly in the future.

PREPARING FOR A LONG WALK

The battered and crumbling alum shale promontory of Saltwick Nab (Day 7 of the Cleveland Way)

There are perhaps a few people who will fill a pack with the most inappropriate gear, tackle a national trail without any previous experience, and suffer no harm at all. Most who adopt this approach, however, will find themselves sore, and sorely inconvenienced, and may regret ever leaving home. Before embarking on something as ambitious as a national trail, spend a few weeks ensuring that you are physically and mentally fit for the trip, and overhaul the gear you plan to carry. Experienced long-distance walkers can skip the following sections, as they will already have evolved strategies and routines that are easily adapted to each and every trip they plan. Beginners will find that a little forethought will make all the difference as the days on the long trail unfold.

General Fitness

Walking long distances in all kinds of weather is always likely to present some difficulties, and those who have never done such a thing previously should be confident of their general health and wellbeing before setting out. The human body thrives on regular exercise, but it would be unwise for the unfit to suddenly shoulder a hefty pack and subject themselves to a long and arduous trek. Start gently and build up your fitness level to the point where a long-distance walk is good for your health, not an ordeal. Unless you can finish a simple day's walk feeling refreshed and positively glowing with health, then you probably need to work at it with a bit more determination.

The next logical step is to discover whether you could also walk all day on the following day and still feel fit and ready for more. Devote a weekend to this kind of exercise and see how you feel on Monday morning. If it is a bank holiday Monday, use the opportunity to take a third day's walk and confirm beyond doubt whether or not you are fit.

Next, you need to determine how well you cope while carrying more than your usual day-sack. If you intend camping along the length of a national trail, you will be carrying a heavy burden all day and every day, and you need to be sure that you are able to do it. Again, try it for two or three days, pitching the tent and making sure that all items of kit are useful and serviceable. If you feel comfortable with the day-in-day-out routine of walking, then you are probably in good shape to embark on any of the national trails.

Once on the trail, look after your health, whether that means eating and drinking wisely, or avoiding stress, strain and injury by trying to do too much. The commonest cause of misery on any long-distance walk is simply blisters, and as blisters are avoidable, it makes sense to deal with any rubbing or 'hot spots' as soon as they are noticed, rather than leaving them till too late. A sensible daily breakdown of the trail should ensure that you don't over-tax yourself, so that you can start relatively fresh each day, rather than suffering aches, pains and fatigue.

You should find that your fitness increases over the duration of a trek, provided you don't cause injury to yourself and compound each injury by continuing when you should be resting. Time for rest and recuperation is just as important as time spent covering the distance. Guard against dehydration by drinking sufficient water or soft drinks, and eat well to maintain health and energy levels. General hygiene is important, too, since sweaty bodies and clothes not only smell unpleasant, but could lead to distressing conditions such as chaffing or prickly heat – get into a routine to deal with washing and drying clothes. Also, take care to maintain equipment on the trail, especially if camping, as failure or loss of equipment could mean a swift end to the walk. For your own health and peace of mind, be sure that your equipment is tried and trusted before wearing or carrying it.

Packing

It either doesn't fit in, or you can't lift it – these are both sure signs that you're packing too much. A pack that is too heavy on a long-distance walk is bound to cause misery, which isn't what you want when you're supposed to be having fun and revelling in the joys of the great outdoors. If you are overburdened, and only tackle the problem too late by posting the excess weight home, you will probably already be carrying injuries that need never have happened. A long-distance trek may be something that happens only once or twice a year, or it may even be the fulfilment of a lifetime dream, so don't spoil it unnecessarily.

Almost everyone who embarks on a long-distance walk for the first time makes the mistake of getting a big backpack. Kit expands to fill the available space and you'll pack far more than you really need. Tents and sleeping bags now tip the scales at less than a kilo each and squash down very small. Modern wicking and waterproof fabrics mean that bulky clothing is a thing of the past. No one really needs more than one change of lightweight clothing for the evening. A good choice of kit will sacrifice little in comfort, but much in weight and bulk.

Food also is the downfall of many – it is heavy and takes up space. Water is a kilo a litre. The lightweight backpacker is easily seduced into packing lots of lightweight meals, then walks past delightful little shops selling wholesome food almost every day on the trail. The obvious thing is to buy food when you need it, and pack only enough to get you to the next shop. On most national trails food can be bought on a daily basis,

A view of Loch Trool, close to the site of Robert the Bruce's famous ambush site (Day 3 of the Southern Upland Way)

so there is no need to carry excess weight, and buying food along the way offers the chance to indulge in regional specialities, which is surely one of the great joys of travel.

A big, heavy, bulky pack is not only a tiresome burden, but an awkward one too. At some point a big pack will stick in narrow stiles, hit low branches, lodge in doorways, catch you off-balance in a gale, and probably clobber your travelling companion if you have one. Sometimes it may be funny, more often it will be annoying, and if you're unlucky it could cause serious injury. Heavy packs also cause the wearer to lean forward, which stresses joints and restricts vision to the sight of feet shuffling monotonously onwards. A smaller, lighter pack leaves the wearer free to stand upright, walk tall and enjoy the splendour of the countryside.

Before choosing to buy, read gear reviews in outdoor magazines, quiz retailers mercilessly, and continually ask yourself whether you really need everything on your list, or whether you can live without some of it. If you plan to trek with someone, a burden shared is a burden halved – a shared two-person tent is lighter than two one-person tents. Obviously you'll still need two sleeping bags, but you won't need two stoves, and coordinated packing means that both of you can carry considerably less than if you were travelling alone.

Baggage-carrying services operate on popular trails, while some companies offering self-guided walking tours arrange for accommodation providers to move baggage to the next night's lodging. All of a sudden there is no need to think light – rather, it becomes very tempting to over-pack and include plenty of extra clothing, footwear and special treats. Having someone else move your pack will be expensive, but many walkers are happy to pay the price in order to be able to travel light.

Best Time of Year

Because many people take a summer holiday, it follows that many walkers who want to follow a national trail will do so in the summer. The weather is usually better and the daylight hours are longer, but bear in mind that some places will be very busy, and if using indoor accommodation it is wise to book well in advance to secure beds.

Most of the national trails could be walked at any time of year, although walkers have been asked not to follow the Hadrian's Wall Path in the winter months, as the wet and muddy ground is easily eroded and this can lead to underlying archaeology being damaged. Those who wish to tackle one of the more remote high-level trails in winter should be aware that weather conditions can be severe – the highest stretch of the Pennine Way, for instance, holds the English records for the highest wind-speeds and most prolonged sub-zero temperatures!

In very general terms, trails in the gentle south-east of England will be easier to walk early in the year than trails further north, or at a higher level. The South West Coast Path can be a problem if attempted too early or too late in the year, since some of the crucial ferries across tidal inlets may not be operating. Heading far north into Scotland, midwinter daylight hours are really very short – as little as six hours. Spring starts early in the south of England and arrives later in northern Scotland, and springtime walkers can enjoy immensely colourful swathes of wild flowers, while deciduous trees gradually come into leaf. Autumn comes earlier in northern Scotland than in the south of England, and again this can be a delightful time to walk, as trees and bracken turn russet and gold. Provided the winter is not too wet and windy, walking a national trail can be enjoyable, but remember that accommodation and services might not be fully available. Deep snow is rare, but will lead to serious problems if progress is reduced to a crawl. On balance, long-distance walking in winter is best left to those with plenty of experience of difficult conditions.

In well-cultivated countryside, which generally means lowland regions, it is interesting to follow the slow rhythm of the seasons from the farmer's perspective. Ploughing and sowing is followed by a period of slow growth where earthy colours are gradually replaced by fresh greens. Sheep give birth to their lambs, and cows to calves. Orchards bloom in spring, while oilseed rape blazes bright yellow in early summer, with wheat and barley turning gold in late summer. Come the harvest, apples and potatoes are picked and packed, cereal crops are mown down to stubble, and the land is prepared for the next crop. Those who walk throughout the year can observe the life and work of country folk, and if you use farmhouse accommodation, you can make further enquiries from those who know best.

Making Time

Most people have busy schedules at home and work, and it may seem almost impossible to pull together the necessary week or two to tackle a long-distance walk, especially if there are others who also have a claim on your precious holiday time. Some people are prepared to wait until retirement to chase their dream of walking a national trail, which is fair enough if you can bear to wait that long, but alternatively, you could clear a space in your diary and let nothing, absolutely nothing, occupy that space. Even if your life is filled with routines and you imagine yourself to be indispensable at home and work, you will find that most routines are easily broken, and you may be nowhere near as indispensable as you might like to think!

If you are the type who worries about whether you left the gas on at home, or cancelled the milk, or put out the cat before hitting the trail, then you probably need to relieve these worries by leaving

Swanlake Bay and West Moor Cliff, seen from East Moor Cliff near Manorbier (Day 11 of the Pembrokeshire Coast Path)

A well-wooded stretch of the Thames Path on the approach to Reading (Day 5 of the Thames Path)

someone in charge of things in your absence. If you like to 'take work with you' on your travels, then constantly phoning the office and chasing people will eat into your time on the trail, and is bound to limit your enjoyment. Moreover, if you intend to be in constant contact with the world while you walk, bear in mind that a mobile phone signal may not always be available when you want one.

My own preferred approach is simply to tidy up any remaining work, leave the house, and think no more about it until I return. Travelling by public transport to the trail, I'm happy to watch the scenery go by and take an occasional peek at my maps to familiarise myself more with the route. Loved ones will receive a postcard and my best wishes, while I make the most of the open trail and enjoy the walk to the greatest possible extent.

Who's Going?

Some people prefer to walk on their own, others prefer company – there are no rules, but obviously anyone walking on their own is entirely responsible for their own safety. The solitary walker is a silent traveller, who probably notices more wildlife, and can please themselves when to walk, how far to walk, where to stay, where to eat, and generally is in control of everything that goes to make an enjoyable trip. On the other hand, walking with a companion is a joy shared, although a companion whose opinions and tastes differ radically to your own can either be a refreshing challenge, or a recipe for disaster.

I'm very much a solitary walker on the national trails, since I prefer the flexibility it gives me with all my arrangements. I meet other solitary walkers, of course, as well as couples and small groups of friends. Very rarely I meet a large group – either friends, or people who have enrolled for a tour offered by a guided walking holiday company. Walkers can be teenagers or senior citizens, and there are occasional families who walk the trails with very young and energetic children.

On the flip side, there are also people who seem entirely unsuited to walking long-distance routes, cursing their ill luck, or lamenting the performance of their companions, partners or children. Often enough, people you meet will be passing travellers, never to be seen again, but sometimes they will be walking your way for days on end and may become firm friends. There is no 'typical' long-distance walker – they come in all ages, shapes and sizes, as rich and varied as humanity itself. Some enjoy the experience, and some – sadly – seem to hate it, but they all share a common purpose on the trail.

Planning

This guide presents all the national trails to prospective walkers in a way that allows ease of comparison and contrast (see also Appendix 2, Route Summaries, for an 'at-a-glance' overview). While some trails are short and easy, lending themselves to completion by beginners, others are much longer, or traverse rugged country, and are more likely to appeal to experienced walkers. Many trails have strong themes: they may follow a river or coastline, or they may traverse ranges of hills.

In this guide, simple location maps show the course of each trail, while gradient profiles show all the ups and downs. Suggested daily route breakdowns are offered, but walkers should feel free to adjust and amend these in any way that suits their particular pace and inclination. Some might split a long day's walk over two days, while others will prefer to keep walking and may cover two days' distance in one long day's walk. As our American cousins would say: 'Hike your own hike!'.

A beginner would do well to underestimate their abilities and plan accordingly. Don't be tempted to cover huge distances in short time spans, but aim for something more leisurely. If you end up with a couple of hours to spare each day, you can be assured that the British countryside has more than enough charm and interest for you to make good use of the extra time. Ambitious schedules that are tied to pre-booked accommodation can result in disastrous trips. You may either feel the need to press on in deteriorating weather, when holding back would be more sensible, or when energy is flagging and your lodging is still a long way off, there is a temptation to call for a taxi or catch a bus, and so break the continuity of the journey.

Try to anticipate things that might go wrong or cause delays, and have some kind of contingency in mind to offset problems – if your overall plan includes a couple of 'spare' hours per day, these can be invaluable. If you think you may need to call on a taxi, or catch a bus at any point, be sure to collect telephone numbers and timetables well in advance, so that you don't waste time searching at the last minute. A carefully made plan leaves you with much better control of your trip.

Public Transport

In this day and age, when most people travel by car, it is easy just to throw your pack into the boot, drive to the start of a national trail and start walking. The problems are, how do you get back to your car at the end of your journey, and will it be safe left for a couple of weeks in the middle of nowhere? In addition, is it a good idea to leave your car cluttering up someone else's view of the countryside while you enjoy walking for days and weeks through wonderful scenery? Leaving a car at one end of a trail usually means a nightmare journey to retrieve it from the other end of the trail. In the case of the Pennine Way, for example, there are no direct services from Kirk Yetholm in the Scottish Borders to Edale in Derbyshire, a journey that would take a whole day to complete, even with good connections.

The view upstream from Victoria Bridge near the Inveroran Hotel (Day 5 of the West Highland Way)

It seems to me that the most practical approach to joining and leaving any national trail is to use public transport, and work out good connections well in advance of travelling. My own preference is to cover the bulk of the outward and return travel using comfortable long-distance trains, such as those provided by Virgin Trains. A good connection with another train, or maybe a local bus service, is usually all that is needed to get me to the start of, or from the end of, each trail. An early morning start might ensure that several hours can be spent walking the trail the same day. At the end of a trail, either spend the last night indoors and devote the following day to travelling home, or finish with a morning walk and leave the afternoon free to travel home. Finishing late, rushing home and suffering poor

connections can make what should be a triumphant return into something fraught with frustration and bad temper!

Some national trails have dedicated public transport services, such as the Hadrian's Wall Bus or Peddars Wayfarer. Other trails, such as the Cleveland Way, run through an area with walker-friendly bus services, such as the Moorsbus. A network of interlinked bus services covers most parts of the Pembrokeshire Coast Path. Walkers on the Great Glen Way from Fort William to Inverness can easily catch buses running parallel. Of course, not all trails are so well supported, and some services may be seasonal at best, but walkers who take the trouble to pick up timetables in advance will always be able to include public transport options in their plans, rather than having to chase details later.

Call on the services of Traveline or Transport Direct to discover if there are any useful public transport services going your way – either telephone 0871 2002233, or check the websites www.traveline.co.uk and www.transportdirect.info. If a taxi is needed at any point and you aren't equipped with any local numbers, call the National Taxi Hotline free, telephone 0800 654321. You will be connected to the nearest operator in the scheme and can negotiate a journey and a fare.

Daily Routine

Walking a national trail means adopting an entirely different routine to that of usual daily life. First thing in the morning you rise from your sleeping bag or hostel bunk, or awake in an unfamiliar hotel or guesthouse room. If self-catering, breakfast is whatever you make of it, otherwise whatever your accommodation provider can offer (any special dietary requirements should be made known well in advance). Wise walkers will already be

Looking to Froward Point from Combe Point on the way to Dartmouth (Day 35 of the South West Coast Path)

aware of the day's weather forecast and will arrange their clothing to suit prevailing conditions.

Generally, most people will aim to start early on the trail, and this is easily arranged if you are camping or hostelling. However, negotiating early breakfasts with hotels and guesthouses requires tact, and consideration for the needs of your host – some will oblige and others will most definitely not!

Walking long distance in high summer means that you can make good use of extended hours of daylight. In the winter months, on the other hand, fewer daylight hours means shorter walks, or you risk continuing in darkness. The important thing to do, day after day, is pace yourself comfortably. Dawdling and dragging your feet will mean finishing late in the day, while rushing like a maniac along the trail could easily result in pain, fatigue and injury. Neither the hare nor the tortoise was right – the best approach lies in between.

Take an interest in your surroundings, especially if it is unlikely you will ever pass that way again. Enjoy the scenery and photograph it if you want a lasting memory. Visit museums and country churches and take note of the vernacular architecture. Support little country shops and pubs wherever possible, and passing the time of day with local people can give access to founts of local knowledge. Mark the changing seasons and the effect this has on trees, flowers and wildlife. Have a chat with other walkers on the trail, especially those coming the other way, since they may have important information about conditions and facilities ahead. If you find a kindred spirit heading in the same direction as yourself, you may even find a friend for life. The daily routine on the trail should not be one of predictable drudgery, but should allow you to keep moving without undue stress or fatigue, leaving you free to savour the sheer joy of being alive and among some of the country's most scenic and interesting landscapes.

Towards the end of each day, honour any advance bookings made with accommodation providers, and most importantly, phone and tell them if anything has upset your plans, making you late or unable to show. Some people worry and may call out the emergency services if they don't hear from you. If you need collecting from the trail, or transporting to and from a pub or restaurant in the evening, be sure to make arrangements in advance, rather than springing this on your host at the last minute.

If the day has been hot and sweaty, you should rinse out clothes and hang them to dry, or if the day has been wet and miserable, be sure to get your clothes dried at the first opportunity, since that will make all the difference to morale in the morning. Those who prefer to camp in the wilds should be scrupulous about being as low key as possible, leaving no trace of their pitches. Also, be sure to pop your head out of the tent on clear nights, as the view of the stars above is often truly remarkable and stirs the soul (of all who walk the national trails, surely those who camp in the wilds are the most blessed).

Emergencies

Getting slightly lost, or suffering a minor cut or scrape, is quite likely to happen at some point on the trail, but is of no real consequence. If you are a rusty navigator, then keep an eye on your map and guide and take every opportunity to improve your skills. If you miss a turning, it is usually better to backtrack to a position where you are certain you are on course, rather than try to cut across country to pick up the trail at some other point. It is very rare that anyone becomes so hopelessly lost on a national trail that they need to be rescued, but walkers have been inconvenienced by straying off-route, losing time and energy while trying to undo their mistakes.

Serious injury is quite another matter. Anyone suffering a bad fall or an accident that leaves them unable to keep walking will need to be rescued. In upland areas, this will doubtless involve the nearest mountain rescue team, while in coastal areas it may involve the coastguard. As many of Britain's national trails run through fairly gentle countryside, the usual

An old marker stone is passed on the descent from Beacon Hill (Day 3 of the Cleveland Way)

ambulance, fire or police services might attend an evacuation. It all depends on the nature of the emergency, and the best thing for anyone to do is simply to alert the emergency services by calling 999 (or the European 112) and giving them full details so that they can make an appropriate response. Better still, walk with due care and attention to avoid emergency situations in the first place.

View across Pendour Cove near Zennor to distant Gurnard's Head (Day 18)

ENGLAND

1 South West Coast Path

Start and Finish	Minehead to South Haven Point
Distance and Time	1016km (631 miles) taking 6 to 7 weeks
Character	A coastal trail of great variety, taking in everything from arduous cliff paths to easy walks along seaside promenades. Some days are much tougher than others and at times the route is quite intricate. Allow plenty of time to explore all the historic towns, huddled villages, museums and heritage centres.
Highlights	The high parts of the Exmoor coast, Hartland Point to Bude, Boscastle to Tintagel, St Ives to Penzance, Mullion to Cadgwith, Dodman Point, Polruan to Polperro, Plymouth Waterfront Walkway, Wembury to Bigbury, Salcombe to Start Point, Dartmouth to Brixham, Beer Head, the Undercliff to Lyme Regis, Golden Cap, Isle of Portland, Osmington Mills to Lulworth Cove and Swanage.

Looking from Poltridmouth to Polruan after walking round Gribbin Head (Day 28)

This is the longest of all the national trails in Britain, twice the length of its nearest rivals in the Pennines. The coast path essentially owes its origin to the 18th-century coastguard paths that were established as part of the fight against the smuggling trade. Following the imposition of excise duty on certain goods, ships began to land their illicit cargoes on remote, unfrequented coastlines, and tales of smuggling and shipwreck abound round the southwest coast. The Coastguard Service was established in 1822 and coastguards pounded beats along the cliff tops, peering into every hidden cove on the lookout for smugglers. In cat-and-mouse fashion, smugglers and coastguards tried to outwit each other, but in due course smuggling declined and less time was spent patrolling the cliffs on foot. Some coastguard paths fell into disuse and were lost, but leisure walking arrived just in time to give many stretches a new lease of life.

A map of southwest England reveals a complex and convoluted coastline between Minehead, in Somerset, and Poole harbour, in Dorset. The crinkly coast adds up to a considerable distance, and where numerous ascents and descents have also to be negotiated, requires a lot of effort to complete. This is no beach walk, but often involves

Walkers climb Bossington Hill, high above Porlock Bay, in the Exmoor National Park

SCHEDULE

Day	Start/Finish	Km	Miles
Day 1	Minehead to Porlock Weir	15	9½
Day 2	Porlock Weir to Lynmouth	20	12½
Day 3	Lynmouth to Combe Martin	21	13
Day 4	Combe Martin to Woolacombe	20	12½
Day 5	Woolacombe to Braunton	25	15½
Day 6	Braunton to Westward Ho!	38	23½
Day 7	Westward Ho! to Clovelly	18	11½
Day 8	Clovelly to Hartland Quay	17	10½
Day 9	Hartland Quay to Bude	25	15½
Day 10	Bude to Boscastle	27	16½
Day 11	Boscastle to Port Isaac	22	13½
Day 12	Port Isaac to Padstow	19	12
Day 13	Padstow to Porthcothan	22	13½
Day 14	Porthcothan Newquay	18	11½
Day 15	Newquay to Perranporth	17	10½
Day 16	Perranporth to Portreath	20	12½
Day 17	Portreath to St Ives	29	18
Day 18	St Ives to Pendeen Watch	22	13½
Day 19	Pendeen Watch to Porthcurno	26	16
Day 20	Porthcurno to Penzance	18	11½
Day 21	Penzance to Porthleven	23	14
Day 22	Porthleven to Lizard	22	13½
Day 23	Lizard to Porthallow	25	15
Day 24	Porthallow to Falmouth	29	18
Day 25	Falmouth to Portloe	22	13½
Day 26	Portloe to Mevagissey	20	12½
Day 27	Mevagissey to Polmear	18	11½
Day 28	Polmear to Polperro	21	13
Day 29	Polperro to Portwrinkle	20	12½
Day 30	Portwrinkle to Plymouth	22	13½
Day 31	Plymouth to Wembury Beach	22	13½
Day 32	Wembury Beach to Bigbury-on-Sea	23	14
Day 33	Bigbury-on-Sea to Salcombe	21	13
Day 34	Salcombe to Stoke Fleming	31	19½
Day 35	Stoke Fleming to Brixham	24	15
Day 36	Brixham to Shaldon	31	19½
Day 37	Shaldon to Budleigh Salterton	23	14
Day 38	Budleigh Salterton to Seaton	28	17½
Day 39	Seaton to Seatown	21	13
Day 40	Seatown to Abbotsbury	20	12½
Day 41	Abbotsbury to Ferrybridge	18	11½
Day 42	Isle of Portland Circuit	25	15½
Day 43	Ferrybridge to Lulworth Cove	23	14
Day 44	Lulworth Cove to Swanage	33	21
Day 45	Swanage to South Haven Point	12	7½
Inland Coast Path	West Bexington to Osmington Mills	27	17

steep paths over rugged cliffs, tight zigzag paths and innumerable steps. Walkers often cross deep, steep-sided, wooded ravines, which separate remote and rocky headlands, and there are also extensive areas of dunes and pebbly storm beaches. Of course, there are also plenty of villages tucked into hidden coves, along with a number of bustling seaside resorts and even a major city. This is an immensely rich and varied coastline with an intensely absorbing history and heritage.

The South West Coast Path was opened in stages between 1973 and 1978, though from the outset the South West Coast Path Association has lobbied tirelessly for improvements, so there are mini openings of short stretches to this day. The route starts at Minehead and traverses Exmoor National Park, then along the rest of its length there are designated areas of outstanding natural beauty, heritage coasts and two extensive world heritage sites. Many stretches of the coast are owned by the National Trust, or preserved as national nature reserves. With this level of protection, it simply has to be good, and no other stretch of English coast enjoys so much attention.

Obviously, walkers who wish to complete the South West Coast Path in one fell swoop will have to walk every day for six or seven weeks. The alternative is to complete

it over a period of time, one or two weeks at a stretch.

Bear in mind that while all facilities are in full swing in the summer months, accommodation options are drastically reduced in the winter, and some of the ferries that provide essential links along the route may be withdrawn. Careful planning is the key to success along this trail, but even at the height of summer, when there is most pressure on facilities, tourist information centres work exceptionally hard to find accommodation for those who need it. If you choose to camp, you don't really need to carry cooking

equipment, as this is a trail where there are shops and cafés at regular intervals.

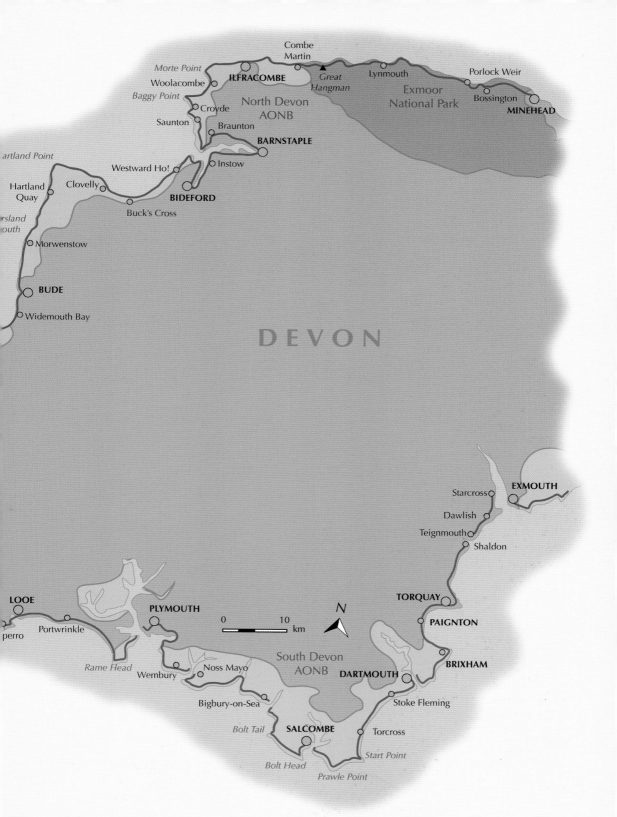

Combe
Martin

Morte Point
Woolacombe
ILFRACOMBE
*Great
Hangman*
Lynmouth
Porlock Weir

Baggy Point
North Devon
AONB
Exmoor
National Park
Bossington
MINEHEAD

Croyde
Saunton
Braunton

Hartland Point
Westward Ho!
Instow
BARNSTAPLE

Hartland
Quay
Clovelly
BIDEFORD

sland
outh
Buck's Cross

Morwenstow

BUDE

Widemouth Bay

D E V O N

Starcross
EXMOUTH

Dawlish

Teignmouth
Shaldon

LOOE
Portwrinkle
perro

PLYMOUTH
0   10
km

TORQUAY

N

PAIGNTON

Rame Head
Wembury
Noss Mayo

South Devon
AONB

DARTMOUTH

BRIXHAM

Bigbury-on-Sea
Stoke Fleming

Bolt Tail
SALCOMBE
Torcross

Bolt Head
Start Point

Prawle Point

Day 1 Minehead to Porlock Weir
15km (9½ miles)

The long journey starts at a monument on the promenade at Minehead, then unexpectedly heads uphill and inland, well away from the coast. Walk across North Hill and Selworthy Beacon, climbing as high as 290m (950ft) to enjoy views over Exmoor National Park. There is an 'Alternative Rugged Coast Path' signposted, which runs closer to the sea, is rather more arduous, but very scenic. It links with the main coast path later on Bossington Hill above Hurlstone Point. Views stretch along the coast to Foreland Point and across the Bristol Channel to south Wales.

walkers could continue to Lynmouth or Lynton, but at the risk of burning themselves out too early in this long trek. Better to take things easy, settle into a sustainable pace and aim for a successful completion in due course.

Day 2 Porlock Weir to Lynmouth
20km (12½ miles)

Start on the Worthy Combe Toll Road, then follow paths and tracks through woods to reach Culbone church, where there is a refreshment cabin. A choice of routes is available: either walk on a wooded slope close to the sea, or follow paths and farm

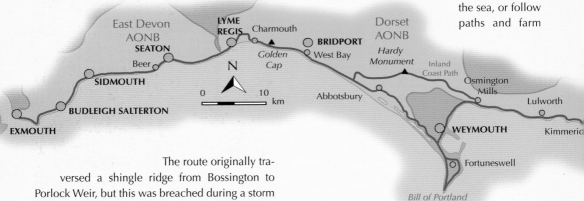

The route originally traversed a shingle ridge from Bossington to Porlock Weir, but this was breached during a storm in 1996 and walkers must now wander through fields and marshes behind the ridge. Porlock and Porlock Weir provide well for walkers, though both villages appear quite early in the day. Stronger

tracks at a higher level, until both routes meet again on Sugarloaf Hill. Shortly afterwards, in

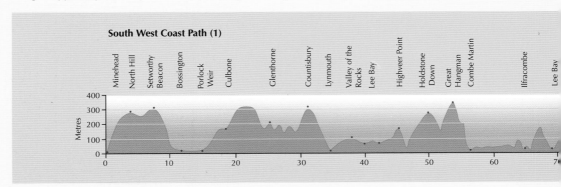

remarkably mixed woodlands, there is access to County Gate and Exmoor National Park Visitor Centre. Somerset gives way to Devon and the coast path finally leaves the woods and traverses a steep and rugged slope on the way to Foreland Point, which is the most northerly point in Devon.

Don't be drawn off-route to the lighthouse, but turn Foreland Point and stay high on the coast path. There is easy access to the tiny village of Countisbury, which has a pub, but most walkers will be happy to start the descent towards Lynmouth. If you have organised accommodation here, it is a good idea to know exactly where you are heading. Lynmouth, naturally, is down by the sea, while Lynton is stacked high up a steep and wooded slope. A cliff lift links both places. Note the Lynmouth Flood Memorial Centre, recalling the devastating floods of August 1952, which resulted in the deaths of 34 people. Also note, after covering the distance from Porlock to Lynmouth, that in January 1899 the Lynmouth lifeboat had to be towed the same distance, in the other direction, during a storm, before it could be launched to aid the stricken vessel *Forrest Hall* off Hurlstone Point.

Day 3 Lynmouth to Combe Martin
21km (13 miles)

After climbing high above Lynmouth, walkers follow a fine path across a steep slope and suddenly reach the Valley of the Rocks. Amazingly complex

Castle Rock rises high above the sea as the coast path heads into the Valley of the Rocks

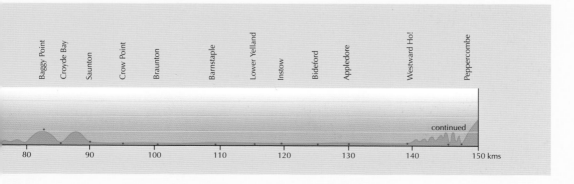

BOURNEMOUTH

South Haven Point

Studland

SWANAGE

St Aldhelm's Head

Baggy Point
Croyde Bay
Saunton
Crow Point
Braunton
Barnstaple
Lower Yelland
Instow
Bideford
Appledore
Westward Ho!
Peppercombe

continued

80   90   100   110   120   130   140   150 kms

rocky outcrops have delighted visitors for decades, so expect the place to be busy. Walk down the road to Lee Abbey, then follow a path across an exceedingly steep and wooded slope at Woody Bay. The precarious 'hanging' oak woods, a refuge for red deer, are preserved as a nature reserve. Cross Hollow Brook at a little waterfall, then turn round Highveer Point to enter a deep and steep-sided valley at Heddon's Mouth. There is access inland to the popular Hunter's Inn.

After climbing steeply from Heddon's Mouth the coast path makes its way towards Holdstone Down, where it suddenly drops into another steep-sided valley at Sherrycombe. The climb uphill leads to the summit of the Great Hangman, which at 318m (1043ft) is the highest point on the entire South West Coast Path. Enjoy the views inland to Exmoor National Park, as the park is left behind on the descent from the Little Hangman to Combe Martin. The village proclaims itself to be the second longest village in England, which begs the question, which is the longest village in England?

Day 4 Combe Martin to Woolacombe
20km (12½ miles)

Take care following the complex and convoluted coast path from Combe Martin to Ilfracombe, or you could find yourself walking round Widmouth Head, which is not part of the route. There is a bird's-eye view of Ilfracombe on the descent from Hillsborough. St Nicholas' Church on Lantern Hill dates from the 14th century, but the town largely developed as a 19th-century resort following the arrival of the railway, now long closed.

Use the popular Torrs Walk to leave the town, looking to see how it has been hacked from the bedrock in places as it works its way round the cliffs. On the descent to Lee Bay a detour could include Lee village, just inland. A fine stretch of cliff coast continues to Bull Point and its lighthouse, then later there is a marked change of direction while turning round Morte Point. The little resort of Woolacombe, which developed from a farming settlement, is reached, with its most notable feature – a broad, golden, sandy surfers' beach.

Day 5 Woolacombe to Braunton
25km (15½ miles)

Walkers who have found the first few days of the South West Coast Path a struggle will be pleased to enjoy a much easier walk today. While it is possible to walk the length of Woolacombe Sands, the route actually stays onshore among scrubby dunes. Leaving Putsborough Sands, a low-lying cliff coast is followed around Baggy Point to Croyde Bay. Another popular golden strand is passed, then the route climbs above a busy coastal road and cuts across Saunton Down to reach the village of Saunton. Walkers who are struggling, or looking

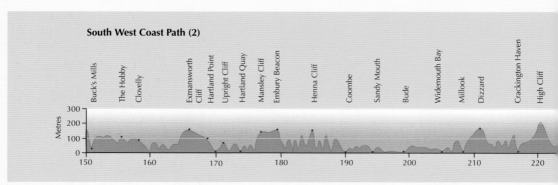

for opportunities to short cut, will be sorely tempted at this point to follow a road or catch a bus to Braunton. The coast path, however, wanders through an area of flowery dunes and scrub woodland, designated as the Braunton Burrows National Nature Reserve. At the very tip of the point, the village of Appledore is close to hand, but will not be reached for another couple of days by those who faithfully follow every part of the coast path. Head inland beside the tidal River Caen, alongside Braunton Marshes, to reach Braunton itself.

Day 6 Braunton to Westward Ho!
38km (23½ miles)

Prepare for level, hard-surface walking along a couple of old railway trackbeds that have been converted into footpath/cycleways. This may seem like a long day's walk, but it is always easy, and can be covered in two days if preferred. (Some walkers actually skip the whole day and catch the bus!) Follow the first old railway trackbed from Braunton to Barnstaple, passing Wrafton Marsh and an airfield at Chivenor, before hugging the shore of the tidal River Taw. Barnstaple has a long and complex history, having been a 10th-century Saxon stronghold against the Danes, and made a borough by King Alfred. In 1068 the town fell to

The Railway Carriage Visitor Centre and old signal box at East-the-Water near Bideford

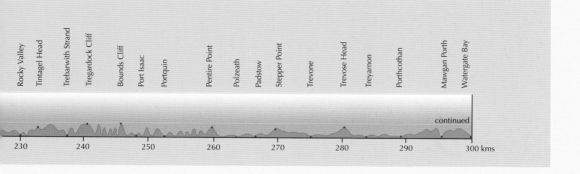

continued

Rocky Valley — Tintagel Head — Trebarwith Strand — Tregardock Cliff — Bounds Cliff — Port Isaac — Portquin — Pentire Point — Polzeath — Padstow — Stepper Point — Trevone — Trevose Head — Treyarnon — Porthcothan — Mawgan Porth — Watergate Bay

230   240   250   260   270   280   290   300 kms

the Normans, then received a succession of royal charters. Although it seems far inland, it developed a fine shipbuilding and naval tradition. Cross the Long Bridge to leave the town.

Another old railway trackbed leads out of Braunton, passing marshes on the southern banks of the River Taw. Fremington Quay was once described as 'the busiest port between Bristol and Land's End' and its old railway station now houses the Fremington Quay Heritage Centre, which has a lookout tower for birdwatchers. Officially, the coast path follows the fringe of the marshland to Instow, but many walkers prefer to stay on the trackbed to reach the village. Depending on seasonal and tidal restrictions, there might be a small ferry operating between Instow and Appledore, otherwise walkers have to keep following the trackbed onwards, crossing the River Torridge at Bideford. In this case, follow the coast path back alongside the river to reach Appledore, another place with a notable shipbuilding tradition. Continue around the dunes of the Northam Burrows Country Park to reach Westward Ho! The resort is named after the novel by Charles Kingsley and always includes the exclamation mark.

Day 7 Westward Ho! to Clovelly
18km (11½ miles)

Easy walking beyond Westward Ho! passes a line of colourful beach huts and quickly gives way to a roller-coaster path along a crumbling cliff line. Expect short diversions whenever a cliff fall has taken place, especially around Babbacombe Cliff. After passing Peppercombe a short detour inland to Horn's Cross could be contemplated if its shop or pub is needed. The undulating coast path becomes more wooded, and a descent into a little valley reveals the village of Buck's Mills, with the slightly larger village of Buck's Cross lying a little further inland.

The route runs inside or alongside Buck's Valley Woods and later joins a fine track known as the Hobby Drive. This well-graded track slices across the steep, wooded slopes and eventually reaches the top part of Clovelly. Although the coast path doesn't actually enter the village, no one should pass by without walking down the high street. If you are spending the night here there is ample opportunity to explore, and once the crowds of tourists depart, the village slips back into a slumber. The steep, cobbled road is barred to traffic, so sleds laden with provisions have to be dragged to the houses, or donkeys are engaged to draw larger loads up and down through the village. The houses, dating from the 14th century, seem stacked so precariously on the slope that a sneeze would send them crashing down into the sea.

Day 8 Clovelly to Hartland Quay
17km (10½ miles)

Paths beyond Clovelly either run alongside or inside woodlands, then comes a zigzag descent to Mill Mouth. The coast path negotiates woods and pasture, rising and falling, before levelling out in fields high above the cliffs. Looking ahead, a prominent 'radome' can be spotted, which is quite close to Hartland Point. The rocky point and its lighthouse mark a significant change of direction, as the coast path swings suddenly southwards. Hartland Point used to be described as 'furthest from the railways', and in poor weather it can seem very bleak and far removed from civilisation, though the scenery is dramatic.

Leaving Hartland Point, one of the most difficult stretches of the coast path begins, featuring several ascents and descents. The first descent is from Upright Cliff, followed by a climb above Damehole Point. Later, a stone bridge crosses the Abbey river, recalling the long-forgotten site of Hartland Abbey that lay further inland. For a brief moment an arch in an old stone tower set behind the next cliff frames a view of Stoke church, then the route descends to Hartland Quay. The old quay, neglected and battered by the sea, crumbled

A twin-spout waterfall at Speke's Mill Mouth near Hartland Quay

away. A few weather-beaten buildings remain, including the Hartland Quay Hotel. Think twice before spurning lodgings, as the cliff path becomes even more severe beyond this point.

Day 9 Hartland Quay to Bude
25km (15½ miles)

This is one of the most dramatic and scenic stretches on the entire South West Coast Path, but also one of the toughest. Leaving Hartland Quay, the route passes a couple of splendid waterfalls spilling into the sea, then embarks on a monstrous roller coaster, climbing high onto the cliffs, only to drop steeply down towards the sea again, time after time. Steps and zigzag paths help to ease the gradient, but walkers should take things slowly and steadily all day. Just before leaving Devon, the path passes Ronald Duncan's Hut, named after the writer who once sought solitude there. The view from the hut looks across Marsland Mouth into Cornwall.

A bilingual sign reading 'Cornwall/Kernow' marks the entry to Cornwall, and the relentless nature of the steep ascents and descents continues unabated. Walkers who need a break from the rigours of the route can detour inland to the Bush Inn at Morwenstow for a break. The coast path, meanwhile, passes Hawker's Hut, which was used as a retreat by an eccentric vicar of the village. After negotiating some particularly rugged parts of the route, the undulations become less severe, and by the time Duckpool and Sandy Mouth are passed, the worst is over. A gentler stretch along lower cliffs leads finally to Bude, where there are broad expanses of sand. Head inland towards the town to cross the first bridge, a stone footbridge, over the River Neet. A small museum explains how this was a thriving little port, especially in the late 19th century.

Day 10 Bude to Boscastle Harbour
27km (16½ miles)

Compass Point, just outside Bude, is crowned with the octagonal Storm Tower, based on the Temple of the Winds at Athens. While cliff coasts can be dangerous in stormy weather, the route south of Bude is never far from a road on the way past Widemouth Bay and Millook. Well-wooded cliffs at Dizzard give way to a succession of ascents and descents on the way to the tiny village of Crackington Haven. This area is often busy with geology students, and the cliffs feature colourful, contorted bands of rock. Climb to the headland of Cambeak, then climb again over High Cliff, which is the highest cliff on this stretch of coast at 223m (732ft). There are some steep and rugged slopes on the way to Boscastle Harbour, and the village remains hidden until you reach Penally Point.

Boscastle Harbour is a splendidly sheltered inlet, but so narrow and crooked that approaches in stormy weather were fraught with danger. Large boats were towed in by rowing boats, with additional steerage provided by men onshore using ropes. On 16 August 2004 a colossal flood swept through Boscastle Harbour, and events were relayed live via television as the disaster unfolded. People were plucked from rooftops by helicopter, and while no one was killed, many properties were left in ruins and recovery was slow.

Day 11 Boscastle Harbour to Port Isaac
22km (13½ miles)

The coast path beyond Boscastle features several rugged and attractive little headlands and coves. The Rocky Valley is particularly scenic, but most walkers will find themselves looking ahead to spot legendary Tintagel Castle on Tintagel Head, reputed to be the birthplace of King Arthur. The promontory has at least 2000 years of history behind it, and is undoubtedly a splendid strategic site, reached by crossing a footbridge over a

Attractive Rocky Valley is passed on the way from Boscastle Harbour to Tintagel Head

crumbling neck of land. The castle has been in ruins since the 16th century. Nearby Tintagel youth hostel also enjoys a fine setting close to the cliff edge.

Slate quarrying has cut into the cliffs over the past five centuries, and broken cast-off slates are incorporated into the zigzag-patterned 'curzy-way' drystone walls and embankments that surround nearby fields. After dropping down to Trebarwith Strand and its pub, note that there are no refreshments until distant Port Isaac, and the coast path includes strenuous ascents and descents. The Headlands Hotel is reached at Port Gaverne, and Port Isaac lies a few minutes beyond. This fishing village has gradually turned to tourism, but fishing still continues and the day's catch can be inspected in an odd-shaped building beside the little beach.

Day 12 Port Isaac to Padstow
19km (12 miles)

Shortly after leaving Port Isaac, a steep-sided little valley is crossed at Pine Haven, then the coast path runs from Varley Head to Kellan Head to reach Port Quin. A tiny settlement stands at the head of the narrow inlet, then a splendid stretch of undulating coast path hugs the low cliffs all the way round Port Quin Bay and Carnweather Point. A complete circuit is made around Pentire Point, then Padstow Bay and the tidal River Camel have to be negotiated. Follow the coast path around Polzeath, then trudge along soft and sandy paths around little Brea Hill.

A ferry runs from Rock to Padstow all year, except winter Sundays, and the nearest bridge is far inland at Wadebridge. Always check ferry

Mother Ivey's Bay, with its golden sandy beach and distant lifeboat station

crossings in advance around the South West Coast Path, taking particular note when several need to be used in quick succession later on the long trail. Padstow's narrow streets are full of charm, and often full of tourists too. Spend the evening exploring if staying here. St Petroc's Church dates from the 6th century. Sir Walter Raleigh lived at the Court House when he was Warden of Cornwall, while Prideaux Place is a fine Elizabethan manor house.

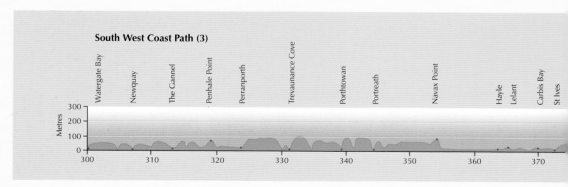

Day 13 Padstow to Porthcothan
Porthcothan 22km (13½ miles)

Fine headlands and sandy bays are passed one after another during this day's walk. The coast path from Padstow passes a sandy beach at Harbour Cove, then turns round Stepper Point to leave Padstow Bay. Pass the deep crater of Pepper Hole and walk round the rocky cove of Butter Hole. The little villages of Trevone and Harlyn offer refreshments, and if you reach the latter at high water, you may have to take a break and wait for the water to recede before you continue along the beach. Mother Ivey's Bay is wonderfully scenic, with its low cliffs and lumpy outcrops rising from the golden strand. A lifeboat station is located at the far end of the bay, but the coast path detours inland before that point, passing a lighthouse on Trevose Head. Booby's Bay and Constantine Bay feature golden sands, then lots of little headlands are passed before the route reaches Porthcothan.

Day 14 Porthcothan to Newquay
18km (11½ miles)

The low cliffs beyond Porthcothan are broken by the narrow inlet of Porth Mear, and the scenery is lovely throughout. All of a sudden, after turning round Park Head, popular Bedruthan Steps are reached and there are likely to be a lot of people

around. The beach is studded with a series of huge and highly individual rock stacks, named, from north to south: Diggory's Island, Queen Bess Rock, Samaritan Rock, Redcove Island, Pendarves Island and Carnewas Island. Enjoy wonderful views before walking round Trenance Point to reach the villages of Trenance and Mawgan Porth.

A climb to Berryl's Point leads back onto the cliffs, where the next break occurs at Watergate Bay – there is a huddle of hotels here. Keep walking along the cliffs to reach Trevelgue Head, which is actually an island connected to the Cornish coast by a footbridge. The coast path negotiates the suburbs of Newquay, which sit high on the cliffs, then after a walk through the town centre the harbour is reached. The original settlement here was called Towanblistra, where a 'new quay' was built in the 16th century. The town developed as a cargo port with a thriving fishing trade, with tourism becoming important following the arrival of the railway. Newquay's 'surf scene' has grown from nothing to assume great importance to the town in recent years.

Day 15 Newquay to Perranporth
17km (10½ miles)

A couple of little headlands are visited on the way out of Newquay, then the long and narrow tidal inlet of the Gannel is reached. At low water there is a tidal footbridge, while at high water a ferry

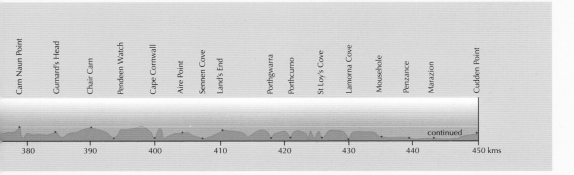

A razor-edged ridge is passed at Ralph's Cupboard on the way out of Portreath (Day 17)

runs from the Fern Pit Café. If neither of these is available, it's a long walk round to Crantock. The coast path turns grassy Pentire Point West and passes a little sandy inlet at Porth Joke. Kelsey Head gives way to a beach walk round Holywell Bay, where the village of Holywell offers refreshments. The path passes the Penhale army training area, where it is essential to follow the route exactly as marked. Beyond Ligger Point, most walkers will stroll along the sands of Perran Beach, but the coast path actually crosses the steep slope above the beach. Either way, the busy little resort of Perranporth is reached at the battered rocky headland of Droskyn Point.

Day 16 Perranporth to Portreath
20km (12½ miles)

Bustling Perranporth is left behind as the coast path continues along bleak and rugged cliffs, passing old mine shafts, crumbling engine houses and gaunt chimneys. Around St Agnes there was once a thriving mining area, and anyone wishing to know more about the industry should visit the Blue Hills Tin Streams. Exhibits show how tin ore was crushed, washed and smelted. Because of its past industry, this area, together with other places along the coast to St Just, has been designated a world heritage site. After passing Trevaunance Cove and its hotel, where the old harbour has been destroyed by storms, the trail runs round rugged St Agnes Head and later drops down to Chapel Porth. Paths climbing direct from this point are dangerous, so head inland as signposted and pick up the cliff path to Porthtowan. Walk from the Unicorn to the Beach Hotel to get back onto the cliffs, and pass a landmark flue chimney. Walk beside an extensive MOD property on Nancekuke Common until diverted onto a road at Lighthouse Hill. Walk down into Portreath, whose little harbour is made of stout stonework.

Day 17 Portreath to St Ives
29km (18 miles)

The cliff scenery beyond Portreath is remarkable, especially around Ralph's Cupboard, where there is an impressive razor-edged cliff. There are several short and steep ascents and descents along the Carvannel Downs and Reskajeague Downs, then the coast path runs close to a road. Deadman's Cove and Hell's Mouth sound fraught with danger, then the trail pulls away from the road to go round Navax Point and Godrevy Point. Godrevy Island is crowned with a lighthouse. The rough and rocky part of the day is over, and the rest is easy, though it is still a long way to St Ives.

At low water a broad strand sweeps round St Ives Bay, and most will be happy to walk along it. The coast path actually weaves about among the extensive dunes of the Towans, which takes longer to negotiate. The tidal mouth of the River Hayle cannot be forded and there is no ferry, so walkers either follow roads to Lelant, or sneak onto a bus or train to avoid the traffic. An intricate coast path runs from Lelant to Carbis Bay and into St Ives. The town's name is derived from St Ia – a 5th-century Irish missionary and daughter of a chieftain. St Ives Head protects a natural harbour and this was developed in the 18th century. The old fishing port is now a thriving tourist resort and a notable arts centre. Spend time exploring its poky alleyways.

Day 18 St Ives to Pendeen Watch
22km (13½ miles)

Some of the most spectacular and dramatic parts of the South West Coast Path are found between St Ives and Penzance, but the way is often quite arduous and may take longer than you expect. There are so many granite headlands and cliff-girt coves that it is easy to lose track of progress. In fair weather or foul, this is a remarkable stretch, but facilities are few. It is necessary to walk all the way to Pendour Cove before there is access inland to the bleak little village of Zennor and its Tinner's Arms. Views ahead take in the humped promontory of Gurnard's Head, but paths are rough and narrow.

The derelict engine houses of old mines are passed near Gurnard's Head. Beyond Porthmeor Cove, the ancient fortification of Bosigran Castle can be visited, and the cliffs nearby are popular with rock climbers. Chair Carn is a tower of rock surmounted by a huge boulder, which looks like the work of Cyclopean masons. After a difficult stretch around Portheras Cove, a little sign may invite wayfarers up to Pendeen Manor Farm for cream teas; otherwise keep walking to pass the landmark lighthouse at Pendeen Watch. This will probably be far enough for most walkers, and a small range of services can be found just inland at Pendeen, among the extensive ruins of old tin mines. Old chimneys, engine houses and winding gear can be seen, and the tin mining theme is explored at Geevor Tin Mine, which worked as late as 1990. Tin was first dug so deep that mines simply flooded, but once mighty pumping engines were developed, ore veins were exploited far beneath the seabed.

Day 19 Pendeen Watch to Porthcurno
26km (16 miles)

Pendeen's mining landscape gives way to breathtaking, beautiful and dramatic scenery on the way

to the prominent hump of Cape Cornwall. Mining remains abound, but they have either been restored, such as the Levant Beam Engine, or merge into the landscape, such as the Old Crowns Mine. Cape Cornwall was once given all the accolades now bestowed on Land's End, though it remains a popular place. Cross the Cot Valley to pick up the coast path at Porth Nanven, then stay above the cliffs all the way to rocky Aire Point. Either stay ashore, or if the tide is out, walk on the beach all the way round Whitesands Bay to reach Sennen Cove. This little fishing village is often a tangle of nets, as well as a centre for arts and crafts.

A short and busy walk leads to Land's End, where hordes of people might be found in high summer. The granite headland is wonderfully scenic, but is sadly attached to something resembling a theme park. However, there is a feeling that a significant point has been turned, and the crowds are quickly left behind in favour of remarkable rocky scenes, such as the pierced granite islet known as the Armed Knight. The coast path is almost level and quite easy as it wanders round Pordenack Point to reach Mill Bay. Pass the National Coastwatch Station on Gwennap Head, as well as a couple of curious 'daymarks', before walking down to the tiny settlement of Porthgwarra. A short cliff path leads onwards, passing the wonderfully romantic Minack Theatre, built into the cliffs near the village of Porthcurno.

Day 20 Porthcurno to Penzance
18km (11½ miles)

The rugged cliff path passes Logan Rock, which can be explored by making a detour; otherwise continue round Cribba Head and drop down to Penberth Cove. Boats are often hauled out onto a paved granite ramp. The path climbs a rugged, bushy slope before dropping down to Porthguarnon. Good views take in blocky cliffs and the path becomes broad and grassy before

dropping down to St Loy's Cove, which has an astoundingly bouldery beach. Climb onto the cliffs to pass Boscawen Point and pass above a lighthouse at Tater-du, where the path is flanked by hedgerows. Refreshments are available at lovely Lamorna Cove, then the path continues round Carn-du and passes the Kemyel Crease Nature Reserve.

A road leads down to Mousehole, where houses huddle round the harbour, and fishing has given way to arts and crafts. The last native Cornish speaker, Dolly Penteath, died here 200 years ago. The language has since been revived, particularly in this part of Cornwall. A long road walk leads from Mousehole to Newlyn and Penzance – easily the most built-up stretch of the South West Coast Path so far. Spanish vessels from France raided all three settlements in 1595. For centuries most visitors arrived from the sea, but in the late 19th century, when the railway reached Penzance, the town began to develop a thriving tourist industry. Naturally, every facility is readily to hand, and many who choose to walk only part of the coast path decide to make Penzance the start or finish of their route.

Day 21 Penzance to Porthleven
23km (14 miles)

The coast path runs along a sea wall, parallel to the railway out of Penzance. When the railway heads inland, the coast path continues to Marazion, an ancient settlement known as early as 308BC. St Michael's Mount rises offshore and can be reached by boat or on foot, depending on the state of the tides. It was crowned with a church in the 12th century, which was the object of a pilgrimage, while a castle was built in the 14th century. A road has to be followed inland from Marazion until the coast path can be regained at Trenow Cove. Pass the little village of Perranuthnoe, where there is a sandy beach, and follow the cliffs to Cudden Point and Prussia Cove.

The path passes above wonderful golden beaches at Kenneggy Sands and Praa Sands – the first being quiet and the second usually quite busy. Look out for layers of clay and peat at Praa Sands, where there was once fenland, before it was eroded by the sea and covered by wind-blown sand. Walk along the cliffs, passing old mine buildings and chimneys around Trewavas Head. After passing a prominent white house, look out for a cross marking a place where unknown seamen were buried. Before the passing of Gryll's Act of 1808, unclaimed bodies from the sea could not be buried in consecrated churchyards, so were often buried in lonely locations such as this. Porthleven has a 19th-century granite harbour and once boasted a thriving cargo trade, but nowadays relies on a little fishing and a lot of tourism.

Day 22 Porthleven to the Lizard
22km (13½ miles)

This day's walk is full of interest and amazing scenery. Shortly after leaving Porthleven, the shingle bank of Loe Bar holds in place a freshwater lake. From Gunwalloe Fishing Cove low cliffs are followed to reach St Winwalow's Church at Gunwalloe Church Cove. This ancient church is embedded into a hillside and has a separate belfry tower. After visiting nearby Poldhu, the cliff path passes a large retirement home, then reaches a monument to one of Marconi's early radio stations,

which operated here from 1900 to 1933. Walk round Polurrian Cove to reach secluded Mullion Cove, whose tiny harbour is guarded by enormous rocky stacks, with Mullion Island further out to sea.

The cliffs and coastal heaths beyond Mullion Cove are part of the Lizard National Nature Reserve, where grazing by rare breeds of sheep and ponies helps a variety of plants to thrive. The landscape of the Lizard is fairly flat, but the cliff coast is remarkably dramatic, with wonderful coves and headlands. Later, particularly around Kynance Cove, the cliffs break up into numerous rock stacks and islets to present a complex and chaotic scene. Flowery grasslands are a feature of the Caerthillian National Nature Reserve, and the coast path turns round Old Lizard Head. Walkers can relax at the Most Southerly Café and ponder that they are at the extreme toe end of Britain.

Day 23 The Lizard to Porthallow
25km (15 miles)

Shortly after passing the lighthouse on the Lizard, the coast path reaches a deep crater called the Lion's Den, which gaped open in 1842. The Lizard Wireless Station is another Marconi site, where signals passed to and from the Isle of Wight in 1901. Lloyds operated a signal station nearby, and the National Coastwatch keeps an eye on shipping these days – testimony to how much traffic passes the point. The coast path

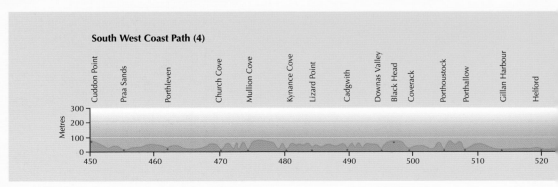

embarks on a roller coaster, and later passes the crater of the Devil's Frying Pan on the way to the village of Cadgwith. There are plenty of ups and downs past Poltesco and Kennack Sands, and onwards to the Downas Valley and Black Head. After passing the promontory of Chynhalls Point the route reaches the village of Coverack.

The coast path stays low around appropriately named Lowland Point, but encounters problems when faced with large, active stone quarries ahead. There is a significant diversion inland, though the beach can be gained at the tiny settlement of Porthoustock. By the time you enter the village of Porthallow, the walk around the South West Coast Path is just about half completed in terms of distance. Celebrate this at the Five Pilchards Inn!

Day 24 Porthallow to Falmouth
29km (18 miles)

Advance planning is needed on this day's walk, since there is a tidal inlet to cross, as well as a ferry journey to make. Indeed, more planning is needed for the following day, when two ferries need to be linked, or onward progress grinds to a halt. First, there is an easy walk from Porthallow to

Rocky stacks fill the sea at Kynance Cove near Lizard Point (Day 22)

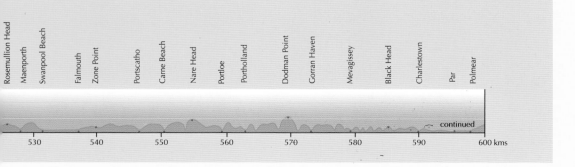

Rosemullion Head, Maenporth, Swanpool Beach, Falmouth, Zone Point, Portscatho, Carne Beach, Nare Head, Portloe, Portholland, Dodman Point, Gorran Haven, Mevagissey, Black Head, Charlestown, Par, Polmear

continued

530 540 550 560 570 580 590 600 kms

Looking back to the tiny village of Portloe tucked into a crooked cove in the cliffs (Day 26)

Nare Point, where Falmouth can be seen in the distance. However, the coast path is by no means direct, and heads towards the tidal inlet of Gillan Harbour. At low tide it is easy to cross the creek, but when the tide is in there is no option but to walk round to St Anthony-in-Meneage. A well-wooded path runs alongside the tidal Helford river to reach the village of Helford. At this point there is a ferry across to Helford Passage, and this is essential as it is too far to walk round. The coast path continues round Rosemullion Head to the little village of Maenporth, then reaches the outskirts of Falmouth at Swanpool.

You can short cut straight through Falmouth if you want, but the coast path goes all the way round the fortified promontory of Pendennis Head. There is a view across the mouth of Carrick Roads to Zone Point before the route heads past Falmouth harbour. Originally ships used to sail to Penrhyn, until Pendennis Castle and its counterpart across at St Mawes were built to protect the harbour in the 16th century. However, Falmouth harbour didn't really develop until the rail link arrived in the mid-19th century, when hundreds of ships used to weigh anchor in Carrick Roads. The town has a splendid range of facilities.

Day 25 Falmouth to Portloe
22km (13½ miles)

This day starts with two ferries rather than a walk. The first ferry is from Falmouth to St Mawes, while the second is a simple, small boat ride from St Mawes to Place. The walking doesn't start until you reach Place, so don't leave it too late. The first stage is a complete circuit around Zone Point, passing a 19th-century battery. The path often runs alongside fields as it progresses towards Portscatho. Take a refreshment break in the village, or continue onwards to pass the National Coastwatch Station on Pednvadan Point. Enjoy a circuit around Gerrans Bay, passing a couple of hotels halfway round near Pendower Beach. A slope covered in gorse bushes leads onto Nare Head, then a succession of little coves and headlands are passed before Portloe is reached. The village and its tiny harbour come into view quite suddenly, and you need to double back to walk down to it.

Day 26 Portloe to Mevagissey
20km (12½ miles)

The cliff path leaving Portloe is quite rugged in places. West and East Portholland are two small settlements with very few facilities, passed on the way to Caerhays Castle and Porthluney Cove. The coast path approaches Dodman Point, often referred to as the Dodman, which bears a stout granite cross on its 114m (375ft) summit. You may have been aware of the Dodman for the past four days, and it will remain prominent for much longer, so views from it naturally extend along a considerable stretch of the coast. The trail later drops down to Vault Beach, then turns round the point of Pen-a-maen to reach the village of Gorran Haven.

Cliff Road takes the coast path back onto the cliffs to reach Chapel Point, although there is no access to the very end of the point. Portmellon's Rising Sun Inn dates from the 17th century, and the busy little town of Mevagissey is reached soon

afterwards. A settlement was recorded here as early as 1313 and it was a shipbuilding centre from 1745. Fishing was once very important, and the first electric generators in town were fuelled with pilchard oil. Although fishing still takes place, the town's biggest earner is tourism and there are plenty of services available.

Day 27 Mevagissey to Polmear
18km (11½ miles)

The way out of Mevagissey is awkward to find, then beyond the town the coast path makes a lot of short, steep ascents and descents, going through the middle of the village of Pentewan before another roller coaster leads to Black Head. From time to time views inland appear to feature snow-capped peaks, but these are in fact the towering spoil heaps of a thriving china clay industry around St Austell. The bedrock granite inland 'rots' and becomes quite crumbly, so that hard minerals are easily sieved out, leaving a creamy white mass ideal for making pottery. The coast path visits the late-18th-century stone-built harbour of Charlestown, which handled much of the china clay trade in the past, but nearby dusty Port of Par has superseded it. Par and Polmear have a small range of services for coast-path walkers, but there are easy links inland to St Austell.

Day 28 Polmear to Polperro
21km (13 miles)

A little harbour at Polkerris is passed as the cliff path heads for Gribbin Head and its prominent red-and-white daymark. Walk down to a little beach at Poltridmouth and continue up and down along the cliffs to reach Readymoney Beach and 16th-century St Catherine's Castle. Follow a road into Fowey, which sits beside a sheltered, deep-water anchorage. Spanish ships attacked the town in the 14th century, so a deterrent chain was

A view of Mevagissey seen from a small park above the harbour (Day 26)

Lantic Bay and Lantivet Bay are passed, the latter having a waterfall at West Coombe. Walk along the top of a scrubby, bushy slope and pass a daymark that, along with a bell out to sea, warns ships away from the Udder Rock. The coast path has a number of ascents and descents on the way to Chapel Cliff, then there is a sudden view of Polperro, crammed into a narrow valley stretching inland from its little harbour. It is a wonderfully atmospheric place, looking like a genuine haunt of smugglers, and there is a Museum of Smuggling and Fishing. Have a look at the fish-landing area, and cross a river at the curious, 16th-century House on Props.

Day 29 Polperro to Portwrinkle
20km (12½ miles)

Leave Polperro by way of the Warren and follow an easy path round to Talland Bay. The path becomes more difficult, but also more attractive, as it turns round the next headland and St George's Island comes into view. The attractive little town of Looe comes in two parts – West Looe and East Looe, with a tidal river between them. Cross a bridge to reach busier East Looe and consider a visit to the Old Guidhall Gaol and Museum. There are occasional boat

stretched across the harbour mouth between two stout blockhouses. Spend a while exploring the narrow streets, which are full of character, then get a ferry across to Polruan.

Bear in mind that the rugged coastal walk beyond Polruan has no facilities until Polperro.

trips out to St George's Island, managed as a nature reserve.

A walk along East Cliff leads away from the town to Millendreath Beach. There is a slight detour from the coast, then the way becomes quite rugged in places. Cross a wooded slope below the Woolly Monkey Sanctuary at Murrayton to reach Seaton. If the tide is in, walk along a road to reach nearby Downderry, otherwise the beach can be used. A fine cliff path leads onwards to Portwrinkle, which has a tiny harbour that is completely dry at low water. Note: if planning to stay overnight, there is only a small range of services.

Day 30 Portwrinkle to Plymouth
22km (13½ miles)

This is the last day's walk on the coast of Cornwall, and there is a military firing range at Tregantle Fort. If firing is taking place, then walk round by road. If the range is open to walkers, as it is during August and on alternate weekends, then follow the path through as directed. Freathy is a peculiar settlement made of highly individual cabins scattered across a steep slope, and the coast path weaves about between them. A grassy track leads onwards, then the coast path climbs round Rame Head, where it is worth making a short detour to have a look at St Michael's Chapel, built in 1397. The route continues to Penlee Point, then drops down to Cawsand and Kingsand. Watch out for a house near the post office, which bears the words 'Devon/Corn', where the old county boundary once ran through the building.

Follow the coast path as signposted to reach Mount Edgcumbe Country Park. Based around the demesne of Mount Edgcumbe House, this has a number of interesting features and is well worth exploring. A ferry runs across the Sound from Cremyll to Admiral's Hard at Plymouth in Devon.

Day 31 Plymouth to Wembury Beach
22km (13½ miles)

In the past, it was common for walkers to catch a bus through Plymouth to avoid the built-up parts of the city and get straight back onto the coast path at Turnchapel. This is now to be discouraged, since the city has made a splendid effort to tidy up its part of the South West Coast Path, so that the Plymouth Waterfront Walkway is presented as a celebration and showcase for the city's heritage. Sculptures and interesting artistic features have been installed, along with plenty of information plaques along the way. Keep an eye open to spot 'acorn' markers on lampposts, or set into the pavement, to keep track of the trail. Explorations are greatly enhanced if you obtain a booklet about the route in advance.

To briefly summarise, there are glimpses of the naval docks and the trail passes the Royal Marines Barracks. Millbay Docks are passed on the way to the Hoe, where Smeaton's Tower stands on a fine green. Don't miss the Mayflower Steps and Barbican on the way to the National Marine Aquarium. Later, a huge navigation beacon has been transformed into an enormous marker post for the South West Coast Path. There is an industrial interlude at Cattedown and a busy road leads to the head of Pomphlett Lake. Wander through the suburbs and pass Radford Castle on the way to Turnchapel. Turn round the end of Mount Batten Point to reach pleasant green spaces at Jennycliff.

The Plymouth Waterfront Walkway ends at Jennycliff, with the South West Coast Path continuing along low cliffs to Staddon Point and Bovisand Bay. Walk all the way round rugged Wembury Point, admiring the pyramidal peak of the Great Mew Stone out to sea. An easy path runs to Wembury Beach, and walkers are advised to spend the evening studying ferry timetables and tide tables, or onward progress to Salcombe could be very awkward.

Day 32   Wembury Beach to Bigbury-on-Sea
23km (14 miles)

Shortly after leaving Wembury, the coast path grinds to a halt at the mouth of the tidal River Yealm. An arrow on a little pier shows which direction you should wave to attract the attention of the ferryman, but only do it at the times when he is likely to be looking! Continue walking from the Noss Mayo shore, through Passage Wood. A fine track is joined, the Revelstoke Drive, which was constructed in the 1880s as a carriage drive for Lord Revelstoke. This leads easily around Gara Point and passes solitary Warren Cottage. If refreshments are needed, they can be obtained at Revelstoke Park in the peak holiday season. Rise around the slopes of Beacon Hill, then follow a path across a valley and pass St Anchorite's Rock. The cliff path eventually reaches the mouth of the tidal River Erme.

There is no ferry across the River Erme, so walkers must turn up at low water, or sit on the shore and wait for the tide to recede. Walking round is possible, but would take a couple of hours. An information board covers all possibilities. Once across, the coast path seems very remote, and there are some considerable ascents and descents, one after the other, before the village of Bigbury-on-Sea is reached. Burgh Island lies offshore and can be reached at low water, but there is also a curious 'sea tractor' that crosses the sands even when the

A view of the Hoe in Plymouth, seen from the Plymouth Walkway at Turnchapel

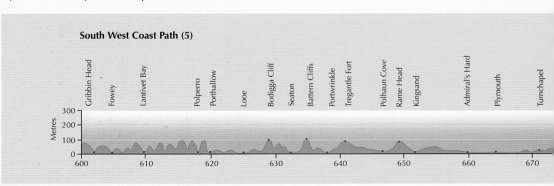

South West Coast Path (5)

tide is in, serving a hotel on the island. Either stay overnight at Bigbury, or seize the chance to cross the River Avon if the ferry is running.

Day 33 Bigbury-on-Sea to Salcombe
21km (13 miles)

The River Avon cannot be forded safely at low water, so yell mightily to attract the ferry stationed on the far shore at Bantham, noting that it may not run on Sundays. The coast path climbs onto the cliffs near Thurlestone, then crosses a long footbridge through a marshy reedbed. Outer Hope and Inner Hope are two little villages passed on the way to the prominent headland of Bolt Tail. The route becomes more and more rugged as it leads onwards to Bolt Head. After dropping down to Starehole Bay, the path climbs steps to pass a fine pinnacle of rock at Sharp Point. Note the 'stare hole' pierced through the rock. There is a fine view of Salcombe ahead, but it takes a while to reach the town as the last stretch is rather convoluted. There is a full range of services here.

Day 34 Salcombe to Stoke Fleming
31km (19½ miles)

First, use the ferry to get from Salcombe to East Portlemouth, then start walking, bearing in mind that this is a long stage. The rugged coast path

Walkers turn around a rock ledge cut into the flanks of Sharp Tor near Salcombe

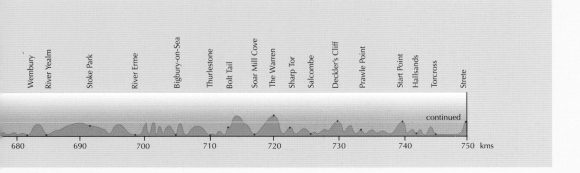

continued

climbs and drops time and time again, but is very scenic and dramatic. Turn round Prawle Point, which is the southernmost part of Devon and features a National Coastwatch Station. A remarkable range of birds can be spotted all the way round the point, and although the path can be difficult in places, overall it becomes easier. Walk around Lannacombe Bay and take care on the part known as the Narrows, where the path does indeed get very narrow. There is a lighthouse on the end of Start Point, but no need for walkers to go out to it. Instead, turn the point and walk towards the sad remains of Hallsands – a coastal village that was wrecked by the sea after its protective beach was destroyed by dredging. A long pebbly beach runs to the neighbouring village of Beesands and a little hill is crossed afterwards.

While high on the hill, enjoy the view around Start Bay, where a long shingle beach curves gracefully from the village of Torcross to distant Strete, separating the sea from the freshwater lake of Slapton Ley. This area was evacuated during the Second World War in preparation for the D-day landings in Normandy. While practice for Operation Tiger was in progress in April 1944, German torpedo boats struck during the night. Almost 750 people were killed, nearly all of them US servicemen.

The coast path doesn't crunch along the shingle beach, but runs along a narrow strip between the coast road and reedbeds alongside Slapton Ley. Climb uphill to the village of Strete, then enjoy a path that was opened in recent years after a long period of lobbying. This leads to Blackpool Sands and Stoke Fleming, which is far enough for today.

Day 35 Stoke Fleming to Brixham
24km (15 miles)

There is a diversion away from the coast on the way out of Stoke Fleming, then the cliffs are regained at Warren Point. Walk round Blackstone Point and drop down to Dartmouth Castle, which is made up of the 14th-century Fortalice, 15th-century Gun Tower, 19th-century Victorian Old Battery and mid-19th-century Castle Light, which is now a tearoom. Head into Dartmouth, built beside a deep-water channel and long favoured as a port. Fleets of ships carried Crusaders to the Holy Land from here, and there was once a thriving fishing industry. Note the huge Royal Naval College, though most of the craft moored in the channel are now pleasure boats. Use a ferry to cross from the Boat Float to Kingswear.

Bear in mind that the rest of the day's walk runs along a remote cliff line with a series of major ascents and descents, and it is likely to take longer than you expect. There are fine views back to the Royal Naval College on the way to the Brownstone Battery, which was built in 1940 to guard Dartmouth's approaches. The cliff path runs round Froward Point and passes Pudcombe Cove on its

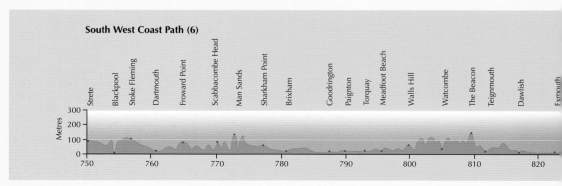

Looking along the roller-coaster cliffs to Sharkham Point and Berry Head near Brixham

way to Scabbacombe Head. After a roller-coaster route along the cliffs to Sharkham Point, walkers who are struggling could short cut into Brixham. The coast path, however, runs all the way round Berry Head before heading for the harbour and town centre. A replica of the Golden Hind is moored here, and a statue of William, Prince of Orange, notes his landing at Brixham in 1688. The town has turned from fishing to tourism and is usually very busy.

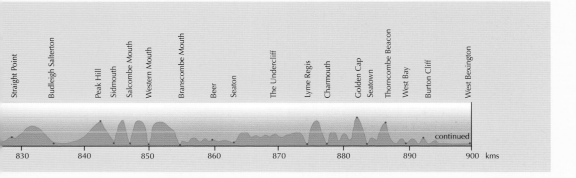

continued

Straight Point Budleigh Salterton Peak Hill Sidmouth Salcombe Mouth Western Mouth Branscombe Mouth Beer Seaton The Undercliff Lyme Regis Charmouth Golden Cap Seatown Thorncombe Beacon West Bay Burton Cliff West Bexington

830   840   850   860   870   880   890   900 kms

A view around Ladram Bay to the distant resort of Budleigh Salterton in Devon (Day 37)

Day 36 Brixham to Shaldon
31km (19½ miles)

Torbay became a tourist destination during the Napoleonic Wars, when its architecture was remodelled to earn it the title of the 'English Riviera', satisfying those who could no longer make the 'grand tour' of Europe. By the mid-19th century a railway ensured easy access for tourists, and all the Torbay towns have grown and merged to become a conglomeration of seaside resorts.

Some walkers catch a bus from one end of Torbay to the other, and there is also a ferry that plies between Brixham and Torquay. In truth,

while the area is very built-up, there are some good coastal paths and green spaces, and the busy promenades through the towns are quickly completed on foot. Look out for bronze 'acorn' disks set into the pavements, as well as signposts. There is a fine coastal path from Brixham to Goodrington, and the red cliffs of Roundham Head are pleasant. Follow the promenade along Paignton's seafront, then follow a busy road most of the way to the harbour in Torquay.

Leaving Torquay, the coast path features some quite good views and the Rock End Walk steers clear of built-up areas. Gradually the suburbs are left behind, and the route becomes a roller coaster as it runs through woods and fields, passing Watcombe and Maidencombe to enjoy more open prospects. The constant ups and downs can be quite tiring at the end of the day, but once the wooded headland of the Ness is passed, the route drops finally to the village of Shaldon at the mouth of the River Teign.

Day 37 Shaldon to Budleigh Salterton
23km (14 miles)

A ferry has operated across the mouth of the River Teign since the 13th century, but there is also a bridge across the river that would take only a few minutes longer to cross. Teignmouth is essentially a 19th-century holiday resort, but it has a long history, having been burnt by the Danes in 800AD, burnt again in 1340, then yet again in 1690, as well as being damaged by the Germans in the Second World War. The coast path out of Teignmouth is subject to tidal restrictions, so either walk seawards of the railway line if the tide is out, or head slightly inland to reach Holcombe. The route plays hide-and-seek with the railway line all the way through Dawlish, a town famous for its colony of black swans. At Dawlish Warren the route runs inland by road to reach Starcross, where a ferry crosses the tidal mouth of the River Exe to reach Exmouth, a journey that could also be made by rail through Exeter.

Exmouth has been a popular seaside resort since the 18th century, and its esplanade carries the coast path out of town, passing a flowery, grassy nature reserve called the Maer. The High Land of Orcombe features a low cliff walk to Sandy Bay, then the route cuts inland behind the red cliffs of Straight Point to avoid a military firing range. There is a fine view of more red cliffs stretching beyond Littleham Cove to Budleigh Salterton. The last few days on the South West Coast Path pass through the Jurassic Coast World Heritage Site.

Day 38 Budleigh Salterton to Seaton
28km (17½ miles)

There is a detour inland at Budleigh Salterton, crossing a bridge over the River Otter to pass through the Otter Estuary Nature Reserve. The gently undulating coast path follows a low cliff, which breaks up into attractive stacks at Ladram Bay. Pass the Three Rocks Inn and climb High Peak, which is only 157m (515ft), and later descend to Sidmouth to walk along its esplanade. Beyond the resort, the high cliffs are cut by a series of valleys, so there are some long and arduous ascents and descents, one after the other, until the top of Weston Cliff is reached. A gentler interlude follows, passing a wildflower meadow, then there is a descent to Branscombe Mouth.

The coast path doesn't cross Hooken Cliffs, but uses a path through the Hooken Undercliff, passing through a chaotic wooded landslip that dates from 1790. A zigzag path later climbs uphill to reach Beer Head, which is a splendid viewpoint. The trail leads down into the lovely little village of Beer, where a vigorous little stream runs alongside Fore Street. Flights of steps climb out of the village to lead walkers over Beer Hill on the way to Seaton.

Day 39 Seaton to Seatown
21km (13 miles)

Extensive woodlands are rare along the South West Coast Path, but the trail from Seaton to Lyme Regis passes through the Undercliff, which is a well-wooded region of old landslips – the last major slip dates from 1839. The problem lies in the thick Gault clay, which deforms under pressure from the hard layers of rock above it. The Undercliff is protected as a national nature reserve and is a jungle world unto itself. There are seldom any views of the sea, or of the cliffs above, as the path weaves between trees and bushy scrub. Ivy creeps over boulders and trees, while damp hollows sprout ferns. Emerging from the Undercliff, the coast path leaves Devon and enters Dorset on the outskirts of Lyme Regis.

A royal charter was granted to Lyme Regis in 1284 and there are many fine old buildings around the town. Essentially a tourist resort, Lyme's chief attraction lies in its bedrock, which is rich in fossils. Anyone can expect to find spiral ammonites or bullet-like belemnites, while the lucky few find the remains of huge ichthyosaurs. Hammers are wielded on the shore, but fossils are also sold throughout the town, and can be inspected in the museum. There are even guided fossil walks for those who want an expert on hand.

Landslips beyond Lyme Regis have caused problems on the coast path, and there is a diversion inland to Charmouth, though at low water it is possible to walk, with care, along the beach. More fossils can be seen at the Charmouth Heritage Coast Centre. Follow crumbling cliffs on a roller-coaster route over Stonebarrow Hill to reach Golden Cap. This is the highest point on the south coast, at 191m (627ft), so enjoy views back along the coast, as well as ahead to the Isle of Portland, then drop down to tiny Seatown.

Day 40 Seatown to Abbotsbury
20km (12½ miles)

The cliff coast remains impressive for a short while beyond Seatown, with some short, steep ascents

and descents around Eype's Mouth and West Bay. Bridport is just inland, and West Bay was its harbour, but trade dwindled when the railway reached the town in 1884. Views from the cliffs reveal the long, bright shingle line of Chesil Beach stretching all the way to the Isle of Portland. If you inspect the pebbles on the beach around West Bay, they are bean-sized, but anyone walking along the ridge will notice that the pebbles increase very gradually over a long distance until they are potato-sized at Portland. You can ponder this curious phenomenon while crunching towards Abbotsbury, though the coast path sometimes plumps for easier conditions underfoot just landward of the shingle bank. Note how the bank encloses marshy reedbeds and pools of water, such as Burton Mere.

At West Bexington a rather curious signpost points out the 'Inland Coast Path', which offers a short cut over chalk downs, avoiding Portland and Weymouth, to reach Osmington Mills (a brief outline of this route is given after the end of Day 45 and before the section headed 'Information'). Chesil Beach is abandoned as the coast path heads inland to Abbotsbury. Only a fragment of the old abbey remains, dating from 1400. The village is pretty and has a few features of interest, but the chief attraction is the Abbotsbury Swannery, where hundreds of mute swans have enjoyed protection since 1393. St Catherine's Church on a nearby hilltop is thought to be 14th

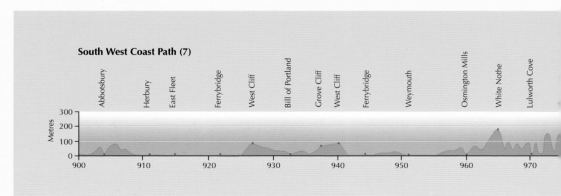

century and can be the subject of a pleasant evening stroll.

Day 41 Abbotsbury to Ferrybridge
18km (11½ miles)

This stretch of the trail is set far back from the sea at the start of the day. First it climbs over Linton Hill, then later reaches saltwater near Langton Herring. However, this is not the open sea, but the long, narrow, shallow tidal lagoon of West Fleet, held in place by the massive shingle bar of Chesil Beach. The lagoon is quite narrow near the Moonfleet Manor Hotel, and when it broadens again it is known as the East Fleet. Tidmouth Army Rifle Range might force a slight detour from the shore, and walkers have to divert round the Wyke Regis training area headquarters. The day's walk concludes at Ferrybridge, where a ferry used to operate to the Isle of Portland, though traffic now hurtles across a busy causeway bridge.

Day 42 Isle of Portland Circuit
25km (15½ miles)

Originally the South West Coast Path headed straight through Weymouth, but a circuit around the Isle of Portland has been added and proves to be a very interesting walk. The island itself is essentially a

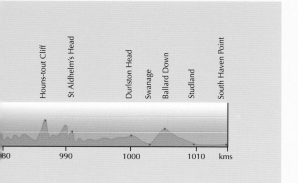

tilted block of limestone, well known for the Portland stone produced here. Old quarry tracks are followed along the western cliff coast of the island, passing a series of imaginative sculptures. The southernmost point is the Bill of Portland, where a slab of rock leans against a sea stack known as Pulpit Rock.

On a very clear day views extend from Start Point in Devon to Durlston Head in Dorset, accounting for 260km (160 miles) of the South West Coast Path, which is over a quarter of Britain's longest trail, and unmatched by any other viewpoint! Follow paths along the eastern cliffs of the island, but take care with route finding among huge fortifications on the high, northern end of the island. Prisons and a military area are passed around the Grove and Fortuneswell, then it is necessary to retrace steps back to Ferrybridge to leave the island.

Day 43 Ferrybridge to Lulworth Cove
23km (14 miles)

The coast path is a rather patchy affair through Weymouth, a busy resort that was popular with King George III. Massive breakwaters flank a huge harbour. Follow the busy promenade to Bowleaze Cove, where things become much quieter once the route reaches the crumbling cliffs. Every so often the path has to move back following landslips, and there is a significant step inland on the descent to Osmington Mills. Pass the popular 13th-century Smugglers Inn to pick up the cliff path towards Ringstead Bay. Climb uphill and walk along the edge of Burning Cliff, where a band of oil shale burst into flames in 1826, and reach the coastguard cottages on top of White Nothe.

A monstrous roller-coaster route follows, starting with a descent into the Warren and a steep climb alongside sheer cliffs to Bat's Head. Drop downhill and climb again to reach Swyre Head,

The coast path makes a complete circuit of the Isle of Portland, famous for its stone (Day 42)

then make another steep descent and enjoy fine views of Durdle Door, where a rock arch looks like a dinosaur taking a drink from the sea. This area is very popular, and the trail continues to the remarkable bay of Lulworth Cove, where a short detour is recommended to peer into rugged Stair Hole. Walkers should also be thinking ahead, however, as the next stretch of the coast path is very scenic and challenging, but part of it lies within the Lulworth Ranges, and access is not permitted during firing.

Day 44 Lulworth Cove to Swanage
33km (21 miles)

This is a long and difficult day's walk, and the first stages must take place while the Lulworth Ranges are open, or walkers will have to detour far inland. Usually the ranges are open during most popular holiday times through the year. Walk round Lulworth Cove and enter the ranges at the Fossil Forest Gate, peering over the cliffs to spot the bulbous remains of fossil trees. Stay on the grassy path indicated by yellow marker posts, and admire the rock stacks in Mupe Bay. Climb steeply on Bindon Hill and drop down to the beach at Arish Mell.

The celebrated rock arch at Durdle Door is an iconic image on the Dorset coast (Day 43)

Climb steeply again to reach the ramparts of an Iron Age hill fort at Flower's Barrow, then drop steeply to Worbarrow Bay. The deserted village of Tyneham lies inland, but the coast path climbs steeply before running along the top of Gad Cliff to reach Tyneham Cap at 167m (548ft). As the descent eases, the coast path runs almost level around Kimmeridge Bay, leaving the ranges at a 'nodding donkey' oilwell.

The landmark Clavell Tower, built in 1830, was dismantled in 2006, moved back from the cliff edge and carefully rebuilt in 2007. A gentle walk above the Kimmeridge Ledges gives way to a steep ascent and descent on Houns-tout Cliff.

Little valleys have to be crossed on the way to St Aldhelm's Head, then there is an easier stretch. Look along the cliffs to see how they have been quarried for Purbeck marble. There are some difficult stretches on the way to Durlston Head, and at that point it is worth visiting the Great Globe – a 40-tonne rock sphere carved to represent the whole world. The coast path runs round Peveril Point on its way to Swanage, but if you have had enough you can short cut directly into the town, with its many facilities.

Day 45 Swanage to South Haven Point
12km (7½ miles)

The last day's walk on the South West Coast Path is short and easy. First the trail leaves Swanage and wanders along the Ballard Cliffs before heading onto the Foreland. Old Harry's Rocks are huge chalk stacks standing offshore, leading the eye to the distant Needles and the Isle of Wight. There are

A view of the Pinnacles on the way out to the end of the Foreland near Swanage

alternative routes through Studland and around Studland Bay. Either walk along the sandy beach, part of which is regularly used by naturists, or follow paths through a sandy heath just inland. Both routes combine at the Shell Bay to approach South Haven Point. A sculpture in the form of a compass and a pair of sails marks the end of the South West Coast Path, though for practical purposes you take a ferry across to Sandbanks to start your journey home.

The Inland Coast Path
27km (17 miles)

This sounds like a complete contradiction, but there is an 'Inland Coast Path' signposted between West Bexington and Osmington Mills. This route cuts out the walk from Abbotsbury to Ferrybridge alongside the Fleet, and so avoids the Isle of Portland and the trail through Weymouth. Instead, walkers are led over a broad chalk downland, crossing Wear's Hill high above Abbotsbury. The route stays high and reaches the Hardy Monument on Black Down at 237m (778ft), which is a splendid viewpoint, but a long way from the coast. The route stays high over Bronkham Hill and crosses a busy road on Ridgeway Hill, then passes the tiny village of Bincombe. Whitehorse Hill, carved with an effigy of King George III on horseback, is crossed before the route descends to Osmington to rejoin the coast path at Osmington Mills, well clear of busy Weymouth.

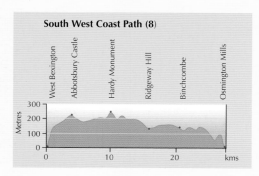

South West Coast Path (8)

INFORMATION

Access to Start	Long-distance Virgin Trains to Taunton link with First buses to Minehead. National Express buses also serve Minehead.
Getting Home	Ferry from South Haven Point to Sandbanks, then bus to Poole or Bournemouth for long-distance Virgin Trains or National Express buses.
Other Public Transport	South West Trains run along most branch lines. First is the main bus operator. Public transport leaflets covering each county in the south west are available from TICs.
Maps	OS 1:50,000 Landrangers 180, 181, 190, 192, 193, 194, 195, 200, 201, 202, 203 and 204
	OS 1:25,000 Explorers 102, 103, 104, 105, 106, 107, 108, 110, 111, 115, 116, 126 and 139, OL9, OL15 and OL20
	Harveys 1:40,000 South West Coast Path (six sheets)
Cicerone Guide	*The South West Coast Path*, by Paddy Dillon
Other Guidebooks	*South West Coast Path, Minehead to Padstow*, by Roland Tarr, Aurum Press
	Padstow to Falmouth, by John Macadam, Aurum Press
	Falmouth to Exmouth, by Brian Le Messurier, Aurum Press
	Exmouth to Poole, by Roland Tarr, Aurum Press
	South West Coast Path Guide, South West Coast Path Association
Tourist Information Centres	Minehead tel 0845 345465, Lynton tel 0845 6603232, Combe Martin tel 01271 883319, Ilfracombe tel 0845 4583630, Barnstaple tel 0845 4582003, Bideford tel 01237 477676, Bude tel 01288 354240, Padstow tel 01841 533449, Newquay tel 01637 854020, St Ives tel 01736 796297, Penzance tel 01736 362207, Falmouth tel 01326 312300, Mevagissey tel 01726 844857, St Austell tel 01726 879500, Fowey tel 01726 833616, Looe tel 01503 262072, Plymouth tel 01752 306330, Salcombe tel 01548 843927, Dartmouth tel 01803 834224, Brixham tel 09066 801268, Paignton tel 01803 558383, Torquay tel 0870 7070010, Teignmouth tel 01626 215666, Dawlish tel 01626 215665, Exmouth tel 01395 222299, Budleigh Salterton tel 01395 445275, Sidmouth tel 01395 515441, Seaton tel 01297 21660, Lyme Regis tel 01297 442138, Weymouth tel 01305 785747, Swanage tel 01929 422885.
Accommodation List	*South West Coast Path Guide*, produced by the South West Coast Path Association
Path Association	South West Coast Path Association, www.swcp.org.uk
Website	www.nationaltrail.co.uk/southwestcoastpath

Cyclists ride down to Whitewool Farm below Old Winchester Hill (Day 2)

2 South Downs Way

Start and Finish	Winchester to Eastbourne
Distance and Time	163km (101 miles) taking up to 1 week
Character	Generally easy underfoot, along clear tracks and paths through open and wooded areas. Bear in mind that villages lie off-route and downhill, so it is necessary to climb back onto the downs after visiting them.
Highlights	Winchester city, Old Winchester Hill, Butser Hill, all the high, open parts of the South Downs and most of the villages along the foot of the downs, the Seven Sisters and Beachy Head.

Walkers trek along the grassy South Downs Way towards Alfriston (Day 6)

When the South Downs Way opened in 1972 it was heralded as the first long-distance bridleway intended for walkers, cyclists and horse riders alike. At the time it ran from Buriton, just inside Hampshire, to Eastbourne in West Sussex, but has since been extended further inland, beyond Buriton, to the wonderfully interesting city of Winchester. The rolling, grassy, flower-rich downs are charming, with many fine wooded areas, delightful river valleys and lovely little villages. Some hilltops are crowned with Iron Age hill forts, while at the seaward end of the range everything comes to an abrupt halt at a series of gleaming-white chalk cliffs. The East Hampshire and Sussex Downs Areas of Outstanding Natural Beauty cover the South Downs, and there are calls for the whole area to be designated a national park.

Those who follow the South Downs Way can expect to walk for about a week, and may be surprised to find very few habitations along the route,

SCHEDULE			
Day	**Start/Finish**	**Km**	**Miles**
Day 1	Winchester to Exton	20	12
Day 2	Exton to South Harting	27	17
Day 3	South Harting to Amberley Station	30	18½
Day 4	Amberley Station to Truleigh Hill	22.5	14
Day 5	Truleigh Hill to Southease Station	31.5	19½
Day 6	Southease Station to Eastbourne	32	20

which often avoids villages as it strives for the elevated, open spaces. The highest parts generally reach just over 200m (655ft), and seldom exceed 250m (820ft), so any sense of being 'on top of the world' is largely illusory. However, it is an illusion that everyone is happy to accept, and such is the nature of the trail that it is easy to stride out and adopt a brisk pace that eats up the distance. Careful planning is needed when searching for accommodation, food and drink, which generally involves detouring off-route, thus increasing the distance. Cyclists and horse riders may occasionally have to follow a different course to walkers, while walkers will be happy to find gates that open and close easily, rather than having to negotiate awkward stiles along the way.

Day 1 Winchester to Exton
20km (12 miles)

Don't leave Winchester without exploring the city, forever associated with King Alfred, as it served as his capital – you could allow all morning if you start with a short day's walk. The 11th-century cathedral is the longest in Europe. The 12th-century St Cross Hospital still hands out the 'wayfarer's dole' to needy travellers, in the form of beer and bread. The 13th-century Great Hall has 'King Arthur's round table' mounted on a wall like an enormous dartboard. The 14th-century Winchester College may be the oldest continuously running

school in the country. The 18th-century City Mill straddles the River Itchen, and there is also a museum and gallery in the city.

The South Downs Way wriggles out of the city, crosses the busy M3 motorway and is suddenly heading through fields to pass the quiet little village of Chilcomb. An easy ascent of Telegraph Hill is followed by a view across a grassy combe, or valley, from Cheesefoot Head. The route then wanders along tracks and paths across the lower slopes of the downs – a rolling, undulating course only passing the odd farm before reaching the Millberrys Inn. Walk alongside a busy road, then take to farm tracks to reach the wooded brow

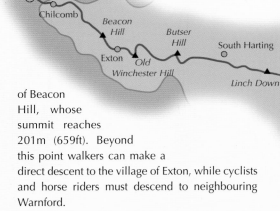

of Beacon Hill, whose summit reaches 201m (659ft). Beyond this point walkers can make a direct descent to the village of Exton, while cyclists and horse riders must descend to neighbouring Warnford.

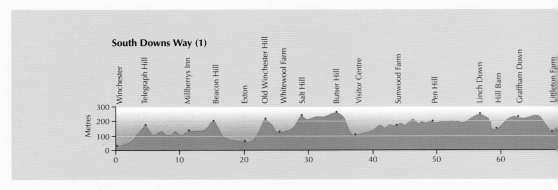

Day 2 Exton to South Harting
27km (17 miles)

The River Meon is followed out of Exton, then field paths lead up onto 197m (646ft) Old Winchester Hill. Iron Age settlers surrounded the hill with a wrinkled rampart, which now offers extensive views of the surrounding countryside. This is a very popular place for walkers, rich in typical chalk downland flowers. Cyclists and horse riders, however, have no access to the hill and must follow Old Winchester Hill Lane out of Warnford, joining with walkers at a road junction. All can then descend to Whitewool Farm, where there are fine old buildings, and a chance to obtain refreshments at a café beside a series of small fishing dams at Meon Springs.

The route climbs from the valley, through fields to

Coombe Cross, then steeply up onto Salt Hill. Former HMS *Mercury*, once a forbidding military site, is now half abandoned and half occupied by the Sustainability Centre, which offers a hostel, campsite, café, and information on 'green' issues. After following a fine track over the gentle slopes of Tegdown Hill, the route swings towards Butser Hill and its prominent masts, touching 250m (820ft). A steep descent of a grassy spur leads to an underpass beneath the busy A3. At this point, in the heart of well-wooded Queen Elizabeth Country Park, a visitor centre and restaurant are available in an area that is usually very busy.

Cyclists and horse riders follow a track parallel to walkers on the ascent of a beech-wooded slope, then all follow the same tracks and farm roads high above Buriton, originally the start of the South Downs Way before its extension to Winchester. The route now follows the high crest of the South Downs, sometimes through fields and sometimes through woods, passing attractive copper beeches at Sunwood Farm. Leaving Hampshire for Sussex, the Forty Acre Lane undulates gently before passing above South Harting.

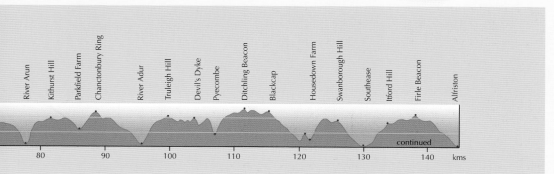

Walking, cycling and horse-riding on the route through the Queen Elizabeth Country Park

Anyone detouring off-route down to the village for accommodation, food and drink would be advised, for safety, to use paths running parallel to the busy road.

Day 3 South Harting to
Amberley Station
30km (18½ miles)

Harting Down is a broad area of rough grassland offering fine views northwards across low-lying countryside, as well as southwards to Portsmouth, the Solent and Isle of Wight. The South Downs Way skirts around Beacon Hill, rather than climbing over the 242m (794ft) summit. Similarly, the route skirts around Treyford Hill, then a clear track follows the rolling crest of the downs, which are well cultivated, over Linch Down at 248m (814ft). The track drops downhill, passing a conspicuous lump of chalk, to cross a busy road above the village of Cocking.

Another clear track climbs up Manorfarm Down, then as the cultivated swathe along the crest of the downs is pinched out, the track continues through Charlton Forest and eventually emerges into fields again on Graffham Down. Apart from Tegleaze Farm, there are no habitations along this stretch until the route drops downhill to pass Littleton Farm and cross another busy road. Climbing again, a fine chalk track crosses Sutton Down at 242m (794ft) and reaches a staggered intersection of tracks. One of the tracks is Stane Street, an old Roman road equipped with a modern signpost pointing to *Londinium* and *Noviomagus* (London and Chichester). The National Trust's Gumber bothy is a handy bunk-barn lying off-route.

Take a clear track over Bignor Hill at 226m (741ft), then zigzag down a wooded slope. Follow a track over Westburton Hill and cross a road high above the village of Bury. Walk alongside Coombe Wood and descend close to the village of Houghton. Accommodation can be found in either Bury or Houghton, before the route follows field paths and crosses the River Arun. As there is a railway station near the Bridge Inn, there is an opportunity to leave the route for Arundel if desired. An interesting industrial museum is situated in an old quarry, while Amberley Castle is a prominent feature nearby.

Day 4 Amberley Station to Truleigh Hill
22.5km (14 miles)

A short, steep climb up Amberley Mount reveals a widening prospect across the lowlands, and a clear path and track leads over Rackham Hill at 193m (633ft). Enjoy striding easily along the high crest of the downs, touching 200m (655ft) on Kithurst Hill, Sullington Hill and Barnsfarm Hill. A clear track runs down to Parkfield Farm, where there is a particularly busy dual carriageway to cross. Horse riders should descend from Barnsfarm Hill to the village of Washington to avoid this crossing, then follow a quiet road back onto the South Downs to continue.

Another good track leads uphill, and a left turn reveals a gently graded track passing Chanctonbury Ring around 230m (755ft). This is another hilltop enclosed by a defensive earthen rampart, made more prominent because of the beech trees that grow all around it. Keep to the track, which stays more or less on the crest of the downs, then walk alongside a road high above the little town of Steyning. Watch for the path running along the brow of Annington Hill and drop down onto tracks around Annington Farm. Cross a bridge over the River Adur, followed by a busy road, then climb up onto the slopes of Beeding Hill and follow a road to Truleigh Hill youth hostel, where it is possible to stay high on the downs at 200m (655ft).

Day 5 Truleigh Hill to Southease Station
31.5km (19½ miles)

This is a long day's walk, but anyone staying at Truleigh Hill is already high on the downs and can make an early start to continue eastwards. Good tracks and paths run over Edburton Hill, Perching Hill and Fulking Hill to reach Devil's Dyke, where an Iron Age hill fort now encloses a modern restaurant. Walk downhill along a bushy, wooded slope to reach the little settlement of Saddlescombe.

Bushes blossom beside the South Downs Way on the slopes of Westburton Hill (Day 3)

Follow paths over West Hill, or Newtimber Hill, and drop down to Pyecombe. Cross a bridge over a very busy road, then either take a break at the Plough Inn, or continue along the South Downs Way as it climbs alongside a golf course. Just off-route, and worthy of a detour, are the Clayton Windmills, known as Jack Mill and Jill Mill. The route runs along the crest of the downs to reach the notable viewpoint of Ditchling Beacon at 248m (814ft). The North Downs, and hence the North Downs Way, is often in view.

Cross a road, where there might be an ice-cream van, then stay on the high downs over Western Brow, Streat Hill and Plumpton Plain. Just before reaching 206m (676ft) Blackcap, turn sharp right and follow a rather muddy track downhill.

Switch to a much cleaner line down Balmer Down, then watch for a right turn to cross a valley and drop down to Housedown Farm. Cross a bridge over yet another very busy road and climb towards Newmarket Hill, swinging left to touch 200m (655ft) on the track called Jugg's Road. Stay high on the downs, first on rough-grazed grasslands, then on more cultivated land over Swanborough Hill. A clear track runs downhill, then paths over Mill Hill pass a house before dropping down a steeper slope. Follow a track to Southease, which has an interesting little church, and cross a bridge over the River Ouse to reach Southease Station, which allows easy access off-route.

A steep-sided grassy valley near the notable viewpoint of Devil's Dyke

Day 6 Southease Station to Eastbourne
32km (20 miles)

The last day's walk may seem long, but it can be broken at Alfriston if desired. Start by crossing a

bridge over a busy road, then climb along a good track and path onto the steep slopes of Itford Hill. The whole morning is spent high on the downs, walking through rough, flowery grasslands offering splendid views in all directions. Cross

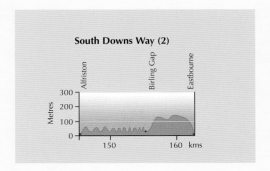

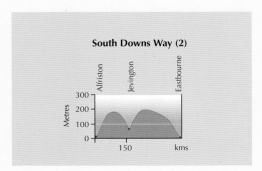

Walkers on the cliffs of Beachy Head, high above the candy-striped lighthouse

Beddingham Hill and enjoy striding along the gently rolling crest to 217m (712ft) at Firle Beacon. Cross over Bostal Hill and link with a clear track that leads down to Alfriston. The village is charming and features many fine old buildings, as well as being one of the few places actually on the South Downs Way offering all facilities.

There are two ways to proceed to Eastbourne. Walkers can choose either way, but horse riders and cyclists must stay inland on a slightly shorter bridleway route.

The **bridleway** route climbs onto Windover Hill, which overlooks the celebrated hillside chalk carving of the Long Man of Wilmington. After making its way down to the lovely little village of Jevington, the route follows a fine track over Willingdon Hill and traverses the top of a wooded brow, passing wind-blasted trees to reach a golf course. After crossing a busy road, a descent along a wooded spur takes the route to a conclusion on the outskirts of Eastbourne.

The **footpath** route runs alongside the Cuckmere river to the village of Litlington, then links field paths and forest paths to reach an interesting visitor centre for the Seven Sisters Country Park. Cross Exceat Hill and descend to the marshes alongside the Cuckmere. After that, one of the most delightful and challenging stretches of the South Downs Way takes a roller-coaster route over the Seven Sisters, the seven prominent chalk cliffs overlooking the English Channel.

After a break at Birling Gap, the coastal path climbs past an old lighthouse at Belle Tout, which was moved back from the cliff, stone by stone, in 1999. Traverse the cliffs of Beachy Head high above a red-and-white candy-striped lighthouse.

All that remains is to follow paths along a high brow, before descending to the Wish Tower on the outskirts of Eastbourne to finish. (Of course, there is nothing to stop keen walkers doubling back along the inland bridleway to finish back in the village of Alfriston!)

INFORMATION

Access to Start	Virgin Trains 'Wessex Scot' serves Winchester from as far away as Edinburgh and there are plenty more trains and buses.
Getting Home	There are plenty of trains and buses away from Eastbourne.
Other Public Transport	The trail is crossed by several useful rail and bus services, and details are contained in a leaflet available from TICs.
Maps	OS 1:50,000 Landrangers 185, 197, 198 and 199
	OS 1:25,000 Explorers 120, 121, 122, 123 and 132
	Harveys 1:40,000 South Downs Way
Cicerone Guide	*The South Downs Way*, by Kev Reynolds
Other Guidebooks	*South Downs Way*, by Paul Millmore, Aurum Press
	Along the South Downs Way, by Harry Comber, South Downs Society
Tourist Information Centres	Winchester tel 01962 840500, Petersfield tel 01730 268829, Chichester tel 01243 775888, Arundel tel 01903 882268, Lewes tel 01273 897426, Brighton tel 09067 112255, Eastbourne tel 09067 112212.
Accommodation List	*South Downs Way Accommodation Guide*, from TICs
Path Association	South Downs Society www.sussexdownsmen.org.uk
Website	www.nationaltrail.co.uk/Southdown

A woodland path fringed with garlic-scented ramsons high on Box Hill in Surrey (Day 3)

3 North Downs Way

Start and Finish	Farnham to Dover
Distance and Time	193–245km (120–152 miles) taking 9 to 11 days
Character	An intricate trail that weaves through wooded and open downs, generally avoiding towns and villages, sometimes running high on the downs and sometimes along the foot of the downs, through fields and orchards.
Highlights	St Martha's Hill, the well-wooded Surrey Hills, Box Hill to Reigate Hill, Otford Mount, Trosley Country Park to Coldrum Long Barrow, Kit's Coty, Detling to Hollingbourne, the Pilgrim's Way to Westwell, Chilham, Canterbury, Wye Downs to Folkestone, White Cliffs of Dover.

An old flint-built church on the North Downs Way in the village of Womenswold (Day 9a)

The original intention was to re-dedicate the long-established Pilgrim's Way from Winchester to Canterbury as a trail for modern-day walkers. It was to be a celebration of the old pilgrim trail, with wayfarers tracing the same shuffling steps as Geoffrey Chaucer, the Pardoner, the Nun's Priest, the Knight, the Wife of Bath, the Miller, and the rest of the 'nine and twenty in a company of sundry folk' earnest on reaching the shrine of St Thomas à Becket at Canterbury. Good intentions, but much of the old pilgrim trail had long been buried beneath the burgeoning road systems of Surrey and Kent. Alternative routes were sought in the surrounding countryside, with the best paths and tracks found at a higher level on the North Downs. As the trail was blazed, it became less of a 'Pilgrim's Way' and more of a 'North Downs Way'. Farnham replaced Winchester as a starting point, but in deference to the original intention, in 1978 the trail was declared open by Dr Donald Coggan, then Archbishop of Canterbury. To this day, most people living along the route refer to it as the Pilgrim's Way, and some claim never to have heard of the North Downs Way!

The prominent south-facing chalk escarpment of the North Downs lies close to the great urban sprawl of London, straddling the 'Surrey stockbroker belt' and more rural Kent, often referred to as the 'garden of England'. The well-wooded Surrey Hills and the open Kent Downs have both been designated areas of outstanding natural beauty and are well used by walkers. While some parts are densely populated and crisscrossed with busy

Day	Start/Finish	Km	Miles
Day 1	Farnham to Guildford	17	10½
Day 2	Guildford to Ranmore Common	18	11
Day 3	Ranmore Common to Godstone	27	17
Day 4	Godstone to Otford	22	13½
Day 5	Otford to Borstal	29	18
Day 6	Borstal to Lenham	24	15
Day 7	Lenham to Boughton Lees	15	9½
Day 8a	Boughton Lees to Canterbury	20	12½
Day 8b	Boughton Lees to Etchinghill	22	13½
Day 9a	Canterbury to Dover	32	20
Day 9b	Etchinghill to Dover	19	12

roads and motorways, wayfarers are led on a meandering course that

strives to make the most of the woods, fields and open downs that remain. The route wriggles through an intricate landscape of greens and earthy tones that constantly change colour with the seasons and needs of agriculture. Towns and villages are often avoided, so detours may be required to obtain food, drink or lodgings. Indeed, detours are to be encouraged, as some nearby settlements are long established and have interesting and intriguing histories.

Many stretches of the North Downs Way are used much more by strollers, dog walkers and day walkers than by long-distance walkers. Those who walk all day and every day along the whole trail must climb onto the downs and descend from them over and over again, sometimes on steep

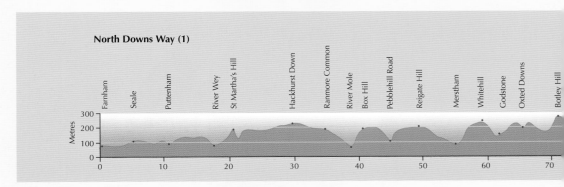

paths that might be muddy and slippery in wet weather. However, the trail generally runs at gentle gradients and is often good underfoot. Hostels and campsites are rare, so most wayfarers use bed-and-breakfast accommodation. While the North Downs Way lies close to London and is within easy commuting distance, it also lies just outside the areas that attract the best discount fares for residents. The full distance from Farnham is quoted as 245km (152 miles), but as the trail ends in an

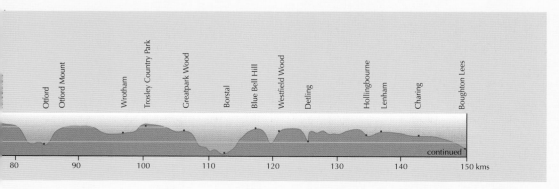

enormous loop, with a choice of routes to Dover, most wayfarers will cover 193–204km (120–127 miles). Keen walkers can cover the full distance by completing the loop to finish back at Boughton Lees.

Day 1 Farnham to Guildford
17km (10½ miles)

Walkers in ages past would have followed the broad crest of the Hog's Back away from Farnham, but the busy A31 runs that way today. The North Downs Way takes a meandering course through low-lying countryside, wandering alongside the River Wye, through woods and fields, to pass a golf course on Furze Hill. A detour into the village of Seale offers the chance for a tea break. The next village along the route is Puttenham, with a pub, camping barn and an old church. A soft and sandy track leads over the wooded rise of Puttenham Heath, then walkers pass beneath the

busy A3. Large crosses erected on the bridge remind motorists of the pilgrim traffic beneath.

The Watts Gallery offers another opportunity for a tea break, then another soft and sandy track, called Sandy Lane, leads onwards. Look at sign-posts along the way, as well as the names of houses alongside, spotting several references to the Pilgrim's Way. A pub is reached on a busy road on the outskirts of Guildford, and this may be far enough for the first day, though strong walkers may wish to continue further. Guildford is well worth considering for an overnight stop. Its Great Tower is a Norman castle keep in attractive grounds. The 16th-century Guildhall has an ornate bracket clock poking well into the High Street, while 17th-century Abbots Hospital stands further uphill. The cathedral is quite modern, being mid-20th century.

Day 2 Guildford to Ranmore Common
18km (11 miles)

The North Downs Way passes St Catherine's Hill, crowned with the ruins of an ancient chapel once frequented by pilgrims. After crossing a footbridge over the River Wey, the route climbs gently along-side a forest at Chantries, then follows a sandy track to the top of St Martha's Hill at 175m (574ft), where another prominent chapel can be inspected. After dropping downhill, the trail shifts from sand-stone to the chalk escarpment of the North Downs proper, following the wooded crest to a busy café at Newlands Corner.

  For the rest of the day, the route is more or less confined to woods and forests, following a clear and almost level track called the Drove Road. This wanders along the wooded top of the downs, occasionally above 200m (655ft), then later a meandering path runs along the brow with occa-sional views across the lowlands. Blatchford Down was named after Alan Blatchford, a founder mem-ber of the Long Distance Walkers' Association. Keep an eye on markers at all path junctions to ensure that you stay on the North Downs Way throughout. The final stretch to Ranmore Common is fairly obvious, and the church of St Barnabas, styled 'the church of the North Downs Way', is a very clear landmark. The simple Tanners Hatch

youth hostel, often used by walkers following the North Downs Way, is signposted off-route.

Day 3 Ranmore Common to Godstone
27km (17 miles)

A descent from the downs passes through Denbies Winery, where vines adorn a south-facing slope. Detour to a subway to cross a busy road, then either cross a footbridge or stepping stones, depending on the amount of water in the River Mole. A steep flight of steps leads onto Box Hill, where yew trees are much more common than box. A stone viewpoint at 172m (564ft) reveals a fine prospect – beyond Dorking and the well-wooded Weald, to the distant South Downs. Traverse around

the slopes above the Brockham Lime Works, which were closed in 1936 and are now being reclaimed by nature.

A good stretch of the Pilgrim's Way is followed along the foot of the downs, often between the wooded escarpment and the gentler, cultivated fields. There are also fine areas of flowery chalk grassland before the route climbs Juniper Hill, again wandering past yew trees. The Reigate Hill Temple, supported on stone columns, dates from 1909 and is a curious structure on an open, grassy part of the downs. Crossing Reigate Hill there are extensive views from around 230m (755ft), stretching north to London. The route later crosses

A field path climbs over a gentle rise on the way to the village of Otford

a footbridge over a busy road and reaches a car park where there is a café.

The route drops from the downs and passes through extensive parklands at Gatton. Here, a modern stone circle features upright slabs inscribed with a selection of famous and thought-provoking quotes. After crossing a golf course on the way down to Merstham, the route crosses the M25 motorway, then later passes beneath the M23, not far from a complex junction of both of them. The roar of road traffic is a constant feature of the day's walk, even when the route climbs back onto the downs and passes Hilltop Farm. A clear track touches 230m (755ft), then a road leads past Whitehill Tower. Good paths meander across a wooded slope, occasionally overlooking a busy motorway junction. Godstone is located on the other side of the junction, and careful map reading reveals safe footpaths to and from the village.

Day 4 Godstone to Otford
22km (13½ miles)

The Godstone Vineyard is passed as the North Downs Way climbs across the slopes of Winders Hill, and for some time the route rises and falls across wooded and open slopes, with a view of a railway vanishing into a tunnel beneath the downs. Pass below a prominent quarry and enjoy the flowery slopes of Oxted Downs. The route suddenly climbs from the bottom to the top of the downs, passing a variety of trees in Titsey Plantation before emerging at over 260m (855ft) near Botley Hill Farmhouse, which offers food and drink.

A network of woodland walks could cause confusion, so keep an eye on the course of the North Downs Way, linking woods, open downs and fields to proceed to Betsom's Hill. The route passes from Surrey into Kent and stays high on the downs, often above 230m (755ft), only occasionally passing farm buildings, and staying well away from the village of Knockholt Pound. After negotiating fields and woods, the route suddenly drops downhill in sight of Chevening House and crosses the M25 motorway. Pass timbered, 15th-century Donnington Manor, now attached to an incongruous modern extension. A short walk over a low hill leads to the bustling village of Otford, built on both sides of the River Darent, with a good range of services. Thomas à Becket, whose name is forever associated with the Pilgrim's Way, lived here.

Day 5 Otford to Borstal
29km (18 miles)

Climb straight uphill from Otford onto the ambitiously named Otford Mount, and pass Otford Manor high above Kemsing. The route is generally over 200m (655ft), but there is a sudden descent to the foot of the downs. A fine stretch of the Pilgrim's Way is followed, rather like walking through a tunnel of trees. Pass the village of Wrotham and cross the M20 motorway, then walk along a road to pass a house called Chaucers. Climb up a wooded slope to reach Trosley Country Park ('Trosley' being the correct pronunciation of nearby Trottiscliffe). A small café is available at a visitor centre.

A broad path leads through the Great Wood, then there is a descent to follow another stretch of the Pilgrim's Way as it makes a tunnel through the trees. It is also worth making a diversion down to Coldrum Long Barrow to see the remains of a 4000-year-old burial chamber. Climb back onto the downs at Holly Hill, around 170m (555ft), then walk through woods, taking great care with the route at a number of junctions of paths and tracks. There are flowery grasslands in these woods, then later the trail crosses a valley containing an old landscaped chalk pit. Cross another valley to reach some attractive timbered houses at Upper Bush, before crossing a field to Cuxton.

Take care with route finding above the village. It is important to follow field paths and farm tracks, then stay on the correct side of busy roads,

in order to be drawn properly onto the Medway Bridge. Although this bridge carries the M2 motorway, there is also a lane for cyclists and pedestrians. There is a good view of Rochester and its castle, though these places are off-route. The North Downs Way only briefly runs alongside the suburb of Borstal. There is food, drink and accommodation here, as well as regular buses into Rochester.

Day 6 Borstal to Lenham
24km (15 miles)

After climbing from Borstal and Nashenden Farm, follow a road over Burham Common, reaching a viewpoint at 182m (597ft) on Blue Bell Hill. Drop downhill and pass the remarkable burial chamber of Kit's Coty, with its massive capstone, then walk beneath the busy A229. Climb steps up a steep, wooded slope, passing the White Horse Stone, emerging at 191m (627ft) in the fields on top of the downs. Stay high on the downs, passing only the buildings at Harp Farm, until the route is signposted down through woods to the village of Detling. Use Jade's Crossing, a footbridge funded by local people following fatalities on the busy A249 (please leave a donation to help cover the cost of the bridge). The Pilgrim's Way runs through Detling, but the North Downs Way climbs back onto the downs, traversing some splendid flowery slopes. The route becomes a roller coaster as it crosses a succession of little valleys, but in due course it makes a sudden descent to Hollingbourne.

There is a pub at Hollingbourne, and also a marked change of theme. The North Downs Way now fulfils its original intention by following a considerable length of the Pilgrim's Way. Although tarmac at first, the route becomes a fine, clear track running through fields at the foot of the downs. Another stretch of tarmac has to be followed past the Marley Works, then the track continues. If seeking accommodation or other

A view from the North Downs above the village of Detling in Kent

services at Lenham, the village is easily reached using a couple of roads or a handful of paths.

Day 7 Lenham to Boughton Lees
15km (9½ miles)

This short day's walk is entirely along the Pilgrim's Way, and it starts by passing a war memorial at the foot of the downs. The route proceeds as a clear track through fields, linking with a tarmac road. After passing Highbourne Park, Cobham Farm and Hart Hill, the route reaches the village of Charing, which has some fine timbered buildings and a full range of services. Follow a road onwards and the Pilgrim's Way again becomes a clear track at the foot of the wooded Westwell Downs. The village of Westwell is off-route, while Eastwell House sits in fine parkland. Pass close to derelict St Mary's Church, overlooking Eastwell Lake, then later pass

close to the Eastwell Manor Hotel. The trail, which is signposted in this area as part of the trans-European E2, leads into the little village of Boughton Lees, neatly arranged around a triangular green featuring a cricket ground. At this point wayfarers are faced with a choice of routes leading to Dover: either (a) via the city of Canterbury, or (b) a slightly more direct route via Folkestone.

Day 8a Boughton Lees to Canterbury
20km (12½ miles)

Leave Boughton Lees and walk across fields to Boughton Aluph and beyond. The route climbs to 157m (515ft) on Soakham Downs, running through woods where the tracks can be rather muddy. Eventually, walk down Mountain Street and head for the village of Chilham. This is a splendid estate village revealing old and interesting buildings at every turn. Walk through the church-yard to leave, then follow roads to the village of Old Wives Lees. The route runs through orchards of apples and pears, as well as passing hop 'gardens' on the way to the village of Chartham Hatch.

The curiously named No Man's Orchard has been preserved for public enjoyment as a traditional orchard in the middle of a wood. Cross a bridge over the busy A2 and pass through one final orchard to reach Harbledown. This is on the outskirts of Canterbury, and roads have to be followed all the way into the city centre. As the River Stour is crossed, stout stone Westgate guards the entrance to the old part of the city, which is a world heritage site. Canterbury is usually very busy with tourists and has abundant features of interest, but most will find themselves drawn, as were pilgrims of old, into the cathedral, where you can pause for a moment of reflection on the spot where Thomas à Becket was slain. (Without his death there would be no Pilgrim's Way, and without the Pilgrim's Way there would be no North Downs Way, and you wouldn't be reading about it in this book!)

Day 8b Boughton Lees to Etchinghill
22km (13½ miles)

Walk through orchards and fields from Boughton Lees to the nearby larger village of Wye. Climb straight towards Wye Crown on the Wye Downs,

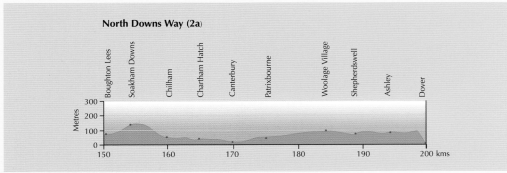

North Downs Way (2a)

The steep-sided grassy valley known as the Devil's Kneading Trough near Wye

around 170m (555ft). The route stays high on the downs, later overlooking a steep-sided grassy valley known as the Devil's Kneading Trough. Stay high to pass Cold Blow, following field paths, tracks and roads over the Brabourne Downs, well away from the village of Hastingleigh. Drop downhill and follow roads through the scattered village of Stowting, passing the Tiger Inn.

Climb steeply up Cobb's Hill and walk alongside a road, then follow a series of paths, rather like a roller coaster, as the route drops into little valleys and climbs up the other sides, narrowly missing the village of Postling. The route skirts a military training area, passing a prominent communication mast, then runs so close to the village of Etchinghill that it requires only a short detour to enter it. Nearby Lyminge has more facilities if required.

Day 9a Canterbury to Dover
32km (20 miles)

Pass the ruins of St Augustine's Abbey on the way out of Canterbury. The Pilgrim's Way is a narrow road running through fields to Patrixbourne and its church. Paths and tracks lead through large fields over Barham Downs, around 100m (330ft). Pass through the villages of Womenswold, which has an attractive church, and Woolage. Shepherdswell, also known as Sibbertwold, offers accommodation, food, drink – and a light steam railway.

Leave Shepherdswell and take a little more care over route finding – there are some fiddly field paths on the way past Waldershare House and a lone chapel to reach Ashley. On leaving Ashley the course of an old Roman road is joined and this leads directly southwards towards

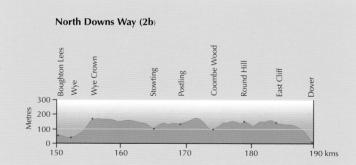

North Downs Way (2b)

Boughton Lees · Wye · Wye Crown · Stowting · Postling · Coombe Wood · Round Hill · East Cliff · Dover

Metres
300
200
100
0
150   160   170   180   190 kms

Chalk cliffs above Samphire Hoe Country Park between Folkestone and Dover

Dover, apart from a lengthy detour to find a bridge over the busy A2. The final descent to Dover is along roads, with a short stretch through Connaught Park. Aim for the town centre, which may be rather shabby, but is rich in history and heritage, having suffered centuries of warfare and military development.

Day 9b Etchinghill to Dover
19km (12 miles)

Drop down from Etchinghill to Combe Wood, then climb up through a grassy valley to reach the top of the downs, around 170m (555ft). The trail turns

a significant corner at Peene Quarry and could be regarded as coastal from this point, although it remains high above the sea all day long. There are fine views of the entrance to the Channel Tunnel – one of the world's greatest engineering accomplishments. Even on a clear day France looks remarkably distant across the English Channel.

Pass Caesar's Camp on Castle Hill, then cross Round Hill before walking alongside a road over Wingate Hill, always with views down to Folkestone. Pass the Battle of Britain memorial, where a couple of Spitfires can be inspected. The Cliff Top Café naturally offers splendid views from its terrace, while the rugged, wooded slopes of the Warren fall to the sea. Later, after walking along

Abbott's Cliff, there are views down onto Samphire Hoe Country Park, made of rubble brought out of the Channel Tunnel. After walking along Shakespeare Cliff, the last of the 'white cliffs of Dover', all that remains to finish is to head inland to the town centre via the Western Heights.

For the Romans this town was *Dubris,* and was enclosed by a wall. The remarkable remains of the Painted House are a reminder of their time here. Dover Castle's curtain wall, drum towers and tall keep form the last of a series of fortifications built throughout the ages on the headland, and there are Napoleonic fortifications and other batteries around the town. The White Cliffs Experience helps the visitor to unravel the complexities of Dover's history.

INFORMATION

Access to Start	Plenty of trains and buses serve Farnham.
Getting Home	Plenty of trains and buses leave Dover, as well as ferries to France and access to the nearby Channel Tunnel.
Other Public Transport	The trail is crossed by several fast and frequent rail services, allowing commuters to get to and from London. There are also plenty of buses and many services link towns and villages near the trail.
Maps	OS 1:50,000 Landrangers 178, 179, 186, 187, 188 and 189
	OS 1:25,000 Explorers 137, 138, 145, 146, 147, 148, 149 and 150
	Harveys 1:40,000 North Downs Way West and North Downs Way East.
Cicerone Guide	*North Downs Way*, by Kev Reynolds
Other Guidebooks	*North Downs Way*, by Neil Curtis, Aurum Press
Tourist Information Centres	Farnham tel 01252 715109, Guildford tel 01483 444333, Dorking tel 01306 879327, Sevenoaks tel 01732 450305, Maidstone tel 01622 602169, Ashford tel 01233 629165, Rochester tel 01634 843666, Canterbury tel 01227 378100, Dover tel 01304 205108, Folkestone tel 01303 258594
Accommodation List	*North Downs Way Accommodation Guide*, from TICs
Website	www.nationaltrail.co.uk/Northdowns

Ivinghoe Beacon is seen in the distance towards the end of the Ridgeway (Day 6)

4 The Ridgeway

Start and Finish	Overton Hill to Ivinghoe Beacon
Distance and Time	139km (87 miles) taking up to 1 week
Character	Half the trail is a broad and obvious track that crosses open, rolling downs, while the other half is a more intricate route using paths and tracks, featuring several ascents and descents, with more woodland cover.
Highlights	Avebury Stone Circle near the start, the open downs and their ancient hill forts, Goring and the River Thames, Grim's Ditch, the Icknield Way, Coombe Hill, Wendover, Ivinghoe Beacon.

Just off-route, the Avenue is a line of stones leading from Avebury to the Ridgeway

The Ridgeway has been called 'the oldest road in Britain', having been tramped by travellers and traders for over 5000 years. Striding over the Marlborough Downs, passing ancient monuments, one feels a connection with those who came this way a long time ago. Bronze Age traders used it while travelling from Dorset to Norfolk, coast to coast through southern England. The rolling green downs are scored, pitted and pockmarked with long-forgotten structures, while in recent years bizarre 'crop circles' have appeared mysteriously and mischievously overnight. This is very much a ritual landscape, where Neolithic and Bronze Age peoples raised monuments, such as the enormous Avebury Stone Circle and Silbury Hill, that were intended to stand out from the natural landscape. Iron Age settlers stationed themselves in defensive hill forts at intervals along the crest of the downs, suggesting that periods of strife were common.

The Ridgeway is a half-and-half trail. The western half runs along the crest of the downs from Wiltshire into Oxfordshire, through an area designated as the North Wessex Downs Area of Outstanding Natural Beauty. For the most part the trail is a broad track that can, subject to seasonal restrictions, be used by any form of traffic. Walkers may meet cyclists, horse riders, motorcyclists and four-wheel-drive vehicles. However, vehicle access is limited to the summer months, and even then is not particularly common. In the past, when vehicles used it summer and winter in considerably greater numbers, some parts were churned up into appalling mud baths, and have since been resurfaced. The eastern half, by contrast, is largely along footpaths and bridleways, and seldom along

	SCHEDULE		
Day	**Start/Finish**	**Km**	**Miles**
Day 1	Overton Hill to Ogbourne St George	15	9½
Day 2	Ogbourne St George to Ridgeway Centre	31.5	19½
Day 3	Ridgeway Centre to Goring	22.5	14
Day 4	Goring to Watlington	24	15
Day 5	Watlington to Wendover	27	17
Day 6	Wendover to Ivinghoe Beacon	19	12

tracks used by vehicles. It includes the ancient linear earthwork of Grim's Ditch, as well as stretches of the low-lying Icknield Way. The eastern stretches run through the Chiltern Hills, also protected as an area of outstanding natural beauty. The route is sometimes high on the hills and sometimes at the foot of the hills, passing farms and fields as well as woodlands and open downlands.

Day 1 Overton Hill to Ogbourne St George
15km (9½ miles)

The Ridgeway National Trail starts at Overton Hill, but visitors should feel compelled to start at the unique village of Avebury. It is surrounded by a huge and complex stone circle, with associated ditches and earth embankments, constructed over 4000 years ago. Protected as a world heritage site, a walk around the circle makes a fine start to the day, and there is a museum in the Great Barn.

Parallel lines of stones known as the Avenue can be inspected on the way to Overton Hill, adding 3km (2 miles) to the day's walk. The stone Avenue is thought to have linked

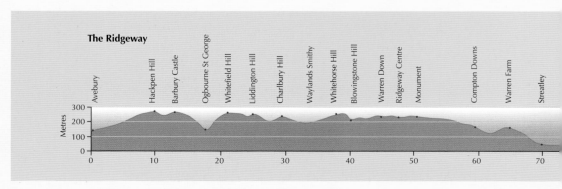

Avebury with the Sanctuary at Overton Hill, another ancient ritual site, and where the Ridgeway actually starts.

A grassy, rutted track climbs gently onto Overton Down. The Grey Wethers are the lumpy grey 'sarsen' stones scattered around the fields on the right, some of which were manhandled downhill to build the Avebury stone circle. The rutted track has been resurfaced as it continues along the crest of the downs to Hackpen Hill. Hidden from sight on the slope dropping north-west is a 'white horse',

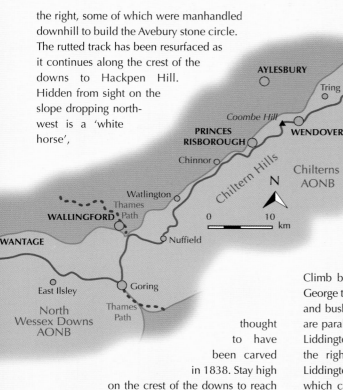

the trail to feature steep slopes on both sides. On the descent at the end of the day, either walk into Ogbourne St George for food, drink and accommoda-tion, or stay faithful to the route a short distance from the village to pass the hamlet of Hallam.

Day 2 Ogbourne St George to Ridgeway Centre
31.5km (19½ miles)

Climb back onto the downs above Ogbourne St George to follow a clear track often flanked by trees and bushes. Some parts may be muddy, but there are parallel paths for walkers. On the approach to Liddington Hill vehicles are required to branch to the right, while walkers keep straight ahead. Liddington Castle is another Iron Age hill fort, which can be reached by making a short detour from the route to a viewing platform at 277m (909ft). A track leads downhill, but a road has to be followed across the busy M4 motorway, then the Shepherd's Rest pub is found at a crossroads.

thought to have been carved in 1838. Stay high on the crest of the downs to reach the rumpled earth ramparts surrounding Barbury Castle at 266m (873ft). This Iron Age hill fort enjoys commanding views over the Marlborough Downs and Swindon. Further along the trail is the Castle Café at Ridgeway Farm, offer-ing food and drink. A grassy track runs along well-defined Smeathe's Ridge, which is the only part of

The Ridgeway climbs back onto the downs via Charlbury Hill, passing close to ancient Celtic field systems near Idstone Barn on the way into Oxfordshire. Cross a road on Ashbury Hill and follow a muddy track to Wayland's Smithy, which is a burial chamber of astonishing size. The track leads onwards and passes close to Uffington Castle, another Iron Age hill fort at 261m (856ft),

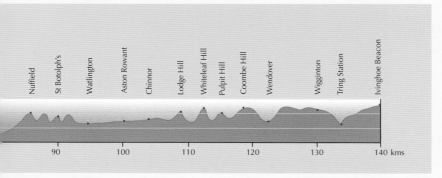

The Ridgeway is a broad, bright, chalk track as it leaves Uffington Castle (Day 2)

and well worth a detour, with splendid views and a most peculiarly shaped 'white horse' carved into its scarp slope, best seen from nearby Dragon's Hill. The broad chalk track continues over Blowingstone Hill, and later looks into the steep-sided valley called the Devil's Punchbowl. One final Iron Age hill fort can be inspected at Letcombe Castle before the trail reaches a main road. The Ridgeway Centre youth hostel is just downhill, with the bustling town of Wantage further to the north.

Day 3   Ridgeway Centre to Goring
22.5km (14 miles)

Be sure to study the displays about the Ridgeway at the youth hostel before leaving, then rejoin the trail on the crest of the downs. Multiple parallel tracks exploit a broad and grassy swathe over the downs, passing the slender stone column of the Wantage Monument. The route runs at over 200m (655ft) and occasionally passes horse gallops on the adjoining fields. After crossing a road on Bury Down the trail uses an underpass to go beneath the busy A34. Take care over route finding, as there are several track junctions that need negotiating over Compton Downs and Lowbury Hill. The Romans chose the latter hill as the site for a temple. On the descent from Warren Farm a clear track and road lead to the village of Streatley. Lodgings and refreshments can be found here as well as at Goring on the other side of the River Thames, on the lowest part of the trail at 50m (165ft). Note how the Ridgeway briefly rubs shoulders with the Thames Path National Trail, overlooking Goring Lock.

The chalk track of the Ridgeway snakes along the crest of the downs high above Wantage (Day 3)

Day 4 Goring to Watlington
24km (15 miles)

Watch for a 'Ridgeway' signpost to leave Goring, then follow tracks and paths through the villages of South Stoke and North Stoke, catching brief glimpses of the River Thames. The Thames Path, meanwhile, follows the opposite bank of the river to Wallingford. The Ridgeway suddenly heads due east, following the ancient earthwork known as Grim's Ditch. Trees, bushes and nettles grow wild along the embankment, forming a wilderness corridor across cultivated fields. No one knows the true age and purpose of the ditch, but it is most likely to be a Dark Ages territorial marker. After climbing through beech woods the route leaves Grim's Ditch for Nuffield and its ancient church.

Cross a valley and climb to the attractive buildings at Ewelme Park, then descend steeply on a wooded slope to Swyncombe House to reach another long-established church – St Botolph's. The trail takes an undulating course, climbing over 200m (655ft) on Swyncombe Downs, then drops down to North Farm and the Icknield Way. A fine stretch of the Icknield Way, an ancient trackway along the foot of the Chilterns, is followed onwards. It can be muddy in places and is open to all forms of traffic in the summer, but there is a parallel path for walkers on some parts. As the trail passes close to Watlington it is easy to detour into the town to make use of its services.

The Icknield Way runs across the foot of Beacon Hill, which is protected as a nature reserve

Day 5   Watlington to Wendover
27km (17 miles)

Once having encountered the Icknield Way, walkers follow it further along the foot of the Chiltern slope. Some stretches may be muddy and rutted, and the old track is often flanked by trees and bushes. There are views of the wooded downs, which later rise steeply from the track on Shirburn Hill. An underpass takes the route beneath the M40 motorway, then the Aston Rowant National Nature Reserve is passed on the slopes of Beacon Hill. Continue along a broad, grassy track flanked by fields, then walk along a sort of ridge between two large, deep quarries near Chinnor. If a detour into the village isn't required, then follow the rutted track round the wooded slopes of Wain Hill, popping out into fields, then aiming for wooded,

bald-topped Lodge Hill. The summit is crossed at 211m (692ft) before field paths and roads lead to the outskirts of Princes Risborough, and another good stretch of the Icknield Way.

For the second half of the day the Ridgeway climbs high into the Chilterns, then becomes a roller-coaster route over Brush Hill, Whiteleaf Hill and Pulpit Hill, mostly wandering along paths through beech woods. Cross the access road near the prime minister's country retreat, Chequers (noting that every step is being watched by security cameras, so do not attempt to approach the house!). Climb back into woods and eventually emerge at a prominent monument on Coombe Hill at 257m (843ft). Enjoy extensive views northwards across the lowlands, then follow a path due east down a wooded slope and walk straight into the centre of Wendover, a most charming little town with a 14th-century church and several notable buildings.

Day 6 Wendover to Ivinghoe Beacon
19km (12 miles)

Leave Wendover by way of the parish church and follow a road to Boswell's Farm, from where a well-made path climbs into woods. Keep high on the wooded brow of the Chilterns and pass through near-level fields touching 250m (820ft). The little settlement of Hastoe is followed by the village of Wigginton. Keep to the edge of a woodland in Tring Park and cross a footbridge over the busy A41. Other bridges cross the Grand Union Canal and the railway at Tring station, where there is a little café.

Pass farm buildings above Tring station and cut across a chalk down to enter a beech hangar, then continue along the top of delightfully grassy downs on Pitstone Hill, featuring extensive views. Cross a road and climb higher along a fine path, eventually reaching a trig point at 230m (755ft) on Ivinghoe Beacon. Take a last long look at the view, as well as looking back along the course of the Ridgeway. Although the trail ends at this point, it is obviously necessary to walk down from the hill, at least to the road at the bottom. A short walk down the road leads to the village of Ivinghoe, which has an adequate range of services, and regular buses to Luton or Tring for onward connections.

INFORMATION	
Access to Start	Buses serve Avebury regularly from Swindon, which has plenty of rail and bus services. It is worth walking from Avebury to Overton Hill.
Getting Home	Walk to the village of Ivinghoe, which has regular buses to Luton, where plenty of onward rail and bus connections are available.
Other Public Transport	Buses and/or trains are easily accessed from a number of places on or near the Ridgeway, including Wantage, Goring, Wallingford, Watlington, Chinnor, Princes Risborough, Wendover and Tring.
Maps	OS 1:50,000 Landrangers 165, 173, 174 and 175
	OS 1:25,000 Explorers 157, 170, 171 and 181
	Harveys 1:40,000 The Ridgeway
Cicerone Guide	*The Greater Ridgeway*, by Ray Quinlan
Other Guidebooks	*The Ridgeway*, by Anthony Burton, Aurum Press
Tourist Information Centres	Swindon tel 01793 530328, Avebury tel 01672 539425, Wantage tel 01235 760176, Wallingford tel 01491 826972, Princes Risborough tel 01844 274795, Wendover tel 01296 696759, Tring 01442 823347.
Accommodation List	*The Ridgeway National Trail Companion,* from TICs
Path Association	Friends of the Ridgeway, www.ridgewayfriends.org.uk
Website	www.nationaltrail.co.uk/Ridgeway

Weeds thrive in the bed of the shallow River Thames at Castle Eaton (Day 10)

5 Thames Path

Start and Finish	Thames Barrier to Thames Head
Distance and Time	294km (183 miles) taking up to 2 weeks
Character	An easy riverside trail using roads, tracks and paths, climbing very gently from sea to source, with only occasional slopes. The route passes through the heart of London, but also includes sparsely inhabited countryside.
Highlights	The city of London, Kew and Richmond, Kingston and Hampton Court Palace, Runnymede and Windsor, Marlow to Henley, Sonning, Goring, Abingdon, Oxford, King's Lock to Lechlade, Castle Eaton, Cricklade through the Cotswold Water Park to the source at Thames Head.

Flowery riverside meadows are preserved as nature reserves beyond Cricklade

The River Thames is England's 'royal river', threading its way through English history in a way that is just as leisurely as its meandering course through the English countryside. The earliest settlers used it to penetrate deep into England's ancient wildwoods, just as Romans and Normans found it to be a useful waterway for conquest. As a ready-made transport artery, the navigation was improved over the centuries and horse-drawn barges hauled goods up and downstream. A continuous towpath evolved, free from all obstructions, all the way between London and Wiltshire. Jerome K Jerome's *Three Men in a Boat* inspired generations of tourists to explore the Thames, and all manner of pleasure craft are now found on its waters.

With the development of roads and railways, transport along the Thames slumped, and there was no longer a need to maintain the towpath, so the river margins sprouted trees and bushes along some stretches, and the path simply became overgrown in others. As the old towpath used to switch from one side of the Thames to the other, some paths ended abruptly when faced with the loss of a strategic ferry to the other bank. The conversion of the old towpath into the Thames Path National Trail involved erecting footbridges where ferries had been lost, and creating alternative routes and new footpaths to ensure continuity. It was expensive, but it was money well spent, and the results are very much appreciated by walkers.

To walk any river from sea to source, or vice versa, is a splendid journey. The Thames is a world-famous river, boasting a variety of scenes, a complex and entertaining history, bustling towns, quiet little villages, and charming riverside pubs, so the journey is one of great interest throughout its length. No other national trail traverses such a vast,

SCHEDULE			
Day	**Start/Finish**	**Km**	**Miles**
Day 1	Thames Barrier to Putney	32	20
Day 2	Putney to Kingston	22	14
Day 3	Kingston to Windsor	30	18½
Day 4	Windsor to Marlow	23	14
Day 5	Marlow to Reading	29	18
Day 6	Reading to Wallingford	29	18
Day 7	Wallingford to Abingdon	23	14
Day 8	Abingdon to Bablock Hythe	32	20
Day 9	Bablock Hythe to Lechlade	32	20
Day 10	Lechlade to Cricklade	19	12
Day 11	Cricklade to Thames Head	23	14½

complex and intensely absorbing city such as London, nor does any other

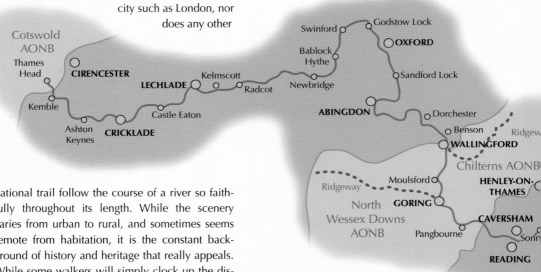

national trail follow the course of a river so faithfully throughout its length. While the scenery varies from urban to rural, and sometimes seems remote from habitation, it is the constant background of history and heritage that really appeals. While some walkers will simply clock up the distance and be happy with their physical achievement, others will want to spend time exploring castles, palaces, ancient cathedrals and churches, art galleries, museums and historic houses, ending their journey with a richer appreciation of England's complex history.

Obviously, from a practical point of view, London has the most extensive range of services and facilities of any national trail, but as the route progresses upstream, bear in mind that accommodation, food and drink can be absent on long stretches. Forward planning is, as always, the key to a successful walk, and the stretch between Oxford and Lechlade has only occasional riverside pubs offering lodgings and refreshments. As walkers plod along the old towpath trail, they will be passed by pleasure barges and cruisers, often seeing the same craft day after day. (It is unlikely that anyone will repeat Lewis Gordon Pugh's long-distance *swim* along the Thames during the summer of 2006. He began by running from Thames Head

The Thames Path passes Shillingford Bridge and the Shillingford Bridge Hotel (Day 7)

to Lechlade, then swam downstream, through the Thames Barrier, to finish at Southend-on-Sea!)

Day 1 Thames Barrier to Putney Bridge
32km (20 miles)

The Thames Barrier is a remarkable flood-control

MARLOW
Cookham
O Hurley
MAIDENHEAD
N
ETON
WINDSOR **STAINES**
10
km
LONDON
WESTMINSTER
RICHMOND
Hampton
Court
BATTERSEA
Thames Barrier
GREENWICH
Teddington Lock
KINGSTON UPON THAMES
WALTON-ON-THAMES

device whose effectiveness will be tested as global warming increases and sea levels rise. Pass through a tunnel beside the barrier, noting how the walls have been inscribed with a long line to represent the course of the Thames. Study the line carefully, watching it step up through a series

of locks as it proceeds to Thames Head. This is your route for the next couple of weeks, but for the time being, follow the tidal Thames towards London, with the huge Millennium Dome prominently in view most of the time. Greenwich is a complete contrast, displaying old buildings and historical features, and designated a world heritage site, while nearby areas undergo massive regeneration. Beyond Greenwich walkers can follow either the south or north bank of the river, and of course can cross from side to side whenever the opportunity arises. Most will probably enjoy walking along the south bank, however – views are generally more colourful, as the buildings on the other side catch the light well. Walking exclusively on the north bank is also slightly longer.

As the route traces the vast meanders of the Thames through London, iconic features come into view, recognised worldwide by millions of people, but there are also many less well-known places of interest to catch the attention along the way. Regeneration continues to transform the riverside, but over the years it has become more walker-friendly, often including areas of greenery, with heritage features incorporated into new developments. Tower Bridge, the Tower of London, Southwark Cathedral, the Globe Theatre, Tate Modern, St Paul's Cathedral, the South Bank Centre, London Eye, Houses of Parliament, Lambeth Palace and Tate Britain – points of interest come thick and fast, and the humble walker who intends visiting them all needs to find accommodation for at least a week!

Always, there are busy bridges spanning the Thames, and the river itself is also teeming with

A patch of greenery in the heart of London, as the Thames Path passes Tower Bridge

pleasure craft and transport barges. Tourists from around the world augment London's cosmopolitan population, but as the trail progresses upstream, things become a little quieter. Tick off the bridges to keep track of progress along the riverside, and watch for markers showing where

the route temporarily moves away from the flow. On the south bank, this happens at Battersea, but is followed by a leafy walk through Battersea Park. Whatever course is followed, walkers who can cover the distance from the Thames Barrier to Putney Bridge in a day are doing very well. Those

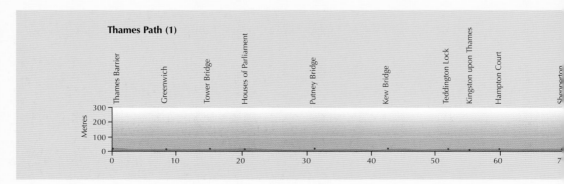

who need time to explore more thoroughly might allow two days for this stretch. There is a feeling that the throbbing city is left behind at Putney Bridge, but in fact the route simply moves into the suburbs for a couple of days.

Day 2 Putney Bridge to Kingston upon Thames
22km (14 miles)

The south bank of the River Thames is accompanied by a fine track from Putney Bridge, though trees and bushes often screen the river from view. There is a route along the north bank, but this is more built up and has fewer green spaces. There are rowing clubs on the river, and a wetland centre is passed on the way to Hammersmith Bridge and Barnes. The Royal Botanic Gardens at Kew, which have been designated a world heritage site, are glimpsed, but there is no direct access from the Thames Path. After passing the Old Deer Park, Richmond presents an elaborate waterfront façade. After walking within sight of the National Trust's Ham House, the tidal limit of the River Thames is reached at Teddington Lock. The river seems more placid, and as a consequence barges and cruisers use it, as well as ferries that run for varying distances from town to town. Finish the day with a short walk along the old towpath to Kingston upon Thames.

Day 3 Kingston upon Thames to Windsor
30km (18½ miles)

While both banks of the Thames have been available to walkers between Greenwich and Teddington, the route now switches from one side to the other and back again, and it's important for walkers to anticipate crossings in advance, and not assume that any old riverside path will be of use. The day starts by following the river around Hampton Court Park. There is a glimpse of Hampton Court Palace, built by Cardinal Wolsey and given to Henry VIII. After passing Molesey Lock the trail passes riverside reservoirs, waterworks and Sunbury Lock, to reach Walton-on-Thames.

Beyond Walton Bridge follow the south bank only if you know that the Shepperton Ferry is running, otherwise walk along the alternative route, mostly along roads, through Shepperton. Head through grassy Chertsey Meads and go under the M3 motorway. At Penton Hook, note how a lengthy meander has been bypassed by a short channel equipped with a lock. The trail continues through built-up Staines, then wanders through pleasant riverside meadows. Runnymede is famous as the location where the Magna Carta was signed, after pressure was brought to bear on King John in 1215. In the charter, the River Thames was declared to be a highway, and awkward fish weirs had to be removed to improve the navigation. Further upstream there is no access to the Thames

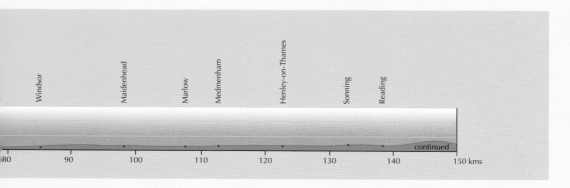

Windsor   Maidenhead   Marlow   Medmenham   Henley-on-Thames   Sonning   Reading

continued

80   90   100   110   120   130   140   150 kms

A placid stretch of the River Thames on the approach to Maidenhead

through the Home Park at Windsor, so walkers have to pass through Datchet instead. Windsor's main attraction is the huge castle that dominates the town, while nearby Legoland naturally features smaller buildings.

Day 4 Windsor to Marlow
23km (14 miles)

The day's walk starts across the river from Windsor, where time could be spent having a look at Eton College. The riverside trail runs through a grassy meadow, then after Boveney Lock it passes a rowing centre used by Eton College. Pass under the M4 motorway to follow the river to Maidenhead, studying a remarkably wide and flat brick-built railway arch. A road has to be followed out of the town to Boulter Lock, then the old towpath beside the river leads onwards. There is a diversion away from the flow into Cookham, a pretty village with an interesting church. Back on the riverside path, walk through the grassy expanses of Cock Marsh and cross the footbridge attached to a railway bridge to reach the village of Bourne End. The trail continues through riverside meadows and eventually goes under a busy road bridge. There is a detour from the river on the way into Marlow, which has a long history, although its 12th-century church was flooded so often that it had to be demolished. Izaak Walton wrote *The Compleat Angler* here. Marlow Regatta takes place before Henley Regatta and is a smaller event.

Day 5 Marlow to Reading
29km (18 miles)

Walk through Thames-side meadows, then cross and recross the river at Hurley, where there are locks, weirs and a number of channels crossed by footbridges. Later, a curious short cut away from the riverside avoids an excellent view across to Medmenham Abbey. Formerly a Cistercian abbey, it was later made infamous by the Hell Fire Club, who performed blasphemous rituals there. Another detour away from the river leads to Aston and the Flower Pot Hotel, followed by a rapid return to the towpath. The trail passes Hambleden Lock, then, after a pronounced meander, Temple Island sits in the middle of the Thames, and a straight stretch of

A rowing team pass the attractive white-painted house and ruins at Medmenham Abbey

the river is marked out into racing lanes for the Henley Regatta.

Henley-on-Thames can be visited, or walkers can simply continue along the riverside path to leave the town. Curious long, bent footbridges have to be crossed at Marsh Lock, then there is a detour from the flow to get through the straggly village of Shiplake to Shiplake Lock. Broad and often flowery meadows are traversed on the way to Sonning, which is a charming village. More meadows lie beyond, but the sprawling suburbs of Reading are often in view ahead. Either cross the Horseshoe Bridge to reach Reading Bridge and Caversham Bridge, or follow a short canal into the town centre. Reading has a full range of services and is a major transport hub. An abbey was founded here in 1121, and although much of it is in ruins, portions can be visited in the town centre. Reading Museum holds a replica of the Bayeux Tapestry.

Day 6 Reading to Wallingford
29km (18 miles)

Leave Reading and walk upstream until the trail is directed up a flight of steps to cross a railway at Tilehurst station. After wandering through a housing estate, the riverside path is regained at Mapledurham Lock. Grassy meadows are traversed on the way to Pangbourne, where a toll bridge, free for walkers, gives access to Whitchurch on Thames. There is another detour from the river, starting with a climb up a road and a walk through Coombe Park, before a path leads across a wooded slope. This is one of the few times that steep slopes flank the river. At length the riverside path leads to Goring, crossing the Thames while overlooking attractive Goring Lock, in common with the Ridgeway National Trail.

The Thames Path follows the western bank of the river from Streatley, passing Runsford Hole and later diverting from the river at the Wedge and Beetle at Moulsford. After walking through

the village, head back onto the riverside path and go under a railway arch. Continue through grassy meadows and eventually pass under a busy road bridge. Follow the path as marked, which begins to pull away from the riverside as it heads into Wallingford. This is a splendid market town at a strategic crossing once protected by 11th-century Wallingford Castle, now in ruins. The town has a long and colourful history, as well as several old buildings.

A pleasure barge noses its way carefully into Goring Lock while heading upstream

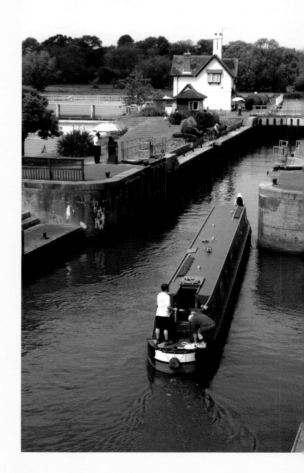

Day 7 Wallingford to Abingdon
23km (14 miles)

Follow the Thames Path to Benson Lock, where the trail crosses the river to the village of Benson. Pick up the towpath at a boatyard and walk through riverside meadows to reach the splendid span of Shillingford Bridge. Leave the riverside and squeeze between gardens to enter Shillingford. Follow a busy road out of the village and get back onto the riverbank to continue through meadows. Cross over the River Thame, where Dorchester is signposted across fields, and note that the Thames, from this point onwards, is often referred to locally as the Isis. There is a pronounced bend in the river just before the route crosses Day's Lock.

More meadows flank the river on the way to Clifton Hampden, then further upstream a large meander has been severed from the navigation by the straight canal of the Clifton Cut. Pass under a railway arch, where Appleford can be seen across the river, then the next bridge offers access to the village of Culham. Another meander has been chopped from the navigation by the straight line of the Culham Cut. On the approach to Abingdon, a footbridge spans the Swift Ditch, which is an old canal cut in 1052 by workers employed by Abingdon Abbey. The abbey itself was originally founded in the year 695, and the town has a long and colourful history inextricably linked to its position on the river. County Hall is an ornate, centrally located building supported on stone arches.

Day 8 Abingdon to Bablock Hythe
32km (20 miles)

The towpath trail from Abingdon to Oxford runs through meadows, passing beneath a railway bridge, running close to Lower Radley to pass Sandford Lock. The surroundings become more urban as the city of Oxford closes in on both banks. Either follow the river straight through, or make a diversion into the city centre and explore the famous colleges. Oxford dates from the 11th century, was blessed with an Augustinian abbey in the 12th century, followed by the first of its colleges in the 13th century, and indeed a structure can be found to represent every century until the present day.

Leaving Oxford, cross the river by way of Fiddler's Island and later pass Godstow Lock and the rather plain ruins of Godstow Abbey. Note how the locks are manually operated from this point. After going under a main road bridge, the Thames Path enters its most remote stretch, where facilities are generally limited to a handful of riverside pubs that offer food, drink and accommodation. Obviously, walkers need to book their beds ahead, or must face long detours from the river to reach distant towns. After passing King's Lock, look across the river to see where the River Evenlode augments the flow. Pass through Wytham Great Wood at the foot of a slope, followed by Swinford Lock. The trail runs through meadows, but is diverted through Bossom's Boatyard and briefly follows a road. Cross the river at Pinkhill Lock, then gradually drift away from the banks, through fields of sheep and cattle, approaching Bablock Hythe and the Ferryman Inn by the road.

Day 9 Bablock Hythe to Lechlade
32km (20 miles)

The Thames Path continues its journey through the meadows, passing a handful of pubs and never coming close to any towns or villages until the end of the day. The first pub of the day is the Rose Revived at Newbridge, which is actually the second oldest bridge on the river, dating from the 13th century. The path onwards may feature long grass, which will lead to soaked legs if wet. The Shifford Cut avoids a big loop in the river. Later, pass the humped footbridge of Tenfoot Bridge and continue upstream to Tadpole Bridge and the Trout Inn. A narrow road leads to Rushey Lock, then a path through meadows passes Old Man's Bridge and

Radcot Lock. Radcot has had a bridge since the year 958, which makes it the oldest known bridging point on the Thames. The Swan is another riverside pub alongside.

The riverside path runs through more meadows and passes Grafton Lock. Later, consider making a short detour into Kelmscott, which is the only village close to the river. There is a pub, but the main attraction is Kelmscott Manor, an attractive old building that was once home to William Morris. Although well preserved for visitors, in Morris' time, when he used to fly into one of his frequent rages, he threw furniture around and broke the wooden panelling! Gentle walking though the meadows leads past Buscot Lock, then later a stepped footbridge crosses the river. St John's Lock is the last lock on the river, and the navigation ends at Lechlade, where at last there is a pretty little town boasting a full range of services for wayfarers.

Day 10 Lechlade to Cricklade
19km (12 miles)

The Thames Path alters markedly on leaving Lechlade. The trail leaves the riverbank and follows a road to Upper Inglesham, then takes its time wandering through fields before it runs close to the river again. Even so, the water is often out of sight, best seen by making short detours onto Hannington Bridge and Castle Eaton Bridge, where the flow is remarkably shallow and the riverbed is a mass of straggly weeds. The Red Lion pub at Castle Eaton has a riverside garden, and the curious old village church overlooks the river too.

Follow a road out of the village, then watch for a signpost pointing the way back to the riverside. The river is followed closely and there are a couple of footbridges to cross on the way to Cricklade. The town is revealed quite suddenly after the trail passes under a busy road bridge with low headroom. St Sampson's Church has an imposing stone tower, while St Mary's, at the other end of town, retains a Norman chancel arch. Other Thames-side towns may have regattas, but the river at Cricklade is narrow and shallow, and features instead an annual rubber duck race!

Day 11 Cricklade to Thames Head
23km (14½ miles)

To the source! The final day on the Thames Path begins by following the diminutive river away from Cricklade. The flowery North Meadow gives way to extensive flooded gravel pits that attract all manner of waterfowl. Bird hides are available and the area around Ashford Keynes and Somerford Keynes has been designated the Cotswold Water Park, mixing recreation and conservation. As the river continues narrowing, there are places where it might be possible to jump across. Walk from Neigh Bridge Country Park to the little village of Ewen, where the river often looks like a flooded field. As the route skirts the village of Kemble, it is

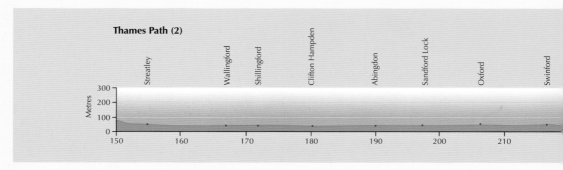

likely that the last flow of water will be passed, and the final stretch through fields to Thames Head is usually quite waterless. A simple stone monument stands at Thames Head, a position occupied by a statue of Old Father Thames from 1958 to 1974, until it was moved to St John's Lock at Lechlade for safekeeping. The trail is over, but for practical purposes it will be necessary to back-track, maybe to Kemble, to catch a train or bus out of the area.

INFORMATION

Access to Start	London is a transport hub, served by long-distance trains from as far away as Scotland and Cornwall, as well as many other rail services, and National Express buses. Frequent trains and buses run close to the Thames Barrier.
Getting Home	Walk back from Thames Head to Kemble for trains and buses, or walk a little further to Cirencester for a greater range of connections.
Other Public Transport	There are plenty of rail and bus services close to London, and plenty more services at every town along the river, though these do become less frequent further along the trail.
Maps	OS 1:50,000 Landrangers 163, 164, 174, 175, 176 and 177
	OS 1:25,000 Explorers 160, 161, 162, 168, 169, 170, 171, 172, 173 and 180
Cicerone Guide	*Thames Path*, by Leigh Hatts
Other Guidebooks	*The Thames Path*, by David Sharp, Aurum Press
Tourist Information Centres	City of London tel 020 73579168, Richmond tel 020 89409125, Kingston tel 020 85475592, Windsor tel 01753 743900, Maidenhead tel 01628 796502, Marlow tel 01628 483597, Henley-on-Thames tel 01491 578034, Reading tel 0118 9566226, Wallingford tel 01491 826972, Abingdon tel 01235 522711, Oxford tel 01865 726871, Farringdon tel 01367 242191, Cirencester tel 01285 654180.
Accommodation List	*The Thames Path National Trail Companion*, from TICs
Websites	www.nationaltrail.co.uk/ThamesPath and www.visitthames.co.uk

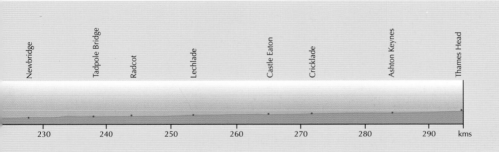

The Devil's Chimney is a curious stump of rock left by quarrymen on Leckhampton Hill (Day 3)

6 Cotswold Way

Start and Finish	Chipping Campden to Bath Abbey
Distance and Time	164km (102 miles) taking 1 week
Character	The contrasting open and wooded scarp slopes of the Cotswold Edge are criss-crossed by paths and tracks, involving some stretches with wide-ranging views, but also plenty of ascents and descents.
Highlights	Beautiful medieval villages and prehistoric sites, Cleeve Hill, Leckhampton Hill, Haresfield Hill, Cam Long Down, Stinchcombe Hill, Tynedale Monument, Wotton Hill, Sodbury Hill, Hanging Hill and the heritage of the city of Bath.

The Cotswold Way follows a grassy track down towards the city of Bath (Day 7)

A long-distance walk along the Cotswold Edge was first proposed back in 1950, and while the route became popular through the 1970s and 1980s, it was only declared fully open as a national trail in 2007. The attraction is obvious, since anyone following the Cotswold Edge will be able to enjoy wide-ranging views from certain points across the low-lying plains, stretching across the River Severn to south Wales, while filling their lungs with fresh air. The edge is well wooded in many places, so views may be limited. Also, the escarpment is broken, so that there are lots of short ascents and descents. Almost the entire trail lies within the Cotswold Area of Outstanding Natural Beauty. Americans love this region, as it fits their view of what England *should* be like, with green fields, rolling countryside and charming old villages.

The Cotswold Way is essentially a walk through lovely English countryside with occasional dramatic views, or at least, that's the sort of walk it is at face value. Walkers with an interest in history could view the Cotswold villages through medieval eyes, since so much remains intact from

SCHEDULE

Day	Start/Finish	Km	Miles
Day 1	Chipping Campden to Winchcombe	29	18
Day 2	Winchcombe to Seven Springs	23	14
Day 3	Seven Springs to Painswick	24	15
Day 4	Painswick to Dursley	26	17
Day 5	Dursley to Hawkesbury Upton	23	14
Day 6	Hawkesbury Upton to Cold Ashton	23	14
Day 7	Cold Ashton to Bath	6	10

those times. There are plenty of sites associated with the Romans too. With more imagination, walkers on the Cotswold Edge could catch a glimpse of life in the Iron Age, as they pass defensive hill forts. Looking even further back, as much as 5000 years or more, there are amazing Neolithic burial chambers dotted around the country-side. Underlying all this is the actual oolitic limestone bedrock of the Cotswolds, which makes the land-scape what it is, and con-tributes so much to the agriculture and architec-ture of the region.

Day 1 Chipping Campden to Winchcombe
29km (18 miles)

Try to spend your first night at Chipping Campden, ensuring that this delightful Cotswold market town can be fully explored. The 'warm' stone used for most of the buildings can be worked into almost any shape, so that many structures are finished off with elaborate and intri-cate carvings. The Cotswold Way climbs straight

uphill, crosses Dover's Hill, then makes a bee-line for prominent Broadway Tower. Built in 1798, the tower is a splendid view-point and its topmost part, at 332m (1089ft), is the highest point in the Cotswolds. However, bear in mind that Cleeve Common, crossed later on the trail, has a higher land surface without a man-made adornment. Drop down to Broadway, which is another remarkably attractive Cotswold village.

Climb through Broadway Coppice to get back onto the Cotswold Edge, then follow tracks up onto Shenbarrow Hill before dropping down to Stanton and the Mount Inn. Low-level field paths link this pretty little 16th-century village with Stanway, which is dominated by Stanway House.

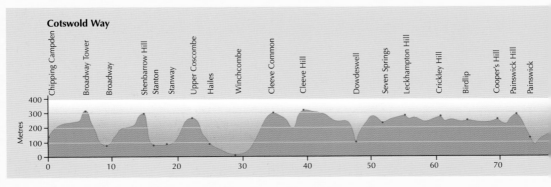

Cotswold Way

Broadway Tower stands high on the Cotswold Edge and was built in 1798

After passing the imposing gateway to the house, continue to Wood Stanway, where a muddy track leads back uphill, linking with Campden Lane on a broad hilltop. The trail drops through Hailes Wood and catches a glimpse of Hailes Abbey, dating from the 13th century. Field paths lead onwards to Winchcombe – a large village crammed with many fine buildings, some of Cotswold stone and others with massive timber frames. Spend the evening in careful exploration.

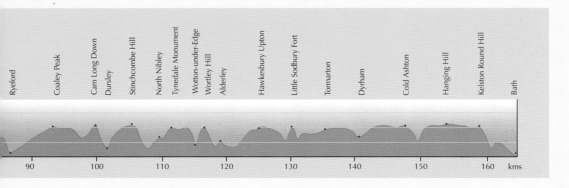

Day 2 Winchcombe to Seven Springs
23km (14 miles)

Leave Winchcombe via attractive Vineyard Street, then follow field paths before climbing uphill past Wadfield. This is the site of a Roman villa, though it can't be seen from the Cotswold Way. Further uphill, and much older, is Belas Knap Long Barrow, one of the best-preserved Neolithic burial chambers on the trail, tucked in beside a wood at 300m (985ft). Tracks and paths lead onto the broad, grassy slopes of Cleeve Common, which is mottled with areas of bracken and dotted with trees and bushes. Take care over route finding, as the trail wanders in a loop around the common, rising and falling, and getting tangled up in a network of paths that run in all directions. The highest point is 330m (1083ft), but this isn't visited. A view indicator can be inspected at 317m (1040ft) on Cleeve Hill, as well as the ramparts of a hill fort on Cleeve Cloud. Views stretch beyond Cheltenham and the River Severn to Wales.

The route shifts downhill by degrees, running south across rugged slopes, later heading through fields, and eventually dropping more steeply down alongside a wood to pass Dowdeswell Reservoir. The Waterside Inn stands beside a busy road. Climb uphill and cut through Lineover Wood, then climb again up the steep slopes of Ravensgare Hill. Walk alongside a road to reach the Seven Springs and a pub of the same name. Most roads leading down to Cheltenham have buses, if a full range of city services is required.

The Cotswold Way runs along the flanks of Cleeve Common high above Cheltenham

Day 3 Seven Springs to Painswick
24km (15 miles)

The route traverses the abrupt and often rocky edge of Leckhampton Hill, reaching a quarried area where a curious tower of rock, known as the Devil's Chimney, has been left as a landmark. Roads and tracks pass Salterley Grange and Ullenwood Manor, then the route enters Crickley Hill Country Park. This was an important hill fort occupied in the Bronze Age and Iron Age. The Air Balloon is a nearby pub, located at a busy road junction.

The Cotswold Way stays faithful to the Cotswold Edge, either running along the top, or cutting across the steep slopes. The predominance of woodlands means that there are only occasional views. The village of Birdlip could be visited by making a short detour. After wriggling round the lower slopes of Cooper's Hill, famous for cheese rolling, the trail climbs to Cranham Corner above Prinknash Abbey, then makes a beeline for Painswick Hill. The summit isn't visited, but is enclosed by the ramparts of yet another hill fort. The route descends to the little market town of Painswick, where a cream-coloured stone has been used extensively and the buildings are most attractive. Spend time in St Mary's churchyard, which is crammed full of ancient clipped yews and elegantly carved monumental tombstones.

Day 4 Painswick to Dursley
26km (17 miles)

Painswick is built on a slope, so the day's walk starts by heading downhill through fields to cross a valley. Climb uphill and cross a busy road near the Edgecombe Inn, and continue over Scottsquar Hill onto a wooded slope. The Cotswold Way describes a circuitous loop around Haresfield Hill, staying above 200m (655ft), and those who short cut will miss some exceptionally charming and extensive views. A spur from the hill narrows at Haresfield

Beacon, where the remains of a fine promontory fort can be inspected. There is another splendid viewpoint before the route runs through Standish Wood. Emerging from the wood along Thieves Lane, walkers head down through fields, threading a way between Stroud and Stonehouse, crossing the railway, roads, river and canal that run through a valley.

Climb past King's Stanley and walk through the village of Middleyard, then skirt round the wooded slopes of Pen Hill to continue through Stanley Wood. The trail climbs as it traverses steep, wooded slopes, eventually reaching Neolithic Nympsfield Long Barrow, perched on the brow of Frocester Hill. Enjoy fine views across the lowlands from Coaley Peak, then consider a diversion above a wooded slope to visit Hetty Pegler's Tump, an excellent Neolithic burial chamber. Flat-topped Uley Bury, also a little off-route, is crowned by the wrinkly ramparts of an Iron Age hill fort. Cross a valley and make a short, steep ascent, then follow the crest of Cam Long Down, followed by the hump of Cam Peak. Enjoy the views, then walk down into the wool town of Dursley, which offers a good range of services for passing wayfarers.

Day 5 Dursley to Hawkesbury Upton
23km (14 miles)

The Cotswold Way makes a complete circuit around Stinchcombe Hill above Dursley, enjoying fine views from its 219m (718ft) summit. After passing above Hollow Combe the trail drops down through woods and fields to cross a valley, then climbs through the village of North Nibley. The tower of the Tyndale Monument is prominently in view, and once there, walkers can climb onto its parapet and enjoy even more extensive views. Raised in 1866, the monument commemorates William Tyndale, who translated the Bible into English in the 16th century, an act that was to cost him his life.

A fine monument to William Tyndale stands on the Cotswold Edge above North Nibley

The route stays high on the Cotswold Edge, passing an Iron Age hill fort in woodlands before dropping down from Wotton Hill to the bustling little town of Wotton-under-Edge. Although dating from at least the year 940, Wotton was burnt and rebuilt in the 13th century. The parish church and nearby almshouses are worth visiting, and a heritage centre offers more information. On leaving town the Cotswold Way climbs over Wortley Hill, then brushes past the hamlets of Wortley and Alderley

before following a valley to Lower Kilcott. Staying above the Long Combe, the route climbs gradually to the Somerset Monument, raised in 1846 in honour of General Lord Somerset. The nearby village of Hawkesbury Upton offers lodgings, food and drink.

Day 6 Hawkesbury Upton to Cold Ashton
23km (14 miles)

The Cotswold Edge seems somewhat diminished on this day's walk, starting along lanes that touch 200m (655ft) a couple of times before dropping downhill. Horton Court, at the foot of the escarpment, dates from the 12th century, and successive occupants have added to it since. Horton village is followed by Little Sodbury, a place associated with William Tyndale. The Cotswold Way climbs uphill to visit Sodbury Hill Fort, which is an Iron Age site, then drops downhill again to proceed to Old Sodbury. The Dog Inn offers refreshments here, then the trail climbs gradually to Tormarton, an ancient village that sits rather too close to the roaring M4 motorway.

Cross the motorway to leave Tormarton, then gradually pull away from it before wandering down through fields to Dyrham. There is a glimpse of Dyrham House on the way through the village, which has elaborate water gardens. Field paths give way to a path up the wooded escarpment to take walkers back onto the Cotswold Edge, reaching a tiny village called Pennsylvania. Follow a field path to Cold Ashton, passing the White Hart on the way into the village, and take note of a splendid Elizabethan manor house.

Day 7 Cold Ashton to Bath
16km (10 miles)

Follow the Greenway Lane from Cold Ashton, walking down into a valley. Climb up through fields on the other side of the valley and pass Beach Wood to reach the top of Hanging Hill at 235m (771ft). Monuments and interpretative panels record a Civil War battle in 1643 on these slopes. The trail stays quite high, passing alongside a golf course and Bath Racecourse. Enjoy the views from Prospect Stile before a long descent to Weston. Watch carefully for signposts and markers on the way through the suburbs of Bath, as the route heads to its final destination in the heart of the city at Bath Abbey.

The walk can be completed in the morning, leaving the whole afternoon free to explore Bath.

Even on the last stages, there are several attractions and distractions, such as the Botanic Gardens, or the Georgian architecture of the Royal Crescent and the Circus. Bath is easily one of the most attractive cities in Britain and repays careful exploration. Tucked away behind Bath Abbey are the Roman Baths and the Pumproom, from where the city's fame and fortune sprang. The River Avon encircles the city centre in a natural defensive moat, and even in that limited area there is plenty of interest to explore.

INFORMATION

Access to Start	Cheltenham is served by long-distance Virgin Trains and buses link with Chipping Campden.
Getting Home	Plenty of trains and buses from Bath, particularly to Bristol to link with long-distance Virgin Trains.
Other Public Transport	A useful public transport leaflet covers all services in the Cotswolds and is available from TICs.
Maps	OS 1:50,000 Landrangers 150, 151, 162, 163 and 172
	OS 1:25,000 Explorers 167, 168, 169 and OL45
	Harveys 1:40,000 Cotswold Way
Cicerone Guide	*The Cotswold Way,* by Kev Reynolds
Other Guidebooks	*The Cotswold Way,* by Anthony Burton, Aurum Press
Tourist Information Centres	Chipping Campden tel 01386 841206, Broadway tel 01386 852937, Winchcombe tel 01242 602925, Cheltenham tel 01242 522878, Painswick tel 01452 813552, Stroud tel 01453 760960, Wotton-under-Edge tel 01453 521541, Chipping Sodbury tel 01454 888686, Bath tel 01225 477101.
Accommodation List	*The Cotswold Way Handbook and Accommodation List,* from TICs
Website	www.nationaltrail.co.uk/Cotswold

Small boats moored in a tidal creek close to Wells-next-the-Sea (Day 6)

7 Peddars Way and Norfolk Coast Path

Start and Finish	Knettishall Heath to Cromer Pier
Distance and Time	149km (93 miles) taking 1 week
Character	Gently rolling countryside is traversed by a long and ancient track, giving way to a varied, low-level coastal trail passing dunes, reedbeds, salt marshes and crumbling clay cliffs. Some parts seem remote from the coast.
Highlights	Breckland heaths, Castle Acre, Ringstead, Hunstanton's cliffs, Holme Dunes Nature Reserve, coastal creeks, salt marshes and pretty coastal villages, Cley next the Sea, the cliffs near Sheringham and the Roman Camp.

A straight stretch of the Peddars Way runs through fields near Swaffham

The end of one national trail is often fairly close to the start of another, but not in Norfolk. The Peddars Way and Norfolk Coast Path is far removed from the network of national trails, and is the only such route in East Anglia. As the name suggests, this is very much a trail of two halves. The Peddars Way is a long, straight, ancient trail through the countryside, while the Norfolk Coast Path has been cobbled together with beaches, sea walls and cliff paths.

While the ruler-straight Peddars Way is usually associated with the Romans, it was originally the eastern end of a Bronze Age trading route from Dorset to Norfolk, crossing gently rolling countryside on its way to the North Sea. The coast path passes sand dunes and marshland, with crumbling cliffs appearing only in a couple of places. Birdwatching is a popular pursuit along the coast, which features a series of marshy nature reserves, and boat trips facilitate visits to more remote shingle points where birds and seals gather. Always, in Norfolk, the low-lying landscape provides exceptional 'big sky' views.

The Peddars Way and Norfolk Coast Path was opened in 1986 by Prince Charles, and remains one of the quieter national trails. Walkers who start planning their trip may wonder how they are supposed

SCHEDULE			
Day	**Start/Finish**	**Km**	**Miles**
Day 1	Knettishall Heath to Merton	18.5	11½
Day 2	Merton to Castle Acre	23	14
Day 3	Castle Acre to Ringstead	27	17
Day 4	Ringstead to Brancaster	25	15½
Day 5	Brancaster to Wells-next-the-Sea	23	14
Day 6	Wells-next-the-Sea to Cley next the Sea	17	10½
Day 7	Cley next the Sea to Cromer	22	13½

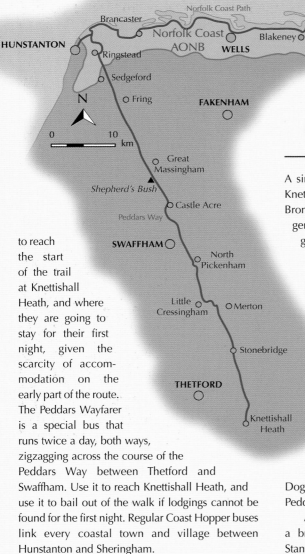

Norfolk Coast Path

Brancaster

Norfolk Coast

HUNSTANTON   Ringstead   **AONB**   **WELLS**

Blakeney   Cley

SHERINGHAM

CROMER

Roman Camp

Sedgeford

Fring

FAKENHAM

N

0   10

km

Great
Massingham

Shepherd's Bush

Castle Acre

Peddars Way

SWAFFHAM

North
Pickenham

Little
Cressingham

Merton

Stonebridge

THETFORD

Knettishall
Heath

Day 1   Knettishall Heath to Merton
18.5km (11½ miles)

A simple signboard marks the start of the trail at Knettishall Heath. A woodland track, formerly a Bronze Age trading route and Roman road, runs gently downhill to cross the Little Ouse River. A gentle ascent leads to a main road, then as the route passes alongside a forest, Thorpe Woodlands campsite is available for those carrying full packs. A meandering board-walk keeps feet dry alongside the River Thet, then after the route crosses another road, there are views across Brettenham Heath to the left, the first of the wild and extensive Breckland Heaths. Cross the busy A11 and a level crossing, then walk through a forest to pass a gas station. A track leads over a gentle rise, passing occasional piggeries and Witsend Farm. Cross a road, then walk beside a disused railway to reach Stonebridge, where the Dog and Partridge offers food and drink, and the Peddars Wayfarer bus stops.

A quiet road leads out of Stonebridge, then later a broad forest track is followed alongside the Stanford Training Area, an extensive military training range to which there is no access. There is a glimpse

to reach the start of the trail at Knettishall Heath, and where they are going to stay for their first night, given the scarcity of accom-modation on the early part of the route. The Peddars Wayfarer is a special bus that runs twice a day, both ways, zigzagging across the course of the Peddars Way between Thetford and Swaffham. Use it to reach Knettishall Heath, and use it to bail out of the walk if lodgings cannot be found for the first night. Regular Coast Hopper buses link every coastal town and village between Hunstanton and Sheringham.

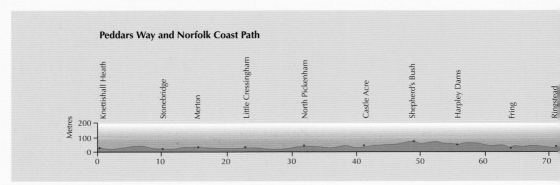

Peddars Way and Norfolk Coast Path

Knettishall Heath — Stonebridge — Merton — Little Cressingham — North Pickenham — Castle Acre — Shepherd's Bush — Harpley Dams — Fring — Ringstead

Metres   200   100   0

0   10   20   30   40   50   60   70

Thompson Water lies close to the Peddars Way between Stonebridge and Merton

of Thompson Water to the right, as well as an opportunity to follow a path to the lake and enjoy views across its surface. While following the track through the forest, notice the inscribed stone sculptures at intervals – modern works with sentiments linked to the trail. After a bendy stretch of the route, the track straightens out to pass Home Farm, where the village of Merton is close to hand, and there is nearby access to the Peddars Wayfarer bus if it proves necessary to leave the route.

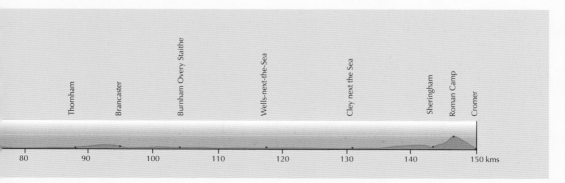

Day 2 Merton to Castle Acre
23km (14 miles)

While most people regard the Peddars Way as a long, straight trail, it does turn a lot of corners as it makes its way from Merton to Little Cressingham. On the way, watch out for All Saints Church, curiously marooned in the fields. After a lengthy walk along a quiet road flanked by cereal fields, there are more corners to be turned in fields on the way to North Pickenham. This village has a pub, the Blue Lion, and is on the Peddars Wayfarer bus route.

The Peddars Way is once again a straight track, but locally it is usually referred to as the Procession Way. Cross over the busy A47 within sight of a McDonalds restaurant on the outskirts of Swaffham. A road leads onwards, zigzagging to cross a dismantled railway. The route runs around 80m (260ft) hereabouts. After passing Palgrave Hall and Great Palgrave, where long-deserted villages once stood, a road leads gradually downhill. Cross a main road and climb gentle Bartholomew's Hills, then walk down to a ford on the River Nar. The ruins of Castle Acre Priory are seen across fields, and the road leads up into the delightful village of Castle Acre, going through the arch of the bailey gate to reach lovely Stocks Green, surrounded by pretty houses. The 11th-century castle ruins feature interpretative panels that reveal how complex and extensive Castle Acre was in its medieval heyday.

Day 3 Castle Acre to Ringstead
27km (17 miles)

A casual glance at the map suggests a road walk away from Castle Acre, but the trail often runs parallel alongside fields, at least to the Wicken. Shepherd's Bush is the high point of the day, a mere 92m (302ft). Follow a track downhill, then walk up a road, continuing along another track from a crossroads. The villages of Great Massingham and Little Massingham are nearby, but the Peddars Way passes only occasional farms and the Harpley

Dams Cottages. A straight and splendid grassy track leads onwards, sometimes flanked by trees, but often with views across nearby fields. Pass a conspicuous tumulus at Bunker's Hill and cross a road, then pass a small wilderness patch that looks odd surrounded by cultivated fields.

The Peddars Way runs more or less in a straight line through gentle countryside, then undulates noticeably as it passes close to the villages of Fring and Sedgeford. A few houses are passed at Littleport, including odd-looking Magazine Cottage. Cross over a dismantled railway and follow the trail to the pretty little village of Ringstead. The Gin Trap Inn, and a shop and lodgings are available here, though some walkers might prefer to add a little more distance to reach the coast and its regular Coast Hopper bus services.

Day 4 Ringstead to Brancaster
25km (15½ miles)

A short walk over a gentle hill leads from Ringstead to Holme next the Sea, the end of the Peddars Way and the beginning of the Norfolk Coast Path. There is a decision to be made, as a spur route leads to Hunstanton, some 5km (3 miles) away, and anyone walking there must return to Holme, either by walking back again, or catching one of the regular Coast Hopper buses. (The distance quoted for the national trail assumes that the spur is only walked in one direction.) The little resort of Hunstanton is certainly worth a visit and has plenty of accommodation, pubs and restaurants. A grassy expanse known as the Green gives way to pleasant gardens, which give way in turn to a striking 'sandwich' cliff of red and white layered rock.

After leaving Holme and the White Horse Inn, the Norfolk Coast Path follows a sandy path that rolls along the crest of sand dunes spiked with marram grass. When a stand of Corsican pines is reached, there is access inland to the Norfolk Wildlife Trust Visitor Centre – a handy source of information about the surrounding nature reserve (and also selling ice cream). The trail overlooks Broad Water and extensive marshes, then follows an embankment round the marshes to reach Thornham, where there is a church and a pub. There is no coastal path to Brancaster, and the busy A149 is not safe for walkers, so follow Choseley Road inland, climbing gently over a rise. A track and path set well back from the coast lead through large fields, then a clear track runs down to Brancaster, reaching a convenient shop on the main road near the church. Brancaster's name derives from *Branodunum,* the name of a Roman fort now marked only by grassy ramparts in nearby fields.

Day 5 Brancaster to Wells-next-the-Sea
23km (14 miles)

A road leading to Brancaster Bay is often closed to traffic at high tide, and a very high tide could well flood parts of the coastal path. The trail runs between extensive reedbeds and a few buildings, and there are stretches of boardwalk to keep feet out of the mud. There is access to Brancaster Staithe and its pubs, then later, access to Burnham Deepdale and its backpacker hostel. Continue along a grassy embankment around Deepdale Marsh, looking across sinuous creeks towards the dunes of the Scolt Head Nature Reserve, which is virtually an island. The embankment swings inland and a prominent old windmill is passed on the way into Burnham Overy Staithe. The Hero pub recalls Horatio Nelson, the local boy who tradition asserts learned to sail here, which seems likely, although there is no proof.

Another grassy embankment runs alongside Overy Marshes, giving way to a boardwalk that leads to a sandy beach. A waymark arrow pointing right may well be buried by shifting dunes. Simply walk along the beach, hugging the dunes if the tide is high, otherwise make the most of the golden sands. More and more people are likely to be noticed as Holkham Gap is approached. Lady Ann's Road could be followed inland to Holkham Hall, where there is food and drink available in a

fine old building set in pleasant parkland. The coast path, however, slips behind the dunes, which are well wooded with Corsican pines, and paths are sandy underfoot most of the way to a large holiday park at Wells Harbour. Simply walk along a stout sea wall to reach Wells-next-the-Sea, a bustling town whose quayside is flanked by tall warehouses. Throughout the summer, holidaymakers line up to fish for crabs (but no need to worry about stocks being depleted, since they are invariably tipped back into the sea afterwards!).

Day 6 Wells-next-the-Sea to Cley next the Sea
17km (10½ miles)

A grassy embankment leaves Wells, giving way to a path running between fields and extensive salt-marshes. There is barely a glimpse of the sea in the distance, but the marshes are full of brackish pools and muddy creeks. A very high tide could flood the whole area, which is mostly a national nature reserve. Pass a car park and campsite at Stiffkey (pronounced Stookey), then follow a track between fields and marshes. At Morston a National Trust information centre features a lookout for birdwatchers, as well as a café. Another sea wall leads to Blakeney, where the quayside can be quite busy. There are plenty of old buildings to explore, including the vaults of an old store. Another prominent grassy sea wall leads onwards, turning angular corners, then making a circuit around a reedy marshland to reach Cley next the Sea. A prominent windmill, which offers accommodation, is just one of many old and interesting buildings in the village.

Day 7 Cley next the Sea to Cromer
22km (13½ miles)

Leave Cley via its towering windmill and follow a sea wall to a beach car park. A long bank of shingle

A prominent landmark windmill rises above reedbeds at Cley next the Sea

protects linear marshland, and the Norfolk Coast Path runs along the foot of it, so the sea is completely hidden from view. It is possible to crunch along the pebbles on top of the bank, but this is quite tiring. A grassy bump is passed halfway along the bank, then the shingle ridge stretches onwards to reach a car park near Weybourne. A short diversion inland leads to a shop, pub and crumbling ruins near the parish church.

Staying on the coastal path, gain height gradually along a crumbling cliff line, enjoying long-ranging views of the coast. Pass some houses that are one day destined to topple over the edge, then pass a golf course before climbing to a prominent National Coastwatch lookout. Walk down to Sheringham and amble along its promenade, maybe detouring into the town centre for a full range of services. Climb uphill, steeply at times, using steps to get over Beeston Hill on the way out of town. The trail abandons the coast and heads inland across a steam railway line. Cross a busy road then head up through woodlands to reach the Roman Camp, the highest point in Norfolk at 102m (335ft). Leave by walking along roads, tracks and paths to reach the busy little resort of Cromer. The trail ends by zigzagging down to the pier, so of course for practical purposes you have to climb uphill again to negotiate the town centre.

Crumbling clay cliffs are crossed on the way to the busy little town of Sheringham

INFORMATION

Access to Start	Trains and buses serve Thetford. The Peddars Wayfarer bus, which runs in the summer, is the only bus from Thetford to Knettishall Heath.
Getting Home	Plenty of trains and buses away from Cromer offer easy links with Cambridge and London.
Other Public Transport	The Peddars Wayfarer bus serves early parts of the trail. Coast Hopper buses run regularly along the coast between Hunstanton and Sheringham.
Maps	OS 1:50,000 Landrangers 132, 133, 134 and 144
	OS 1:25,000 Explorers 229, 236, 250, 251 and 252
Guidebook	*Peddars Way & Norfolk Coast Path*, by Bruce Robinson, Aurum Press
Tourist Information Centres	Thetford tel 01842 820689, Watton tel 01953 884224, Swaffham tel 01760 722255, Hunstanton tel 01485 532610, Wells-next-the-Sea tel 01328 710885, Cromer tel 01263 512497.
Accommodation List	Guide and accommodation list, *Walking the Peddars Way and Norfolk Coast Path* from TICs
Website	www.nationaltrail.co.uk/PeddarsWay

Bright poppies grow profusely among the crops on the way to Stockendale Farm (Day 6)

8 Yorkshire Wolds Way

Start and Finish	Hessle to Filey Brigg
Distance and Time	127km (79 miles) taking up to 1 week
Character	A coast-to-coast walk through the gently rolling Yorkshire Wolds, passing large fields and wooded areas, with steep slopes encountered on the way in and out of dales. Detours may be needed to reach villages.
Highlights	The Humber Bridge, Welton, Brantingham, Goodmanham, Market Weighton, Londesborough Park, Nunburnholme, Millington, Huggate Sheepwalk to Huggate and Thixendale, deserted village of Wharram Percy, Wintringham, Manor Wold, Camp Dale, Filey Brigg.

The Yorkshire Wolds Way runs along the brow of a grassy dale as it heads for Huggate (Day 4)

The Yorkshire Wolds is a chalk upland of no great height, occasionally rising more than 200m (655ft) above sea level, with a gentle but well-defined escarpment to the west and north, while to the east there are cliffs. Geologically, the Wolds continue south into Lincolnshire, but have been severed by the Humber estuary. The chalk upland has been carved by countless deep, steep-sided little dales, and as these grassy slopes cannot be cultivated, they are used for sheep grazing. The high ground is gently rolling and has been divided into huge fields. These are mainly cultivated for cereals, as the soil is too thin and full of flints to support root crops. Villages are few and far between, though in

the past the area had many more settlements, which were abandoned in the Middle Ages.

The Yorkshire Wolds Way runs partly along the escarpment, but also through the very heart of the region, often alongside huge arable fields, but also in and out of grassy dales and woods. In effect, the route is a coast-to-coast through the Wolds, starting on the tidal Humber estuary and finishing on the crumbling cliffs of Filey Brigg. When the trail runs through dales, views are very limited, but when it runs through the highest fields, there are 'big sky' views and often amazing cloudscapes. As crops rotate throughout the seasons, so the colours along the Yorkshire Wolds Way change. Tilled fields produce fresh green shoots in spring, oilseed rape blooms blinding yellow in early summer, then wheat and barley turn gold later in the year (in hot weather farmers may need to spray water onto fields when the soil dries out). After the harvest, the plough turns the earth (exposing masses of angular flints), ready for another cycle of crops.

A 'Wolds Way' was first suggested by local Ramblers' Association members in 1969, and while it gained approval in 1971, the route wasn't declared open until 1982. Always a quiet trail, it was rebranded in 2004 as the Yorkshire Wolds Way, in an effort to establish it on the map. Walkers need to be aware that food, drink and accommodation are sparse in some areas, so

	SCHEDULE		
Day	**Start/Finish**	**Km**	**Miles**
Day 1	Hessle to South Cave	21.5	13½
Day 2	South Cave to Market Weighton	19	12
Day 3	Market Weighton to Millington	14.5	9
Day 4	Millington to Thixendale	23.5	14½
Day 5	Thixendale to Sherburn	29	18
Day 6	Sherburn to Filey Brigg	23.5	14½

careful planning is needed, as well as advance booking at busy times. However, there are usually villages not far from the route that can be visited for their services.

Day 1 Hessle to South Cave
21.5km (13½ miles)

Hessle is one of the least salubrious places for starting a long trail, but thankfully it is quickly left behind. Study a stone sculpture on the shore of the Humber and take note of the placenames carved deeply around it – they will become familiar and much loved as the week unfolds. A short coastal walk runs past one of the towers that support the graceful span of the Humber Bridge. Continue along a narrow strip sandwiched between the muddy shore and a railway line. Later, depending on the state of the tide, there is a choice of routes – either along the shore before cutting inland to the busy A63, or along the streets of North Ferriby if the shore walk is flooded. Either way, cross the busy dual carriageway using a footbridge for safety.

The trail crosses Melton Hill and passes a chalk quarry on the way to the charming village of Welton, where highwayman Dick Turpin was arrested in 1739 at the Green Dragon Inn. Walk through wooded Welton Dale and pass Wauldby Manor Farm, moving

into typical Wolds countryside, with large fields bounded by hedgerows, along with prominent clumps of trees and small woodlands. A broad track leads over Brantingham Wold, touching 140m (460ft). The route just misses the charming little village of Brantingham, but passes the isolated parish church. Well-wooded Ellerker North Wold and Mount Airy are crossed, before the route runs down a steep slope. A short detour leads into the village of South Cave, which has everything a walker needs.

Day 2 South Cave to Market Weighton
19km (12 miles)

Climb past Little Wolds Plantation and catch a glimpse back to the Humber estuary before wandering down into grassy Comber Dale. An old railway trackbed is crossed in Weedley Dale, then the trail climbs up a wooded valley to emerge in fields. Pass High Hunsley Beacon at 162m (532ft) and walk beside large fields before

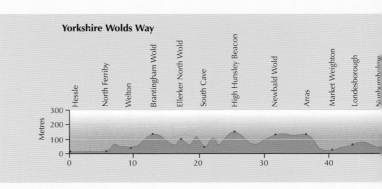

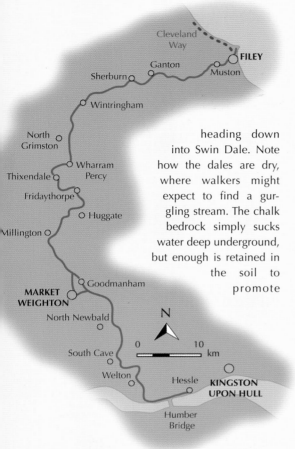

heading down into Swin Dale. Note how the dales are dry, where walkers might expect to find a gurgling stream. The chalk bedrock simply sucks water deep underground, but enough is retained in the soil to promote

a lush covering of grass.

North Newbald and its pub are half an hour off-route, and most wayfarers simply climb over Newbald Wold at 144m (472ft) and head straight for Hessleskew. After crossing a busy road the route passes the isolated farm of Arras, then runs gently downhill beside huge fields to reach another old railway trackbed. Here there is a

choice of routes. The main course of the Yorkshire Wolds Way goes up a narrow road to the village of Goodmanham, while an alternative loop runs along the trackbed to the bustling little town of Market Weighton. The town's most famous inhabitant was William Bradley (1792–1820), at the time the tallest man in the country at 2.36m (7ft 9ins).

Day 3 Market Weighton to Millington
14.5km (9 miles)

In the morning, walkers from Goodmanham follow a slightly higher route than those from Market Weighton, and soon meet again at the lovely estate village of Londesborough. The road leaving the village has remarkable views stretching across the plains to the distant Pennines, then field paths lead down to the pretty village of Nunburnholme. There was a priory here, and an Anglo Saxon stone cross can be seen in the parish church. The site of a 12th-century manorial complex has been identified, but pleasant though the place is, there is nothing to hold the attention of walkers for long.

Climb through Bratt Wood and pass Wold Farm around 130m (425ft) on the chalk escarpment. There is a glimpse of Kilnwick Percy Hall, first mentioned in the Domesday Book, although the present structure dates from the 18th century. It is now a Buddhist centre, with beautifully restored gardens. Services are sparse in this part of the

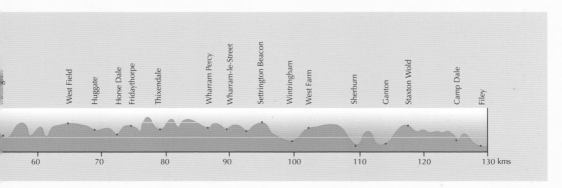

A fine little pond in the heart of Londesborough Park attracts a variety of wildfowl (Day 3)

Wolds, so most walkers will divert off-route into the beautiful village of Millington and visit the Ramblers Rest tearoom at weekends.

Day 4 Millington to Thixendale
23.5km (14½ miles)

This day's walk leads into the very heart of the Yorkshire Wolds, starting with some short but steep ascents and descents. Stretches of an ancient earthwork are traced along the high ground overlooking the grassy dale known as the Huggate Sheepwalk. Gradients are gentler as the route runs through West Field, then there is a descent towards

Huggate. The whitewashed Wolds Inn is popular with walkers and the village has all sorts of interesting corners to explore.

Leave Huggate by road, then notice the line of the ancient earthwork again on the descent into Horse Dale. The grassy floor of Holm Dale leads up to Fridaythorpe, where a notice on the green celebrates the opening of the Wolds Way, as well as its rededication as the Yorkshire Wolds Way, and highlights the fact that this is the halfway point. Note the curious box-like church in the village, and the large feed mill on its outskirts. The trail drops into a steep-sided dale and passes Ings Plantation, then after passing Gill's Farm at 210m (690ft) drops into another dale to reach

Thixendale. This long and straggling village is full of charm and is a notable sheep-rearing location.

Day 5 Thixendale to Sherburn
29km (18 miles)

Several dales cluster round Thixendale. The Yorkshire Wolds Way climbs over Cow Wold at 210m (690ft) to cross another dale, then runs along the brow of Deep Dale before dropping into it. The deserted village of Wharram Percy, which was originally omitted from the route, deserves a thorough exploration. There are helpful notices around

Wharram Percy is the most famous of the deserted villages in the Yorkshire Wolds

the site, which contains traces of prehistoric and Roman settlement, as well as Saxon remains. Apart from the ruined church, which was in use until 1949, the only building remaining is a relatively recent house occupying the site of an 18th-century farmstead.

The trail passes through the crossroads village of Wharram-le-Street and climbs through fields. A descent from the Peak leads into a dale drained by a stream, then a farm road is followed up to a wooded hilltop. Emerging from the woods, there is a splendid view of Wintringham, though when the trail reaches the village, it sneaks round the outskirts to reach the parish church. After climbing uphill, the route runs along the northern escarpment of the Wolds, occasionally featuring views of the North York Moors. After rising to 180m (590ft) on Manor Wold, the trail descends gently, then more steeply, and runs close to Sherburn, which offers a small but adequate range of services.

Day 6 Sherburn to Filey Brigg
23.5km (14½ miles)

The Yorkshire Wolds Way climbs uphill from Sherburn, only to run back down to Potter Brompton and Ganton. It climbs again and often makes right-angled turns as it negotiates the edges of huge fields. A military installation is passed at 178m (584ft) on Staxton Wold, then the trail embarks on a roller-coaster route through more fields. After reaching Camp Dale the route climbs past Stockendale Farm, then descends towards Muston, where the pub is called the Ship Inn, and the coast will already have been in view for some time.

A short walk leads to the busy little seaside resort of Filey, but this

Some of the steepest parts of the Yorkshire Wolds Way are found near Millington (Day 4)

A clear track at the foot of the Wolds near Potter Brompton

is not the end of the trail. Continue along the coast to reach the crumbling clay promontory of Filey Brigg, where a stone monument marks the junction of the Yorkshire Wolds Way and the Cleveland Way. Obviously, keen trailblazers could continue onwards, but those who set out only to walk through the Wolds can simply celebrate their achievement by enjoying a fine coastal view, then retrace footsteps to Filey to catch a bus or train home.

INFORMATION

Access to Start	Hull Trains run from London to Hull and there are plenty of trains and buses between Hull and Hessle.
Getting Home	Filey has plenty of trains and bus services.
Other Public Transport	East Yorkshire Motor Services buses crisscross the trail.
Maps	OS Landrangers 100, 101 and 106
	OS Explorers 293, 294, 300 and 301
Cicerone Guide	*The Cleveland Way and the Yorkshire Wolds Way*, by Paddy Dillon
Other Guidebooks	*Yorkshire Wolds Way*, by Roger Ratcliffe, Aurum Press
Tourist Information Centres	Hull tel 01482 223559, Humber Bridge tel 01482 640854, Malton tel 01653 600048, Filey tel 01723 518000.
Accommodation List	*Yorkshire Wolds Way Accommodation and Information Guide*, from TICs
Website	www.nationaltrail.co.uk/yorkshirewoldsway

The lovely little fishing harbour of Staithes is associated with Captain Cook (Day 6)

9 Cleveland Way

Start and Finish	Helmsley to Filey Brigg
Distance and Time	176km (109 miles) taking about 1½ weeks
Character	Rugged moorland walking contrasts with a striking cliff coast path, passing round the fringes of the North York Moors National Park and involving plenty of ascents and descents. Well-worn paths have been paved in stone.
Highlights	Helmsley, Rievaulx Abbey, Sutton Bank, the Drove Road, Osmotherley, the Cleveland Hills, ancient stone crosses, Captain Cook's Monument, Roseberry Topping, Boulby Cliff and Staithes, Whitby to Robin Hood's Bay, Ravenscar to Hayburn Wyke, Scarborough and Filey Brigg.

The Cleveland Way follows a roller-coaster route on its way to Hasty Bank (Day 3)

The Cleveland Way is a trail of two parts, featuring an inland moorland stretch that contrasts markedly with a rugged cliff coast path, and most of it runs through the North York Moors National Park. Here you will find the most extensive areas of heather moorland in England, flushed with purple each summer, and managed as a habitat for red grouse. The moors have attracted long-distance walkers for

decades and there are a number of classic routes available apart from the Cleveland Way. The arduous Lyke Wake Walk and the Coast to Coast Walk both run concurrent with the Cleveland Way National Trail for some distance, and the relentless pressure of booted feet practically destroyed the trail, and the worst parts had to be completely rebuilt in stone during the 1990s.

Many days along the Cleveland Way have distinct individual themes. The route starts gently in a quaint medieval setting at Helmsley, then traverses a splendid escarpment offering extensive views across the plains to the distant Pennines. Next come the Cleveland Hills, one after another, up and down all day long. Broad moorlands give way to explorations in 'Captain Cook country'. A designated heritage coast features fishing villages, smuggling coves and Victorian seaside resorts, all linked by rugged cliff paths. The trail ends with a grand finale on the battered promontory of Filey Brigg. At that point, keen wayfarers could continue along the Yorkshire Wolds Way, through gentler agricultural countryside.

The Cleveland Way is quite popular and in the summer months there can be a lot of pressure on accommodation. Small villages on the moorland stages of the trail can run short of lodgings, while the busy little resorts along the coast can also come under pressure, particularly at summer weekends, so it is wise to book beds in advance to

Day	Start/Finish	Km	Miles
Day 1	Helmsley to Sutton Bank	17	10½
Day 2	Sutton Bank to Osmotherley	18.5	11½
Day 3	Osmotherley to Clay Bank	18	11
Day 4	Clay Bank to Kildale	15	9½
Day 5	Kildale to Saltburn-by-the-Sea	24	15
Day 6	Saltburn-by-the-Sea to Sandsend	27	17
Day 7	Sandsend to Robin Hood's Bay	16	10
Day 8	Robin Hood's Bay to Scarborough	23.5	14½
Day 9	Scarborough to Filey	18	11

avoid disappointment. The Moorsbus could prove useful in case of difficulty, allowing walkers to join and leave the route in awkward places by using a network of special minibus services.

Day 1 Helmsley to Sutton Bank
17km (10½ miles)

Spend the night in honey-coloured Helmsley so that all its nooks and crannies can be explored properly. It was an Anglo-Saxon foundation and its imposing Norman castle keep dates from 1200. An easy walk through fields and woods leads close to Rievaulx, so a detour easily includes the towering arches of the 12th-century abbey beside the River Rye. A wooded dale and a gentle climb through fields leads to the village of Cold Kirby, then field paths and woods lead to Sutton Bank

and a very popular visitor centre around 300m (985ft).

There is a spur from the trail at Sutton Bank, wandering along an abrupt edge where extensive views lead the eye across the Plain of York to the distant Pennines. The path leads to the 'eye' of the Kilburn White Horse, which was carved on the hillside in 1857, though it really needs to be seen from below. Backtrack along the path to return to Sutton Bank, where nearby lodgings are very sparse. However, there are buses back to Helmsley if they are needed.

Day 2 Sutton Bank to Osmotherley
18.5km (11½ miles)

The Cleveland Way runs along a splendid escarpment from Sutton Bank. Sometimes there is a sheer

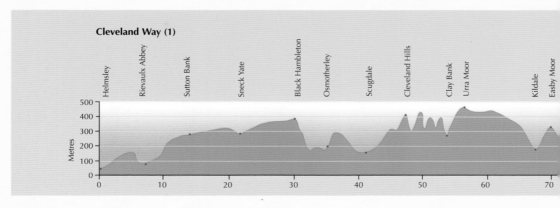

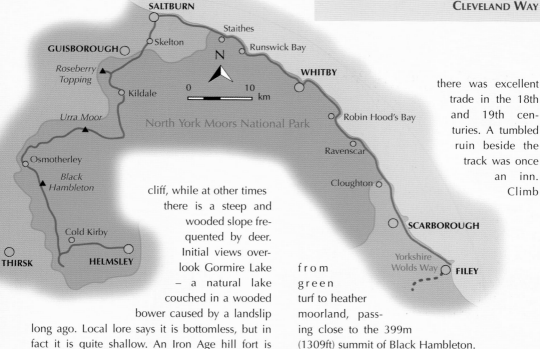

there was excellent trade in the 18th and 19th centuries. A tumbled ruin beside the track was once an inn. Climb

cliff, while at other times there is a steep and wooded slope frequented by deer. Initial views overlook Gormire Lake – a natural lake couched in a wooded bower caused by a landslip long ago. Local lore says it is bottomless, but in fact it is quite shallow. An Iron Age hill fort is passed at Boltby Scar, where rumpled earthworks enclose an area of land close to the cliff edge. The trail continues across Sneck Yate Bank, then shifts away from the escarpment to follow the Hambleton Drove Road.

The Drove Road may well have been a prehistoric ridgeway route, used at a time when the plains were completely impassable due to dense forests and extensive swamps. In more recent times, when the lowlands were enclosed and cultivated, and travellers on turnpike roads were required to pay tolls, Scottish drovers kept to the high ground while moving cattle to London, and

from green turf to heather moorland, passing close to the 399m (1309ft) summit of Black Hambleton.

Walk down to a small reservoir in wooded Oak Dale, then take care while following fiddly field paths to Osmotherley. This fine stone village has a good range of facilities – including award-winning public toilets, which are well worth a visit – and has provided for the needs of walkers for generations.

Day 3 Osmotherley to Clay Bank
18km (11 miles)

An easy climb from Osmotherley crosses the top of Beacon Hill at 299m (891ft) in the company of

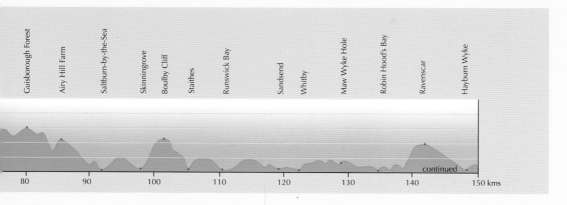

both the Lyke Wake Walk and Coast to Coast Walk. In effect, three very popular trails run concurrently down a moorland slope and through woods to Scugdale. The whole day's walk is a joyful romp over one hill after another in fine weather, crossing Live Moor and Holey Moor. From the top of Carlton Moor at 408m (1338ft) there are superb views of sprawling moors, gentle green dales and patchwork plains. Drop down to the Lord Stones Café, which is open all year, but look carefully for it, as the building lies half-buried underground!

The next series of hills is a little higher, steeper and rockier, starting with Cringle Moor, where the trail is stone-slabbed at over 420m (1380ft). After steep-sided Cold Moor come the awesome jagged Wain Stones on Hasty Bank. Walkers stop and admire them, while rock climbers grapple with them. An easy walk along a flagstone path gives way to a steep drop to a road on Clay Bank. Lodgings lie a long way off-route in both directions, so if you can time your arrival to catch the Moorsbus, you can save extra walking.

Day 4   Clay Bank to Kildale
15km (9½ miles)

A steep climb from Clay Bank gives way to much gentler paths and tracks running across Urra Moor. The highest point in the North York Moors National Park is very close to hand, where the ancient burial mound on Round Hill stands at 454m (1490ft). The Lyke Wake Walk continues eastwards across the high moors, in the company of the Coast to Coast Walk for part of the way, but the Cleveland Way heads roughly northwards along a broad track. The remains of the Rosedale Mineral Railway can be seen, which from 1861 to 1929 carried iron ore high over the moors from Rosedale to Middlesbrough.

Be sure to have a look at some of the old stone 'crosses' dotted around the moorlands, many of which are deeply carved with route directions, albeit with rather bizarre and archaic spellings

looking back along the cliff coast path from Skinningrove to Hunt Cliff

(one of them often has a handful of coins on top, left there for needy travellers!). The trail follows a road down from the moorlands to reach the little village of Kildale. Lodgings are very limited here, but this is no problem, since there is a railway station from where regular trains run to places with more accommodation.

Day 5 Kildale to Saltburn-by-the-Sea
24km (15 miles)

After climbing through forest, the trail emerges on Easby Moor, a small heath dominated by Captain Cook's Monument. James Cook was born in Marton and educated at Great Ayton, where his old school at the foot of the slope is now a museum. A stirring inscription on the obelisk describes him as, 'A man in nautical knowledge inferior to none. In zeal, prudence and energy superior to most.' Continue towards another landmark – the distinctive hill of Roseberry Topping. The hill is reached by a spur from the trail, sadly omitted by some wayfarers, who thereby deprive themselves of its remarkably extensive views.

Take care with route finding across the moors and through Guisborough Forest. The route leaves the national park at Slapewath, where the Fox and Hounds offers food and drink. Walk through the village of Skelton and cross Skelton Beck in a deep, wooded ravine beneath the towering arches of a monumental railway viaduct. Climb up to Saltburn-by-the-Sea, which has a history of fishing and smuggling, and became a quintessential Victorian seaside resort. A water-powered cliff lift runs between the town and the pier.

Day 6 Saltburn-by-the-Sea to Sandsend
27km (17 miles)

Follow a crumbling cliff coast path from Saltburn, passing close to a railway line on the way to industrial Skinningrove. A steelworks still operates here,

Lobster pots stacked beside the beach at the village of Runswick Bay

almost the same size as the village, and there is a mining museum. The coast path climbs steeply, then continues, quite rugged in places, as it enters the national park. It reaches 203m (666ft) at Boulby Cliff, the highest cliff on the eastern coast of England. The cliffs were torn apart at the Loftus Alum Quarries, and a row of former alum workers' cottages are passed at Boulby. Looking inland, the Boulby Potash Mine has shafts dropping 1500m (4900ft) and leading out 7km (4½ miles) beneath the North Sea. The quaint fishing harbour of Staithes, another place associated with Captain Cook, appears quite suddenly. Whitewashed and stone houses are piled in confusion, half stacked against the cliffs and some literally half in the sea (their foundations are on the seabed in the harbour), with colourful fishing boats alongside.

The cliff path runs high above Port Mulgrave, where the battered little harbour has no access road, since it was served by tunnels from ironstone mines far inland at Grinkle. Runswick Bay has a charming arrangement of houses on a steep slope, but in 1664 the entire village, barring one house, was lost in a landslip one night, fortunately without loss of life. The same happened further along the coast at Kettleness in 1829, with the inhabitants being plucked to safety aboard a ship awaiting a consignment of alum. The route passes areas being reclaimed by nature after 250 years of quarrying alum shale, and at length reaches Sandsend. This village housed the alum workers and was once served by a railway, but quarrying ceased in 1867 and the line closed in 1958. There is accommodation here, as well as in nearby Whitby.

Day 7 Sandsend to Robin Hood's Bay
16km (10 miles)

Whitby has a long history, and its sheltered harbour has attracted settlers for centuries. Whitby Abbey dates from the 7th century, though the current ruins largely date from the 12th century. The town was a notable whaling port in the 18th and 19th centuries and Captain Cook started his seafaring career here. Whitby has some wonderfully poky alleys, but is largely overrun by tourists. Climb the famous 199 stone steps to pass close to the abbey, then continue to Saltwick Bay, where there are yet more extensive old alum quarries.

The cliff path leading onwards is particularly impressive. Pass a lighthouse and foghorn, then cross some steep-sided valleys at Maw Wyke Hole. The Coast to Coast Path accompanies the Cleveland Way around Ness Point to reach Robin Hood's Bay. While Robin Hood had no connection with the area, there is still plenty of history and heritage to take on board. The houses are tightly packed on a steep slope, and were reputedly connected by secret doorways and cupboards, so that goods could be passed unseen from ships, all the way to the top of the village, where they could be smuggled inland.

Day 8 Robin Hood's Bay to Scarborough
23.5km (14½ miles)

The Flagstaff Steps lead out of Robin Hood's Bay and the coastal trail leads to Boggle Hole, where there is a youth hostel in an old corn mill. A steep climb from Stoupe Beck leads onto a fine cliff path, then the trail shifts inland as it climbs through fields to reach Ravenscar. This odd cliff-top settlement, at 190m (625ft), was planned as a tourist resort in 1890, but few investors bought plots or

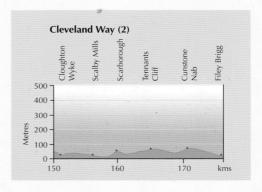

built houses. The Raven Hall Hotel stands on the site of an ancient Roman signal station, connected by line of sight to other stations along the coast. The Lyke Wake Walk, last seen on the other side of the North York Moors, ends in the village after hardy walkers cover 65km (40 miles) across rugged moorlands in 24 hours.

The cliff path overlooks dense, bushy scrub on Beast Cliff and gradually descends towards Hayburn Wyke. A short detour down to the beach reveals a slender waterfall spilling into a rock pool. Inland is a hotel offering food and drink. The route turns around the bay of Cloughton Wyke, where the cliffs are made of chunky slabs, and the national park is left behind on the approach to Scalby Mills. Ahead lies Scarborough, with its 12th-century castle perched strategically on a headland overlooking the harbour. The town was the earliest seaside resort in Britain, when in 1626 a local doctor extolled the virtues of its spa waters. Today, the air is filled with the scent of fish and chips and the busy streets seem to attract tourists throughout the year.

Chunky cobbles are piled high on the beach around lovely Hayburn Wyke

Day 9 Scarborough to Filey
18km (11 miles)

The last day on the trail starts with a fiddly bit of route finding to leave town, passing the site of the Holbeck Hall Hotel, which slid slowly into the sea while watched by TV viewers in the summer of 1993. The cliff path passes above Cornelian Bay, where semi-precious stones can be plucked from the beach. Complex woodland paths are followed at Knipe Point. Walk along Tenants Cliff to reach Lebberston Cliff and Cunstone Nab, passing caravan sites along the way. The last stretch of cliff path runs alongside fields to reach the crumbling clay promontory of Filey Brigg. A monumental stone is deeply inscribed with placenames from along the Cleveland Way, as well as from the Yorkshire Wolds Way. In fact, the final short walk to nearby Filey is along the Wolds Way, and of course keen walkers might like to continue all the way to the Humber estuary.

INFORMATION	
Access to Start	Helmsley is served by regular East Yorkshire Motor Services buses from Scarborough.
Getting Home	Filey has plenty of trains and bus services.
Other Public Transport	East Yorkshire Motor Services cover the southern parts of the trail, while Arriva buses and trains cover the northern parts. Moorsbus provides a useful network of special buses serving remote parts of the trail.
Maps	OS Landrangers 93, 94, 99, 100 and 101
	OS Explorers OL26, OL27 and 301
Cicerone Guide	*The Cleveland Way and the Yorkshire Wolds Way*, by Paddy Dillon
Other Guidebooks	*Cleveland Way*, by Ian Sampson, Aurum Press
Tourist Information Centres	Helmsley tel 01439 70173, Sutton Bank tel 01845 597426, Great Ayton tel 01642 722835, Guisborough tel 01287 633801, Saltburn-by-the-Sea tel 01287 622422, Whitby tel 01947 602674, Robin Hood's Bay tel 01947 885900, Scarborough tel 01723 373333, Filey tel 01723 518000.
Accommodation List	*The Cleveland Way Accommodation and Information Guide*, from TICs
Website	www.nationaltrail.co.uk/ClevelandWay

The Pennine Bridleway runs below Stoodley Pike, while the Pennine Way runs past it

10 Pennine Bridleway

Start and Finish	Middleton Top to Byrness (by 2012)
Distance and Time	195km (121 miles) currently open, taking 1 week
Character	A multi-use footpath, bridleway and cycleway largely following old tracks and quiet roads, mostly along the flanks of hillsides between the valleys and the open moorlands. There is plenty of ascent and descent, but mostly on easy gradients.
Highlights	On the stretch currently open: the High Peak Trail, Derbyshire Dales Nature Reserve, Mount Famine, Hayfield, Cown Edge Rocks, Watergrove Reservoir, Prickshaw to Waterfoot, the Cliviger valley, Gorple and Widdop, Calderdale and Mankinholes.

A fine moorland track crosses a shallow valley holding the Oldham reservoirs (Day 4)

The Pennine Bridleway is an ambitious, multi-use trail running through the Pennines from Derbyshire to Northumberland. The trail is essentially a work-in-progress – at the time of writing (2007) only the southern half is fully open and signposted, stretching from Derbyshire to Lancashire. The projected completion date of the route through the Yorkshire Dales is 2009, while the northern stretch is scheduled for completion in 2012. Walkers, cyclists and horse riders can use the Pennine Bridleway, though for some short stretches different users are required to follow slightly different courses.

This new trail runs roughly parallel to the long-established Pennine Way, though at a lower altitude. While some stretches cross open moorland, much of the route follows firm tracks alongside fields. Many lengths run along the margins between moorland and cultivated countryside, often within sight of old mill towns. The southern half of the trail can be followed from Middleton Top, near Matlock, to Summit, near Rochdale. Leaving Summit, an enormous circular route, called the Mary Towneley Loop, leads onwards

SCHEDULE			
Day	**Start/Finish**	**Km**	**Miles**
Day 1	Middleton Top to Chelmorton	27.5	17
Day 2	Chelmorton to Hayfield	30	18½
Day 3	Hayfield to Uppermill	33	20½
Day 4	Uppermill to Summit	27.5	17
Day 5	Summit to Waterfoot	24	15
Day 6	Waterfoot to Colden	31	19
Day 7	Colden to Summit	22	13½

and is named after the driving force behind the trail.

In future, the Pennine Bridleway will extend northwards from Lancashire, taking a low-level route through the Yorkshire Dales to the Vale of Eden. It will then cross the North Pennines and explore South Tynedale and North Tynedale, before passing though extensive forests to finish at Byrness near the Scottish border. When complete, the trail is expected to measure around 565km (350 miles), which will make it the second longest national trail, exceeded in length only by the South West Coast Path.

Day 1 Middleton Top to Chelmorton

27.5km (17 miles)

The Pennine Bridleway starts at Middleton Top above Matlock and Wirksworth. A visitor centre is immediately to hand, stocked with information and offering refreshments, with cycle hire also available. The first day follows the High Peak Trail, an old railway trackbed that was converted to a footpath and cycleway long before the Pennine Bridleway was established. The trail is very popular and rich in railway heritage, starting with a short tunnel and an incline. For the rest of the day, the route is almost level, though overall it climbs gently uphill. A dark cindery surface leads to Longcliffe and a rock cutting, then the old trackbed has a creamy limestone surface, and is flanked by stout stone buttresses as it runs round Minninglow Hill.

The ribbon-like railway track passes lush green fields, as well as a brickworks at Friden. After passing through the short Newhaven Tunnel, the trackbed reaches a junction with the Tissington Trail, where a spur of the Pennine Bridleway leads to nearby Hartington Station along another old railway trackbed. The High Peak Trail passes a cycle-hire centre with refreshments at Parsley Hay, then later passes a pub at Hurdlow and runs close to another pub at Pomeroy. The railway trackbed ends suddenly near a quarry at Dowlow, but roads and another track are followed northwards, running near the village of Chelmorton and the Church Inn.

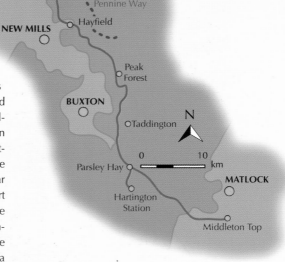

Day 2 Chelmorton to Hayfield
30km (18½ miles)

Shortly after leaving Chelmorton, it is worth making a detour to the burial chamber of Fivewells Cairn. This stands at around 430m (1410ft), enjoying views northwards across Chee Dale. The Pennine Bridleway zigzags down into the deep-cut dale and briefly touches the Monsal Trail, which is another walkway and cycleway based on an old railway trackbed. Climb from the dale to pass the Old Moor Quarry and walk through fields past the little village of Wormhill. A walled path leads down into Monk's Dale, which is one of a handful of lovely wooded valleys making up the Derbyshire Dales National Nature Reserve. The Pennine Bridleway mostly follows roads through the villages of Wheston and Peak Forest, and while cyclists and horse riders must stick to the signposted trail, walkers would doubtless enjoy footpaths through the dales instead.

Roads are followed through Perry Dale to Rushup Edge, and there is a transition from the limestone landscape of the White Peak to the gritstone landscape of the Dark Peak. A clear track wanders down to Roych Clough, where the ford is paved with flagstones. The track climbs over 450m (1475ft) around South Head Hill to cross a gap close to Mount Famine. The sprawling moorland slopes of Kinder Scout dominate as good tracks finally lead down to Hayfield. This village is usually very busy at weekends and holiday periods as hundreds of walkers head to and from Kinder Scout.

Day 3 Hayfield to Uppermill
33km (20½ miles)

An old railway trackbed leads from Hayfield to Birch Vale, then the trail climbs across the heathery slopes of Lantern Pike. There are good views of the

The Pennine Bridleway follows a farm track between Lantern Pike and Cown Edge Rocks

moorland massif of Kinder Scout, whose skyline is traversed by the Pennine Way. Tracks and minor roads lead onwards, then cyclists and horse riders must part company with walkers. The former are largely limited to roads and the course of the Trans Pennine Trail to Tintwistle, while the latter can enjoy a high-level scenic walk over Cown Edge Rocks, taking tracks and field paths to Hollingworth before climbing back towards the moors.

A moorland track leads across a little gap to reach the Swineshaw reservoirs, then a road runs down through the Brushes Valley. Fine tracks are followed easily across rugged slopes, between fields and the fringes of the moors, looking down on mill villages and towns. On the descent to Greenfield, a rocky edge overlooking the village is crowned with the 'pots and pans' obelisk, a notable local landmark. Steep-sided Chew Valley bites deeply into the flank of the Pennines. Yet another old railway trackbed is followed through a pleasantly wooded corridor to Uppermill, which has a good range of facilities.

Day 4 Uppermill to Summit
27.5km (17 miles)

Walk up the valley from Uppermill and Diggle to reach the busy A62 at Standedge. The road passes through a cutting on high, bleak moorland, and the Pennine Bridleway briefly runs in tandem with the

Pennine Way. The course of an old road is followed downhill to Bleak Hey Nook, and the route passes Castleshaw, where the grassy ramparts of an old Roman fort can be distinguished. A network of tracks zigzags, rises and falls, crossing the moors and climbing as high as 420m (1380ft), and passing a series of little reservoirs. A couple of busy roads have to be crossed and the Ram Inn is easily reached from the second of these.

The route passes beneath the noisy M62 motorway, which is supported on tall concrete columns rising from a grassy valley. Hollingworth Lake was built in 1801 to feed the Rochdale Canal. It is also known as the 'weighvers' seaport', as it was popular with workers from nearby mills. Captain Webb practised here before becoming the first person to swim across the English Channel. The reservoir is a venue for all kinds of watersports and is equipped with a visitor centre. Roads and tracks climb once more to the fringes of the moors, crossing another busy road above Littleborough. The Pennine Bridleway reaches Summit, where there is a pub, as well as a main road with regular bus services to nearby towns.

Day 5 Summit to Waterfoot
24km (15 miles)

The Pennine Bridleway includes an enormous circular trail called the Mary Towneley Loop. This

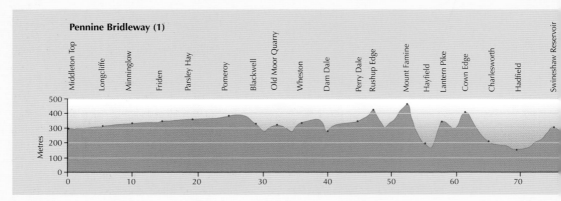

A dusting of snow picks out a moorland track on the slopes of Brown Wardle Hill (Day 5)

would take walkers three days to complete if they returned to Summit. However, once the northern stages of the route are fully open, most walkers will complete only one half of the loop and simply continue northwards, rather than doubling back to Summit.

Good tracks lead to Watergrove Reservoir, where a farming community was evacuated during construction in the 1930s in the interests of maintaining water purity. The ruins of former farmsteads abound, and their names are preserved on wooden boards, while some stonework from the old buildings has been incorporated into the reservoir dam. A fine cobbled road climbs from the reservoirs towards the moors, linking nowhere with nowhere, although once it would have been busy with horses and carts. Tracks leading across the flanks of Brown Wardle Hill can be muddy, but later, down in the wooded valley of Healey Dell, surfaces are

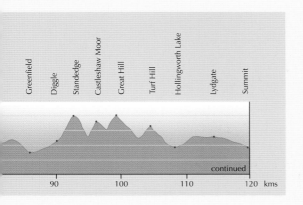

continued

An old farmstead in the Colden valley is covered with snow in the middle of winter (Day 6)

Rossendale Valley, where a succession of mill settlements links to form a ribbon-like urban sprawl. Descend to Waterfoot, which is one of these settlements, enjoying good transport links to the others.

Day 6 Waterfoot to Colden
31km (19 miles)

As the trail climbs from Waterfoot, it remains close to the built-up settlements in the valley, though these gradually give way to farmsteads, fields and moors. Cross and recross the main road that climbs from the valley, reaching 363m (1191ft) on Deerplay Moor. The trail descends close to Easden Clough and passes a monument to the late Mary Towneley, who had the original idea for the Pennine Bridleway. After the long-established Towneley family vacated Towneley Hall near Burnley, they settled at Dyneley Hall in the Cliviger valley. Drop into the Cliviger valley and cross the River Calder to reach Holme Chapel, then the route wriggles up the other

firm and clean. Another fine cobbled road climbs to the lovingly restored stone hamlet of Prickshaw.

There is no end of well-laid cobbled roads in this part of the Pennines, and another fine example leads from Catley Lane Head as high as 465m (1525ft) at Top of Leach. The old moorland road needed a firm surface, as it once carried heavy loads of building stone and flagstones from a series of high quarries. Enjoy fine views over the

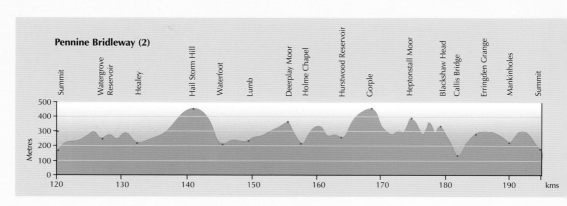

Pennine Bridleway (2)

side of the valley. An old moorland road known as the Long Causeway is crossed near a whirling windfarm, then rugged, hummocky ground is crossed at Shedden. Limestone cobbles were once dug from glacial drift and burnt to make lime to fertilise nearby fields.

The trail passes Cant Clough Reservoir and Hurstwood Reservoir, and it is worth making a short detour to see the old stone houses in the village of Hurstwood. One of these is reputed to have been the home of the Elizabethan poet Edmund Spenser. A fine track known as the Gorple Road crosses rolling moorlands, climbing as high as 431m (1414ft) before dropping to Widdop Reservoir. The Pennine Bridleway touches the Pennine Way a couple of times before running roughly parallel to it across the flanks of Heptonstall Moor. However, the Pennine Way takes a direct line across the Colden valley, while the Pennine Bridleway zigzags and so takes longer to cross.

Day 7 Colden to Summit
22km (13½ miles)

The two national trails continue to pursue parallel courses as they drop steeply to Callis Bridge near Hebden Bridge, then they climb up the other side of Calderdale. While the Pennine Way climbs to the prominent monument of Stoodley Pike, the Pennine Bridleway stays lower, and follows clear tracks to the little village of Mankinholes. A road leads from one pub to another, then a rather rugged route climbs round a spur of moorland before descending to the valley. A very steep cobbled track drops to the Rochdale Canal, where the trail also crosses a busy main road. A steep climb leads to an airy track picking its way along a cliff edge high above the valley, before a descent finally leads back to Summit to bring the Mary Towneley Loop to a close.

INFORMATION

Access to Start	Trains serve Matlock, from where buses lead to Middleton.
Getting Home	Until the route extends further northwards, buses from Summit link with trains at Rochdale and Todmorden for onward travel.
Other Public Transport	Trains run close to the route at Matlock, Buxton, Glossop, Littleborough, Rochdale, Burnley, Hebden Bridge and Todmorden, often with good connections to local bus services.
Maps	OS 1:50,000 Landrangers 103, 109, 110 and 119
	OS 1:25,000 Explorers OL1, OL21 and OL24
	Harveys 1:40,000 Pennine Bridleway South
Guidebook	*Pennine Bridleway South*, by Sue Viccars, Aurum Press
Tourist Information Centres	Matlock tel 01629 583388, Bakewell tel 01629 813227, Buxton tel 01298 25106, Glossop tel 01457 855920, Saddleworth tel 01457 870336, Oldham tel 0161 6271024, Rochdale tel 01706 864928, Rawtenstall tel 01706 244678, Burnley tel 01282 664421, Hebden Bridge tel 01422 843831, Todmorden tel 01706 818181.
Accommodation List	*Pennine Bridleway Holiday Guide*, from TICs.
Website	www.nationaltrail.co.uk/PennineBridleway

The pencil-like pinnacle of Nichol's Chair is seen poking from the cliffs of High Cup (Day 11)

11 Pennine Way

Start and Finish	Edale to Kirk Yetholm
Distance and Time	435km (270 miles) taking 2½ weeks
Character	A long and arduous upland trail, often crossing remote moorlands and hills, suitable for fit and experienced walkers. There is seldom much shelter from inclement weather. Several well-worn stretches have been paved with stone and are much easier to follow than in previous years.
Highlights	Kinder Scout, Bleaklow, Black Hill, Blackstone Edge, Stoodley Pike, Calderdale, Widdop, Brontë country, Lothersdale, Gargrave, Malham, Fountains Fell, Pen-y-Ghent, Ling Gill, Hawes, Hardraw Force, Great Shunner Fell, Thwaite, waterfalls at Keld, Tan Hill Inn, Baldersdale, Lunedale, waterfalls in Teesdale, High Cup, Dufton, Cross Fell, Alston, Hadrian's Wall, Bellingham and the Cheviot Hills.

Cauldron Snout is a furious waterfall tearing down through a twisted rocky gorge (Day 10)

The Pennine Way was the first of Britain's national trails, and for many it remains the best, climbing higher and traversing more remote country than any other. It has a long and convoluted history – the initial idea was proposed as long ago as 1935. Ramblers' champion Tom Stephenson, writing in the *Daily Herald,* called for a 'long green trail' to be established, 'Why should we not press for something akin to the Appalachian Trail?', he asked, 'A Pennine way from the Peak to the Cheviots.' He imagined 'a faint line on the Ordnance Maps which the feet of grateful pilgrims would, with the passing years, engrave on the face of the land.' The route was opened in 1965 and proved immensely popular from the outset.

This challenging trail marches across the bleak moors of the Dark Peak in the northern half of the Peak District National Park. It runs through the South Pennines, where the moors are lower and gentler. High hills and moors, separated by verdant vales, are enjoyed through the Yorkshire Dales National Park. Sprawling moorlands and the highest hills are traversed in the North Pennines Area of Outstanding Natural Beauty. A stretch of Hadrian's Wall leads the route into the Northumberland National Park, then forests and empty moorlands

Day	Start/Finish	Km	Miles
Day 1	Edale to Crowden	26	16
Day 2	Crowden to Standedge	21	13
Day 3	Standedge to Callis Bridge	26	16
Day 4	Callis Bridge to Cowling	26	16
Day 5	Cowling to Malham	29	18
Day 6	Malham to Horton-in-Ribblesdale	24	15
Day 7	Horton-in-Ribblesdale to Hawes	24	15
Day 8	Hawes to Tan Hill Inn	27.5	17
Day 9	Tan Hill Inn to Middleton-in-Teesdale	27.5	17
Day 10	Middleton-in-Teesdale to Langdon Beck	13	8
Day 11	Langdon Beck to Dufton	22.5	14
Day 12	Dufton to Alston	32	20
Day 13	Alston to Greenhead	27.5	17
Day 14	Greenhead to Housesteads	17.5	11
Day 15	Housesteads to Bellingham	22.5	14
Day 16	Bellingham to Byrness	24	15
Day 17	Byrness to Hen Hole	32	20
Day 18	Hen Hole to Kirk Yetholm	13	8

SCHEDULE

are crossed on the way to the remote crest of the Cheviot Hills. The trail steps over the border into Scotland to finish at Kirk Yetholm. This is a long walk and a hard walk, but one that is well worth the effort.

Within a decade of opening, some of the more fragile parts of the Pennine Way, particularly the upland peat bogs, began to look less like a 'long green trail' and more like a hideous black scar. During the 1980s there were calls for action and a number of patchy repairs were inaugurated, but it became clear that a hard-wearing and more expensive solution was needed. In the 1990s, huge stone-built mills were being demolished close to the Pennines, and cages full of thick flagstones were lifted by helicopter onto the remote moors.

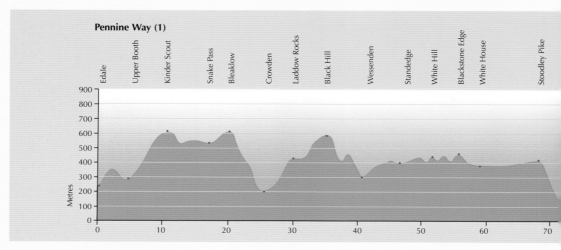

Workers laboured to lay the flagstones end to end in a style reminiscent of Pennine packhorse ways of old. By the time the flagstones bedded in and the vegetation was restored alongside, walkers were able to walk without wallowing in filth, and without contributing to the destruction of the very moorlands they wanted to enjoy.

Facilities along the Pennine Way are well established. There are plenty of campsites for backpackers, and this has long been the traditional way to walk the trail. It was once possible to walk almost the entire route using youth hostels, but many have closed in recent years. There are plenty of bed and breakfasts, along with inns and hotels, but the long and remote stretch through the Cheviot Hills requires advance planning. While tens of thousands of people have walked the Pennine Way, it was claimed, in the early days, that half of all those who failed to complete it dropped out in the middle of their first day's walk!

Day 1 Edale to Crowden
26km (16 miles)

Originally, there were two ways out of Edale – the Pennine Way main route, crossing the forbidding bogs of Kinder Scout, and an alternative route,

A stone-flagged path wanders through pastures as it climbs away from Edale

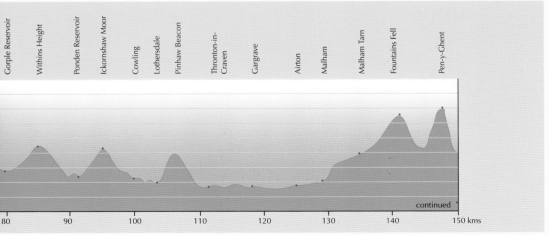

Gorple Reservoir · Withins Height · Ponden Reservoir · Ickornshaw Moor · Cowling · Lothersdale · Pinhaw Beacon · Thronton-in-Craven · Gargrave · Airton · Malham · Malham Tarn · Fountains Fell · Pen-y-Ghent

continued

80   90   100   110   120   130   140   150 kms

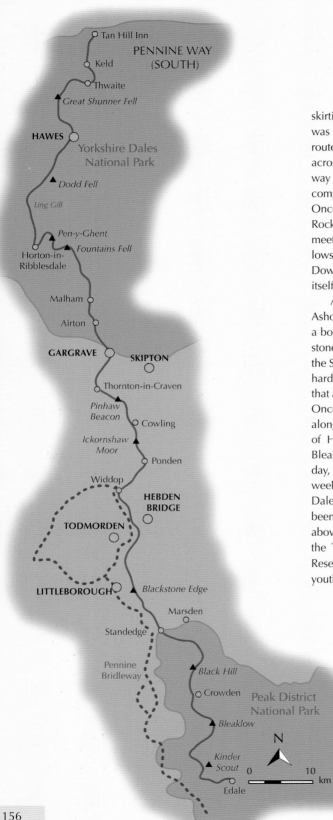

skirting the firmer rocky edge of the plateau. What was once the alternative route is now the main route, and walkers are discouraged from trampling across the top of Kinder Scout. An old packhorse way called Jacob's Ladder, a route that had to be completely rebuilt in stone, is used to gain height. Once at the top, gentler gradients lead past Edale Rocks to Kinder Low, at 633m (2077ft). Black peat meets an abrupt gritstone edge, and as the trail follows this edge it passes a waterfall at Kinder Downfall. On windy days the water blows back on itself, soaking unwary walkers.

After descending from the Kinder plateau at Ashop Head, the Pennine Way used to flounder in a boggy, overtrodden morass, but it now follows a stone-flagged path all the way across the moors to the Snake Road. Some walkers complain about the hard surface, but there is no evidence to suggest that anyone prefers to wallow in the bog alongside. Once across the Snake Road, the trail runs straight along Devil's Dike, then climbs up the streambed of Hern Clough to reach the broad summit of Bleaklow Head at 633m (2077ft). On a really clear day, it is possible to look ahead along a whole week's journey to Pen-y-Ghent in the Yorkshire Dales. Most of the descent from the moors has been resurfaced, picking a way along a brow high above Torside Clough. After a steep descent, cross the Trans Pennine Trail and the dam of Torside Reservoir and walk to Crowden, where there is a youth hostel and campsite.

Day 2 Crowden to Standedge
21km (13 miles)

This used to be a horrible stage, but it's now quite pleasant. Start the day by climbing a rugged path into a wild, steep-sided valley. After passing little waterfalls in Oakenclough Brook, walk along the gritstone edge of Laddow Rocks. The route runs parallel to Crowden Great Brook,

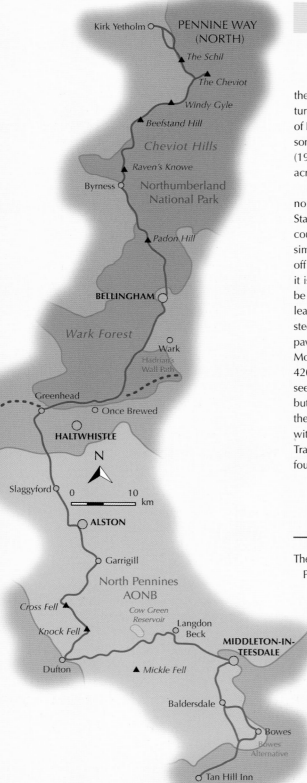

PENNINE WAY (NORTH)

Kirk Yetholm

The Schil

The Cheviot

Windy Gyle

Beefstand Hill

Cheviot Hills

Raven's Knowe

Byrness   Northumberland National Park

Padon Hill

BELLINGHAM

Wark Forest

Wark
Hadrian's Wall Path

Greenhead

Once Brewed

HALTWHISTLE

N

Slaggyford

0   10 km

ALSTON

Garrigill

North Pennines AONB

Cross Fell

Cow Green Reservoir   Langdon Beck

Knock Fell

MIDDLETON-IN-TEESDALE

Dufton   Mickle Fell

Baldersdale

Bowes
Bowes Alternative

Tan Hill Inn

then a flagstone path climbs onto the broad, featureless moorland slopes of Black Hill. The summit of Black Hill used to be a nightmare quagmire, and sometimes it was impossible to reach the 582m (1909ft) summit. Now flagstones lead effortlessly across it, and the bare peat is re-vegetating.

In the past, the main route forged directly northwest across appalling bogs to reach Standedge, and an alternative route took an easier course via Wessenden. Now, the Pennine Way simply heads straight for Wessenden, and coming off Black Hill and going over to Wessenden Head it is paved with slabs. ('Snoopy's' snack van might be parked at Wessenden Head.) A reservoir road leads down to Wessenden, then a path crosses a steep-sided valley. A gentler climb is again largely paved with flagstones and leads between the Black Moss reservoirs. Cross a moorland crest around 420m (1380ft) and walk downhill. A pub can be seen in the distance, close to Redbrook Reservoir, but the Pennine Way follows a moorland track to the crest of the busy A62 at Standedge, intersecting with the course of the Pennine Bridleway National Trail. A couple of bed-and-breakfast places can be found by walking down the bridleway.

Day 3 Standedge to Callis Bridge
26km (16 miles)

The Pennine Way leaves the Peak District National Park at Standedge and traverses lower moorlands throughout the day. The gritstone edge of Standedge peaks at 448m (1470ft) and overlooks Oldham. Good paths run over rugged moorland, crossing a road before climbing White Hill, which is crowned with a trig point at 466m (1529ft). A snack van is usually parked at the next road crossing, near a prominent communication mast at Bleakedgate. A graceful footbridge takes the Pennine Way over the M62 motorway, then a stony path leads up over Blackstone Edge. Rounded boulders and

Stoodley Pike is a prominent monument perched high above industrial Calderdale

outcrops peak at 472m (1549ft) and views stretch into the distance beyond Manchester. An old paved road runs downhill and is often referred to as a Roman road, though this is highly unlikely. A reservoir drain contours across the moorland slope and leads to the White House pub.

Three reservoirs perched on a moorland brow are linked by a broad, firm track running around 375m (1230ft). A more rugged path continues across the moors towards the prominent monument of Stoodley Pike. Before reaching that point, hostellers can descend to Mankinholes for the night. The black obelisk at 400m (1310ft) on Stoodley Pike commemorates the Peace of Ghent in 1812 and has been rebuilt twice. It offers splendid views of Calderdale. Field paths link with a farm road running down through Callis Wood into the dale. At Callis Bridge, a canal, main road and

railway run close together, with mill buildings, industrial sites and terraced houses squeezed cheek by jowl. Hebden Bridge is a nearby town, easily reached on foot or by bus, and offering all facilities.

Day 4   Callis Bridge to Cowling
26km (16 miles)

Climb steeply from Calderdale, then more gently through fields near Blackshaw Head, only to drop down into another wooded valley. Climb again past Colden, passing close to a wonderfully remote shop that offers all kinds of food and drink. The trail touches 375m (1230ft) on the flanks of Heptonstall Moor, then descends into a rugged little valley just below Gorple Lower Reservoir. The remote Pack Horse Inn is nearby and can be reached by making a short detour. The Pennine Way passes two of the three Walshaw reservoirs, then climbs to 450m (1475ft) on a flagstone path over the moors of Withins Height. The ruins of Top Withins, vaguely associated with Emily Brontë's *Wuthering Heights*, incorporate a basic shelter for walkers.

The Pennine Way descends from the moors and drops through fields to reach Ponden Reservoir, where there is a bed and breakfast and basic campsite. After climbing away from the reservoir the route makes a beeline onto Ickornshaw Moor, climbing as high as 438m (1437ft) on a paved path before wriggling downhill. A handful of curious little chalets are passed, then fiddly field paths are linked on the way down to a main road. The long and straggly village of Cowling offers shops, pubs and accommodation.

Day 5 Cowling to Malham
29km (18 miles)

Take care with route finding during this day's walk, which is often confined to fields. The first stage runs from Cowling to Lothersdale, where a mill village is tucked into a steep-sided little valley. The Hare and Hounds provides food and drink. Climb through fields and continue onto heathery Elslack Moor, whose summit is Pinhaw Beacon at 388m (1273ft). Views stretch back to the South Pennines, and ahead across the rumpled green patchwork spread of the Aire Gap through the distant Yorkshire Dales. Descend from the moor, through fields to Thornton-in-Craven, where there is another pub.

The rolling green fields stretching north are low-lying and a meandering course is taken along the towpath of the Leeds and Liverpool Canal. This could be followed all the way to Gargrave, but the Pennine Way takes a more direct line through fields. This large, stone-built village proclaims itself as a gateway to the Yorkshire Dales National Park, and the Dalesman Café has catered for many weary wayfarers over the years. There are good views as the trail climbs gently past Haw Crag,

then easy walking follows the silvery River Aire upstream past Airton and Hanlith. Malham is first seen from a grassy hillside and looks charming, but is often overrun with visitors. If any spare time is available in the evening, Gordale Scar is well worth a visit, and few could fail to be awed by the spectacular overhanging cliffs and waterfalls.

Day 6 Malham to Horton-in-Ribblesdale
24km (15 miles)

A popular path runs to Malham Cove, where a sheer cliff of limestone once had a waterfall pouring over it, and now has a river bubbling up from

Gordale Scar is just off-route near Malham, but is well worth a visit in the evening

its base. Climb uphill and cross a wonderful lime-stone pavement, then walk up the 'dry valley' that once carried a river. The trail passes the Water Sinks, where the river from Malham Tarn simply vanishes into its own bed. One has to wonder what is happening underground, but so far pot-holers haven't managed to penetrate the depths to discover. Malham Tarn is surrounded by permeable limestone, but sits on a bed of impermeable slate, so it remains full of water. Pass Malham Tarn House, which is used by the Field Studies Council. The trail wanders through woods and fields, then meanders across the more rugged slopes of Fountains Fell. It doesn't quite reach the 668m (2192ft) summit, which is pitted with old bell-pits that once produced coal, and while this is the highest point yet gained on the trail, it is soon to be surpassed.

Walk steeply downhill and follow a road past the farm at Rainscar. Pass another farm at Dale Head and take a boardwalk towards the rocky southern prow of Pen-y-Ghent. A limestone rock-step is followed by a gritstone rock-step and this is one of the few times you will feel any sense of exposure on the Pennine Way. Gentler slopes lead to the 694m (2277ft) summit of Pen-y-Ghent, where an old drystone wall has been rebuilt to incorporate an artistic seating area. Follow the path

as it drops steeply from the summit, passing close to the dark slit of Hunt Pot on the lower slopes. A walled lane leads down to Horton-in-Ribblesdale, where the Pen-y-Ghent Café has served pint pots of tea to wayfarers for decades, and thick Pennine Way visitor books can be studied.

Day 7 Horton-in-Ribblesdale to Hawes
24km (15 miles)

Leave Horton-in-Ribblesdale via the Crown and follow a walled track as it undulates through little grassy hills in Upper Ribblesdale. There are several potholes close to the track – some obvious with waterfalls pouring into them, and others hidden or 'dry'. Farm buildings are passed at Old Ing, then a track that was once a highway reaches the wooded gorge of Ling Gill. The trail climbs to Cam End, where it joins an even older highway – a Roman road that once ran through the heart of the Yorkshire Dales. This is Cam High Road, and it runs above Cam Houses, which offers lodgings in this remote spot.

The road serving Cam Houses is a narrow strip of tarmac and the Pennine Way leaves it to follow a track across the slopes of Dodd Fell, contouring around 590m (1935ft) with lovely views

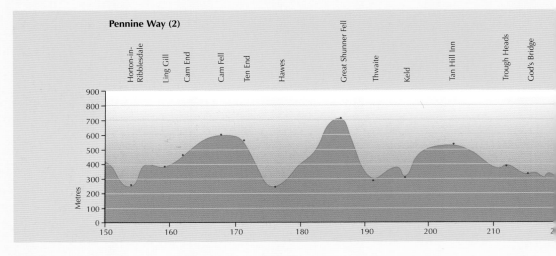

down-dale to Snaizeholme. This track, known as Cam Road, can be followed straight down to Hawes, but the Pennine Way leaves it to follow a path across hummocky ground at Ten End. A descent with fine views along Wensleydale links with Gaudy Lane. Field paths and back alleys lead into the heart of Hawes, which is a delightful bustling market town with every facility for wayfarers. Those with time to spare can have a look at the old station, now a visitor centre, or the Wensleydale Creamery, or simply explore the shops and visit some of the quaint pubs.

Day 8 Hawes to Tan Hill Inn
27.5km (17 miles)

Cross the River Ure on the way from Hawes to Hardraw, then decide whether to detour through the Green Dragon Inn to see the spectacular leap taken by Hardraw

Hardraw Force can be visited after leaving Hawes by detouring through a pub

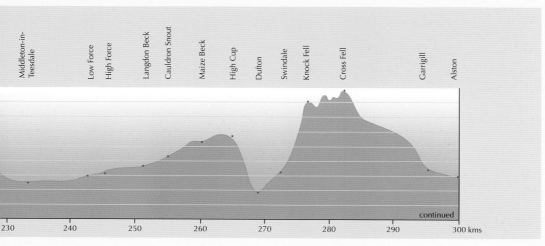

Middleton-in-Teesdale · Low Force · High Force · Langdon Beck · Cauldron Snout · Maize Beck · High Cup · Dufton · Swindale · Knock Fell · Cross Fell · Garrigill · Alston

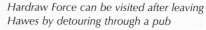

continued

230   240   250   260   270   280   290   300 kms

Force – a waterfall with a single drop of 29m (96ft). Back on the trail, the Pennine Way climbs up a walled lane, then continues up a path on the broad moorland crest of Great Shunner Fell. False summits raise false hopes in mist, but the provision of a paved path means that wayfarers no longer have to wallow in peat bogs as they did many years ago. The top of the whaleback bears a cross-shelter at 716m (2349ft). There is a long moorland descent to the lovely stone-built village of Thwaite, and anyone arriving after a foul crossing will be pleased to find a pub, restaurant and hotel. However, it is no great hardship to continue up and around the steep slopes of Kisdon to reach the nearby village of Keld. Walkers who stay here should make an effort to discover splendid waterfalls on an evening stroll.

Walkers who feel able to continue beyond Keld will climb gradually away from farms up a boggy moorland slope. Looking ahead, there is no sign of habitation, though a road runs parallel some distance below the trail. Stay on the marked path, as the open mouths of old colliery bell-pits await the unwary. All of a sudden, the Tan Hill Inn pops into view, offering food, drink and accommodation in the middle of nowhere at an elevation of 530m (1732ft). At this height it is the highest pub in England, as signs fixed to the wall confirm. The inn is licensed for weddings, and it has happened that walkers following the Pennine Way have been married on the premises!

Day 9 Tan Hill Inn to Middleton-in-Teesdale
27.5km (17 miles)

The Yorkshire Dales National Park is left behind at Tan Hill, and the route enters the North Pennines Area of Outstanding Natural Beauty. Gently sloping Sleightholme Moor proves to be very wet and boggy, but was once much worse. The Pennine

The Tan Hill Inn is the highest hostelry in England and sits in a bleak part of the Pennines

Way used to run along the southern bank of Frumming Beck and became very badly trodden, so it has been transferred to a firmer footing on the northern bank. Some walkers leave Tan Hill and sneak along the Sleightholme Moor Road instead, picking up the trail later. Take care to leave the road beyond Sleightholme and cross the valley to reach the isolated farmstead of Trough Heads. At this point the route splits in two, and you must decide whether to make a beeline for Middleton-in-Teesdale, or take the Bowes Alternative, which is a longer route, but might suit those who started the day walking from Thwaite or Keld.

The main route heads north and crosses God's Bridge, a natural rock bridge over the River Greta. An underpass takes the trail under the busy A66. Rolling moorlands reach 390m (1280ft) at the heap of stones known as Ravock Castle. Broad Deep Dale is followed by sprawling Cotherstone Moor, which reaches 428m (1404ft) at Race Yate. The sense of space is astounding, then the trail leads down into Baldersdale, where reservoirs fill the valley floor. Pass the farm of Low Birk Hatt, made famous after Hannah Hauxwell's life was documented for television. Fields and enclosed patches of moorland are crossed as the route leads over to Lunedale, where a bridge crosses the head of Grassholme Reservoir. A rather fiddly series of field paths takes the trail to 440m (1445ft) across the slopes of Harter Fell, then there is a direct descent to Middleton-in-Teesdale. This former lead-mining town has a splendid central green, fine stone houses and plenty of services for visiting walkers.

The Bowes Alternative, seen leaving the main route at Trough Heads, links a series of farms as it roughly traces Sleightholme Beck and the River Greta to the village of Bowes. The Ancient Unicorn pub and limited accommodation are available, and a ruined castle and old church are worth exploring. Leaving Bowes by road, the route crosses Deepdale Beck and stays fairly low as it crosses the moors, barely touching 370m

(1215ft) as it passes the distinctive gritstone outcrop encircling Goldsborough. The Bowes Alternative rejoins the main Pennine Way route in Baldersdale to continue to Teesdale.

Day 10 Middleton-in-Teesdale to Langdon Beck
13km (8 miles)

Many walkers will welcome one or two easy days along the Pennine Way, and the journey upstream beside the River Tees is little more than a half-day walk. A cattle mart stands across the river from Middleton-in-Teesdale\ and a level, easy path leads straight through fields. The River Tees describes broad and scenic meanders and the Pennine Way clips one bend before settling down to follow the river faithfully. Pass Scoberry Bridge, but pause at Wynch Bridge, an attractive suspension footbridge giving access to the pretty little whitewashed village

High Force is a powerful waterfall pounding into a dark gorge at Forest in Teesdale

of Bowlees. The bridge dates from 1830, but replaces an earlier bridge of 1704, both of which were strung up by local lead miners. Bowlees has a visitor centre in an old chapel, helping people to understand and enjoy the wonderful range of wild flowers and wildlife of Upper Teesdale.

Just upstream from Wynch Bridge are the powerful rapids of Low Force, and the river often flows across bare rock as it is followed further upstream. Pass Holwick Head Bridge and follow the path through masses of juniper, possibly the greatest spread of juniper in England. A short detour through the bushes reveals a good but precarious viewpoint for High Force – the most powerful waterfall in England, where the water breaks halfway down a dark gash in a dolerite cliff and pounds into a turbulent pool. After this dramatic scene the river seems tamer upstream, and a large quarry blights the scene. However, after climbing beyond Bleabeck Force, the broad flowery pastures and hay-meadows of Upper Teesdale delight the eye, dotted with attractive whitewashed farmsteads.

The Pennine Way abandons the River Tees and wanders alongside Langdon Beck instead. At this point there is a three-way split, depending on the night's lodgings. Backpackers can camp at Sayer Hill, while hostellers head in the other direction, and anyone staying at the Langdon Beck Hotel can continue a little further upstream.

Day 11 Langdon Beck to Dufton
22.5km (14 miles)

The Pennine Way regains the banks of the River Tees soon after leaving Langdon Beck, following it upstream past Widdybank Farm. Cronkley Scar and Falcon Clints are rugged cliffs with bouldery slopes that frown on the river. All of a sudden, after turning a rocky corner, the furious, foaming falls of Cauldron Snout are seen and heard. Hands have to be used to grapple with the rock, then at the top of the falls, the massive dam of Cow Green Reservoir appears. Follow a farm road to the isolated farmstead at

Birkdale, then continue onto the open moors. A gradual ascent past old mine workings, alongside an enormous military firing range, crosses the moorland slopes of Rasp Hill at 583m (1913ft). Descend a little to walk beside Maize Beck and cross it using a footbridge built in recent years.

The sight of High Cup breaking into view after the long moorland plod is truly memorable. All of a sudden, cliffs fall precipitously ahead, and stretch away in an arc either side of a deep and rugged valley. On a clear day the fells of the Lake District form a dramatic distant backdrop. The trail picks a way along the rim of the cliffs, decreasing in width at the appropriately named Narrowgate. The way ahead is usually obvious, down a slope to Peeping Hill, then down a fine track that becomes a walled lane. At the end of the day, the charming red-sandstone village of Dufton stands four square around an extensive green. The Stag Inn offers food and drink, while lodgings include a campsite, youth hostel and a handful of bed and breakfasts.

Day 12 Dufton to Alston
32km (20 miles)

Hope and pray for good weather on this day's walk, which crosses the highest and most remote terrain on the whole of the Pennine Way (which also happens to hold the English records for both the highest wind-speeds and most prolonged frosts!). The trail climbs very gently as it leaves Dufton, but the gradient steepens on the way to Swindale Beck. From there, climb straight up rugged and often bouldery slopes, with no clear view of the top until at fairly close quarters. A huge cairn is passed shortly before the 794m (2605ft) summit of Knock Fell is reached. Views take in exceptionally wild and rugged moors, which have earned the region the nickname 'England's last wilderness'.

Walk on the very crest of the highest Pennines to continue, aiming first for the distinctive 'radome' of the weather station on top of Great Dun Fell. Pass close to the 848m (2782ft) summit and drop down the other side. A fine stretch of paved pathway crosses a boggy gap, then another climb leads to the summit of Little Dun Fell at 842m (2762ft). Follow the flagstone path across a broader boggy gap, then climb up a wet slope to the very source of the mighty River Tees, maybe taking a sup from the highest and most refreshing spring. A bouldery slope gives way to a broad and virtually pathless plateau, and the cross-shelter on top of Cross Fell is not immediately apparent. It stands at 893m (2930ft) – the highest point on the Pennine Way, and indeed, the highest point on any of the national trails in Britain. On a clear day, views encompass the bleak North Pennines, then stretch into the distance to include the Yorkshire Dales, Lake District, southern Scotland and the Cheviot Hills.

Take care to descend correctly, hitting a good path that leads down to an old mine building called Greg's Hut. This offers the only hope of shelter in foul weather, and is equipped for basic overnight lodging. An old mining track leads away from Greg's Hut, undulating at a high level across the bleak and exposed northern slopes of Cross Fell. When it finally drops below 600m (1970ft) as it leaves Pikeman Hill, the Pennine Way follows a walled lane down to the village of Garrigill. Walkers who have had enough will find limited lodgings here, while there is also a shop and pub offering food and drink.

A tall cairn on the edge of Cross Fell

The last stretch is easy, but can seem never-ending at the close of such a long day's walk. Simply follow a path heading downstream beside the River South Tyne. This climbs a little above the river at Bleagate and eventually reaches Alston, the highest market town in England. The market cross, only halfway up the steep and cobbled main street, stands at 300m (985ft).

Day 13 Alston to Greenhead
27.5km (17 miles)

The River South Tyne flows northwards from Alston and the Pennine Way very roughly follows its course. Early in the day, the route drifts well away from the flow and climbs through rough pasture to pass the rumpled ramparts of Whitley Castle, an old Roman fort. The trail runs through fields, but it is easy to be drawn along an old railway trackbed on the way to Slaggyford. Beyond this little village there is a pub just off-route at Knarsdale, then the route follows the course of an old Roman road known as the Maiden Way. It is now little more than a narrow footpath along the edge of moorland, almost reaching 300m (985ft) at one point.

The trail leads down into a valley to cross Hartley Burn, and careful route finding is required,

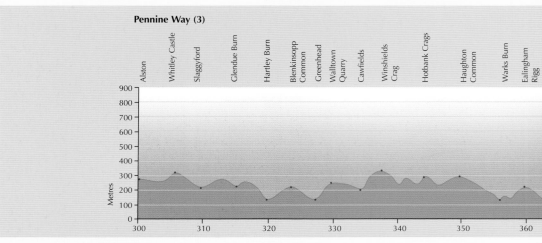

Pennine Way (3)

Moorland slopes are always in view as the Pennine Way runs though South Tynedale

first through fields, then over gentle moorlands. The line of a wire fence proves a useful guide around 275m (900ft) on the crest of Wain Rigg. The way down to Greenhead is anything but direct, and by the time the village is reached, the Pennine Way runs concurrent with the popular Hadrian's Wall Path National Trail. This leads to extra pressure on limited services, but anyone needing to look elsewhere for lodgings can make use of the Hadrian's Wall Bus.

Day 14 Greenhead to Housesteads
17.5km (11 miles)

This is a short and relatively easy day's walk, entirely along the course of Hadrian's Wall. However, the wall pursues a roller-coaster route over several steep-sided little hills, and there are many interesting sites worthy of careful exploration, so any spare time can be quickly consumed. Climb uphill from 14th-century Thirlwall Castle, whose walls are built of stone plundered from Hadrian's Wall, so the actual wall isn't seen until the route is high above Walltown Quarry. An excellent length of the wall writhes along a cliff edge, passing a turret and a milecastle. On a lower stretch, explore the ruins of an extensive Roman fort at Great Chesters.

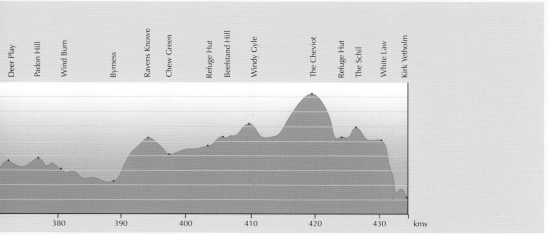

At nearby Cawfields Quarry, there is another excellent stretch of wall climbing from a milecastle, and a fine turret foundation is passed above Caw Gap.

The highest point on Hadrian's Wall is reached on top of Winshields Crag at 345m (1132ft), where extensive views stretch from Cross Fell to the Cheviot Hills. Many Pennine Wayfarers head off-route to the Once Brewed Youth Hostel or the Twice Brewed Inn for the night, but it is worth continuing further along the wall, crossing Peel Crags and Highshield Crags above the lovely lake of Crag Lough. Continue along the top of Hotbank Crags to follow an excellent stretch of the wall to Housesteads Roman fort, which lies a little off the Pennine Way and so isn't always visited by wayfarers. The site is extensive and amazingly complex, with a museum nearby offering help and assistance. There is a guesthouse at Beggar Bog, or the Hadrian's Wall Bus could be used to reach the Once Brewed Youth Hostel, or any other available lodgings in the area.

Day 15 Housesteads to Bellingham
22.5km (14 miles)

Pick up the course of the Pennine Way in the morning and follow it away from Hadrian's Wall, across a low, rolling moorland in sight of Greenlee Lough and Broomlee Lough. The trail is confined to forest on three occasions, and these are just three little corners of the immense Keilder Forest. Watch carefully for waymarks on the crossing of Warks Burn, then continue through fields and along a road, passing farms and crossing Houxty Burn. The Pennine Way makes a beeline for the low gritstone outcrop of Shitlington Crags, passing a bunkhouse that has a basic foodstore. After wandering across Ealingham Common the trail crosses the River North Tyne and enters the stout, stone-built little town of Bellingham. An evening stroll through an interesting, well-wooded valley to visit the waterfall of Hareshaw Linn is highly recommended.

Day 16 Bellingham to Byrness
24km (15 miles)

A gradual climb from Bellingham passes a farm called Blakelaw, then the trail cuts across a moorland slope to reach Hareshaw House. Another gradual ascent on rugged paths takes the route over the summits of Lough Shaw, Deer Play and Whitley Pike, the latter standing at 356m (1168ft). A reconstructed path leads across the slopes of Padon Hill, whose summit is crowned with a prominent pepperpot cairn. Scottish Covenanters, who met to pray in remote locations to avoid persecution, raised the cairn in the 17th

The route above Crag Lough follows Hadrian's Wall

Day 17 Byrness to Hen Hole
32km (20 miles)

Some walkers start early and aim to traverse the whole of the Cheviot Hills in a day, while others take advantage of the (very limited) options to break the journey over two days. There are two basic shelter huts that occur at the 13km and 32km (8 mile and 20 mile) marks. There is also a remote farmhouse bed and breakfast well off-route at Uswayford, which must be booked in advance. Some of the bed and breakfasts in Kirk Yetholm will, by advance arrangement, pick up walkers who descend to Cocklawfoot. You need to choose an option, pack food accordingly, then set out on the most remote part of the whole trail.

Climb a steep and forested slope above Byrness, then enjoy gentler gradients along a moorland crest, crossing Byrness Hill, Houx Hill and Ravens Knowe, the latter standing at 527m (1729ft). The route passes a forest and briefly steps across the Border Fence into Scotland, before stepping back into England to pass the complex earthworks of a Roman marching camp at Chew Green (there are still armies in the area – a vast military training range lies to the south). A flagstone path leads back to the high moorland crest and the line of the Border Fence is followed for a while. The trail pulls away from the fence across a broad and boggy depression, then the fence appears again as the route reaches the first basic shelter hut at 450m (1475ft) on Yearning Saddle.

Follow the Border Fence closely over Lamb Hill, Beefstand Hill and Mozie Law, then cross a broad saddle and climb to the sprawling summit burial cairn on Windy Gyle at 619m (2031ft). Remarkably extensive views stretch back along the trail to Cross Fell in the North Pennines, as well as embracing the huge heathery humps of the Cheviot Hills and extensive stretches of the Southern Uplands of Scotland. Another stone-slabbed path accompanies the Border Fence along a broad and boggy crest, then there is a long and gradual climb to West Cairn Hill at 743m (2438ft).

century. The Pennine Way runs alongside another extensive forest, climbing over the moorland hump of Brownrigg Head at 365m (1198ft). Heading into the forest, the trail follows a long, undulating forest road and eventually descends to the hamlet of Blakehopeburnhaugh. Stay low in the valley to pass Cottonshopeburn Foot, then head for the little forestry village of Byrness, where facilities for walkers are very limited. This is, however, the last place to buy food supplies before the long and arduous walk through the Cheviot Hills.

It has to be said that at this point, most walkers who aim to cross the Cheviot Hills in a day turn a corner and make a beeline for Kirk Yetholm. The Pennine Way, however, includes a spur to the summit of the Cheviot, returning to West Cairn Hill. In the past, this was an appallingly messy bog-trot, but now there is a firm flagstone path the whole way, so the detour is easily made to the 815m (2674ft) summit. Returning to West Cairn Hill, follow a boardwalk path to Auchope Cairn, then drop steeply to a saddle. A short ascent leads to the second shelter hut on a little hump at 497m (1631ft), but you need to be self-sufficient if staying here. Water is available down at Hen Hole.

Day 18 Hen Hole to Kirk Yetholm
13km (8 miles)

Leave the hut and follow the Border Fence along the moorland crest before climbing the rugged slopes of the Schil, passing close to the rocky summit at 605m (1985ft). On the slopes of Black Hag, the Pennine Way steps across the Border Fence into Scotland, and used to descend to Halterburnhead, but this path became badly eroded and is now marked as an alternative route, suitable for use in poor weather. The main route now stays high along a crest, climbing one last hill at White Law, just short of 450m (1475ft). The

Descending from the Cheviot as the Pennine Way finally crosses the border into Scotland

Pennine Way runs concurrent with the course of St Cuthbert's Way as it drops into a valley to ford Halter Burn. All that remains is a short road walk over a gap to finish in the charming little village of Kirk Yetholm. The Border Hotel stands just off a fine green, where bona fide Pennine Wayfarers can claim a free celebratory drink at the bar!

INFORMATION

Access to Start	Transpennine trains regularly serve Edale between Manchester and Sheffield.
Getting Home	Occasional buses from Kirk Yetholm, or a few more from nearby Town Yetholm, go to Kelso, which has good bus links to towns with railway stations for onward travel.
Other Public Transport	The trail is crisscrossed by bus and rail services with varying frequencies. Full details are contained in the *Pennine Way Accommodation and Public Transport Guid*e, available from TICs.
Maps	OS 1:50,000 Landrangers 80, 86, 91, 92, 98, 103, 109 and 110
	OS 1:25,000 Explorers OL1, OL2, OL16, OL21, OL30, OL31, OL42 and OL43
	Harveys 1:40,000 Pennine Way South, Central and North
Cicerone Guide	*The Pennine Way*, by Martin Collins, Cicerone
Other Guidebooks	*Pennine Way South and Pennine Way North*, by Tony Hopkins, Aurum Press
	Pennine Way Companion, Alfred Wainwright, Frances Lincoln
Tourist Information Centres	Castleton tel 01433 620679, Glossop tel 01457 855920, Saddleworth tel 01457 870336, Marsden tel 01484 845595, Rochdale tel 01706 864928, Hebden Bridge tel 01422 843831, Haworth tel 01535 642329, Malham tel 01729 830673, Horton-in-Ribblesdale tel 01729 860333, Hawes tel 01969 667450, Middleton-in-Teesdale tel 01833 641001, Alston tel 01434 382244, Haltwhistle tel 01434 322002, Bellingham tel 01434 220616, Kelso tel 01573 223464.
Accommodation List	*Pennine Way Accommodation and Public Transport Guide*, from TICs
	Pennine Way Accommodation and Camping Guide, from Pennine Way Association
Path Association	Pennine Way Association www.penninewayassociation/co/uk
Website	www.nationaltrail.co.uk/PennineWay

The Roman fort near Gilsland was built on a curious sloping site (Day 4)

12 Hadrian's Wall Path

Start and Finish	Wallsend to Bowness-on-Solway
Distance and Time	135km (84 miles) taking up to 1 week
Character	An intensely absorbing archaeological trail that often runs through very gentle, low-lying countryside, but includes several short, steep, rugged ascents and descents in its central and more elevated parts.
Highlights	Wallsend, city of Newcastle upon Tyne, Heddon-on-the-Wall, Chesters Fort, the whole stretch of Hadrian's Wall from Walwick to Banks, including its associated museums, Carlisle and the Solway coast.

Milecastle 39 sits in a little gap and its north gate leads straight over a steep edge (Day 3)

122AD, he ordered the construction of a frontier defence from coast to coast. No other part of the Roman Empire boasted such a stout defence, which ran for 80 'Roman' miles, but over time much of the wall was plundered for stone and parts were completely levelled. Only mere fragments remain today, but there is more than enough to satisfy anyone with an interest in archaeology and a keen imagination, and the interpretative facilities along the way are excellent. The rolling landscape flanking Hadrian's Wall has been designated a world heritage site, to recognise the historic importance of this former frontier zone. The central parts are within the Northumberland National Park, while the westernmost stretch runs through the Solway Coast Area of Outstanding Natural Beauty.

The Romans had largely conquered Britain by the 1st century, but the northern territories were difficult to control and their armies fell back after battling the Picts. When Emperor Hadrian visited in

Walkers have followed the course of Hadrian's Wall for decades, but previously their enjoyment was marred because long stretches followed roads. The Hadrian's Wall Path runs as close as possible

SCHEDULE			
Day	**Start/Finish**	**Km**	**Miles**
Day 1	Wallsend to Heddon-on-the-Wall	23	14
Day 2	Heddon-on-the-Wall to Chollerford	25	15½
Day 3	Chollerford to Once Brewed	20	12½
Day 4	Once Brewed to Walton	26	16
Day 5	Walton to Carlisle	18	12
Day 6	Carlisle to Bowness-on-Solway	23	14

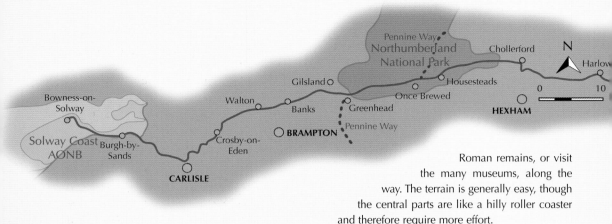

Roman remains, or visit the many museums, along the way. The terrain is generally easy, though the central parts are like a hilly roller coaster and therefore require more effort.

to the course of the wall, but also avoids roads as much as possible, and the feet of today's walkers rejoice as a consequence. Ever since the trail was officially opened in 2002, it has proved immensely popular, attracting walkers from all over the world. In fact, visitors were requested not to follow the route during the winter months, as the ground became rather soft, and constant pressure was causing damage to the underlying archaeology.

Accommodation is sparse outside Newcastle upon Tyne and Carlisle, but there is a dedicated Hadrian's Wall bus service, imaginatively numbered the AD122, which allows walkers to reach distant lodgings, or even operate from a base and therefore travel lightweight (at certain times the bus even carries an informative guide dressed as a Roman soldier!). Walkers are advised to allow plenty of extra time if they wish to explore in detail the many

Day 1 Wallsend to Heddon-on-the-Wall
23km (14 miles)

Wallsend is an appropriate name for the eastern terminus of Hadrian's Wall. A viewing tower allows a bird's-eye view of the Roman fort of Segedunum, as well as a vista across the city of Newcastle upon Tyne. The original course of Hadrian's Wall lies buried deep beneath the busy city, so the route follows a cycleway called Hadrian's Way, running roughly parallel to the River Tyne. The whole day's walk is essentially urban, but is fringed with greenery, and there is plenty of interest in the city centre, where several bridges of remarkably varied design span the Tyne. Watch carefully to spot where the Romans built a bridge across the river, marvelling at

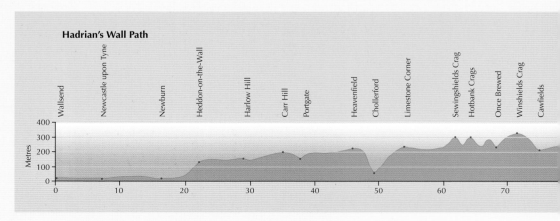

their achievement.

After leaving the city, the route follows part of the Wylam Waggonway, a horse-drawn precursor to the railway systems that now span the world. The riverside path is followed by a gentle climb up to the village of Heddon-on-the-Wall, where a well-preserved short stretch of Hadrian's Wall can be inspected, and the imagination is fired for further discoveries along the trail.

The sites of Roman forts at Rudchester and Halton Shields are simply rumpled grassy fields. Remote pubs or tearooms pop up at Wallhouses, Portgate and St Oswald's Hill. The latter is close to the battle ground of Heavenfield, where a Christian army from Northumberland defeated a pagan army in the year 734AD. On the descent towards the village of Wall, a fragment of Hadrian's Wall excites the imagination, and on leaving Wall, a fine turret site can be inspected. Also worthy of a detour is the remains of the old Roman bridge abutment at Chollerford, which can be made the subject of an evening stroll. Note how the river has shifted course since the bridge was erected.

Day 2 Heddon-on-the-Wall to Chollerford
25km (15½ miles)

Leaving Heddon-on-the-Wall via the B6318 gives walkers a taste of what following Hadrian's Wall was like before it was designated a national trail. The road is straight, hard and unyielding, and walkers have to share it with the traffic. However, this is only for a short time, as paths run parallel on one or the other side of the road. Hadrian's Wall was torn down in the middle of the 18th century to lay the foundations of a military road. Throughout this day's walk, there is nothing to see of the wall, although its course is followed faithfully.

Day 3 Chollerford to Once Brewed
20km (12½ miles)

The day starts with an exploration of Chesters Fort, which overlooks the point where the Roman bridge once spanned the River Tyne. Climb uphill beyond Walwick and Tower Tye to enter the Northumberland National Park, where fine stretches of Hadrian's Wall can be inspected. A defensive ditch was cut into hard rock at Limestone Corner, where views begin to open up splendidly across empty countryside. The site of a Roman fort can be inspected at Brocolitia, with a splendid Mithraic temple alongside. Visitors are in the habit of leaving coins on one of the altars.

Gradually, the complexity of Hadrian's Wall becomes apparent as the route begins to pull away from the B6318. Milecastles were built every Roman mile, with two turrets between each, and these can be inspected on the way up to Sewingshields Crag, where the wall begins a roller-coaster journey over a series of rugged little hills. Allow plenty of time to visit Housesteads, which is the most remarkable of all the Roman forts, and enjoy following

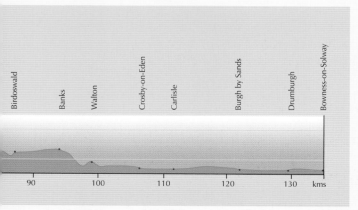

The ruins of a Mithraic temple lie beside the Roman fort of Brocolitia

A host of interesting fragments of the wall survive around Gilsland and Birdoswald, including splendid milecastles, turrets, bridge abutments and a fine fort. Birdoswald youth hostel is completely enclosed by the walls of a Roman fort, and splendid stretches of Hadrian's Wall can be followed either side of it. Gradually, the stone remains of the wall peter out, with occasional turrets and a signal station being passed near Banks. The line of the wall can be followed faithfully along field paths, and the last remaining fragment of stonework has been covered with earth and grass for protection on the climb towards the village of Walton.

some of the best-preserved parts of the wall onwards, now in the company of the Pennine Way National Trail. There are views of Broomlee and Greenlee loughs, before the route runs along Highshield Crags above Crag Lough. A short diversion off-route leads to the Once Brewed Youth Hostel, Twice Brewed Inn and a Northumberland National Park information centre.

Day 4 Once Brewed to Walton
26km (16 miles)

Another splendid day starts by following Hadrian's Wall over its highest point at 345m (1132ft) on Winshields Crags. After crossing Caw Gap, a well-preserved stretch of the wall is suddenly severed at a quarry edge, though an excellent milecastle has been spared. The site of Great Chesters Fort is passed as the route gradually gains height again, and another quarry has abruptly severed the wall at Walltown. A diversion off-route could include the Roman Army Museum at Carvoran. Stone from Carvoran Fort and the wall was used to build Thirlwall Castle. At this point the Pennine Way parts company with the Hadrian's Wall Path.

Day 5 Walton to Carlisle
18km (12 miles)

Every effort is made to stay true to the course of Hadrian's Wall, but there is no more masonry to be seen as the route follows field paths from farm to farm and village to village. Placenames continue to remind walkers of past features, as they pass Oldwall and Wall Head. As the route approaches the city of Carlisle, the line of the wall is a less attractive proposition, so there is a diversion to Crosby-on-Eden in order to follow paths close to the River Eden instead.

Riverside paths and field paths prove pleasant to follow, and a couple of neat parks are linked close to the very centre of Carlisle. There should be enough time to explore the city, where the Tullie House Museum is a fine source of information about the Roman period. The red-sandstone edifices of Carlisle Castle and the little cathedral are notable features, along with the imposing drum towers of the courts.

Day 6 Carlisle to Bowness-on-Solway
23km (14 miles)

The River Eden is followed downstream from Carlisle, so that the urban sprawl is largely hidden from sight. The route occasionally traces the course of Hadrian's Wall, from Grinstead to Kirkandrews, then Beaumont to Burgh by Sands. The church at Burgh was largely constructed from Roman masonry. A long and straight road runs alongside Burgh Marshes, and this can flood at high tide, so take note of the tide times posted beside the road, and bear in mind that a long grassy embankment running parallel to the road offers an escape (the embankment once held a canal, and later a railway, but both fell into disuse). The route moves inland from Drumburgh to Glasson, but reaches the coast again at Port Carlisle.

A short road walk leads to Bowness-on-Solway, where a fort once marked the western terminus of Hadrian's Wall, although Roman forts were also built all the way along the coast to Ravenglass, protecting this part of the country from invasion from the sea. To leave Bowness, the AD122 Hadrian's Wall bus, which is essentially a summer service, can be used to reach Carlisle, or even return all the way to Wallsend.

INFORMATION

Access to Start	Newcastle upon Tyne is served by long-distance Virgin Trains. Frequent metro and bus services link the city with Wallsend.
Getting Home	Occasional Stagecoach bus services link Bowness-on-Solway with Carlisle, which is served by long-distance Virgin Trains.
Other Public Transport	The Hadrian's Wall Bus, or AD122, runs regularly along the central parts of the trail, and occasionally runs all the way between Wallsend and Bowness-on-Solway. Northern Trains run between Newcastle and Carlisle, along with Arriva and Stagecoach buses.
Maps	OS 1:50,000 Landrangers 85, 86, 87 and 88
	OS 1:25,000 Explorers 314, 315, 316 and OL43
	Harveys 1:40,000 Hadrian's Wall Path
Cicerone Guide	*Hadrian's Wall Path*, by Mark Richards
Other Guidebooks	*Hadrian's Wall Path*, by Anthony Burton, Aurum Press
Tourist Information Centres	Newcastle upon Tyne tel 0191 2778000, Hexham tel 01434 652220, Haltwhistle tel 01434 322002, Carlisle tel 01228 625600.
Accommodation List	*Hadrian's Wall Country, Walking and Accommodation Guide*, from TICs
Websites	www.nationaltrail.co.uk/hadrianswall and www.hadrians-wall.org

The Strumble Head lighthouse sits on a small island connected to the mainland by a bridge (Day 3)

WALES

13 Pembrokeshire Coast Path

Start and Finish	Poppit Sands to Amroth Castle
Distance and Time	299km (186 miles) taking up to 2 weeks
Character	A complex cliff coast punctuated by coves and beaches, along with a succession of towns and villages. Plenty of short, steep, rugged ascents and descents, often on narrow paths exposed to the elements.
Highlights	Cemaes Head to Newport, Dinas Island, Strumble Head, St David's Head, St David's, Solva, the Deer Park and Marloes Sands, the Green Bridge and cliff coast to Stackpole Head and onwards to Freshwater East.

Looking back along the rugged cliffs towards Solva on the way to Newgale (Day 5)

Sandwiched between southwest England and southeast Ireland, the gentle Pembrokeshire countryside has a window on the Atlantic Ocean, so wild weather brings heavy seas pounding the rugged peninsulas, sending furious, foamy waves scouring the beaches and bays. On fine days, the colours and contrasts of the coast are remarkable. Golden strands and serpentine tidal creeks punctuate a low cliff coast of rocky promontories and hidden coves. Multi-coloured cliffs expose their geological bones, while seabirds nest on rocky ledges, or soar on the breeze. A mere handful of towns and a scattering of coastal villages ensure that some stretches of the coast are well removed from habitation, but the coast path also runs round the industrial inlet of Milford Haven, with its pervasive whiff of petro-chemicals.

When the Pembrokeshire Coast National Park was designated in 1952, one of the park authority's first acts was to look at the possibility of establishing a long-distance coastal path. The cliff coast is usually quite low, but is also incredibly convoluted, with countless headlands and bays. The sea is filled with rocky stacks, and the many intriguing little islands are protected as nature reserves for the benefit of seabirds. If you could unravel this convoluted coast path, crumpled tightly into a corner of southwest Wales, you might be amazed to discover it is much longer than the Offa's Dyke Path, which runs the full length of Wales. The trail was opened in 1980 by Wynford Vaughan Thomas of the Council for the Preservation of Rural Wales, and has proved to be very popular even from its earliest years.

There are some things that walkers should be aware of while making their plans. The southern coast of Pembrokeshire is remarkably scenic, but lies within the confines of a military firing range – be sure to time your arrival to coincide with a period when the range is open to walkers. There are also two tidal creeks that need to be crossed on the northern shore of Milford Haven, so either arrive at low water, or be prepared to make a longer detour round. Accommodation is sparse in some places, but there are helpful bus services to and from almost every coastal settlement, so walkers can easily detour off-route. Get a copy of the Pembrokeshire

SCHEDULE

Day	Start/Finish	Km	Miles
Day 1	Poppit Sands to Newport	22.5	14
Day 2	Newport to Goodwick	22.5	14
Day 3	Goodwick to Trefin	3	20
Day 4	Trefin to St Justinian	22.5	14
Day 5	St Justinian to Newgale	27.5	17
Day 6	Newgale to Marloes	24	15
Day 7	Marloes to Sandy Haven	28	17½
Day 8	Sandy Haven to Pembroke	24	15
Day 9	Pembroke to West Angle Bay	24	15
Day 10	West Angle Bay to Broad Haven	26	16
Day 11	Broad Haven to Tenby	28	17½
Day 12	Tenby to Amroth	18	11

Coastal Bus Services timetable before you start planning, so that you are aware of your options. Walkers will find bilingual signposts reading 'Llwybr Afordir / Coast Path', and might also note that most stiles and gates are numbered, and that there are over 700 of them to be negotiated!

Day 1 Poppit Sands to Newport
22.5km (14 miles)

Buses run from Cardigan to Poppit Sands, where commemorative stones near a café mark the start of the Pembrokeshire Coast Path. Follow a road uphill, passing a youth hostel and campsite before a track like a green carpet leads onto the bracken slopes of Cemaes Head. Views of Cardigan Island are lost as the coast path turns around the headland at 170m (560ft). This is the highest part of the trail, and the cliffs reveal tightly contorted layers of rock, battered and beaten by the waves. Walkers need to be self-sufficient on this day's walk, unless they plan to divert inland from Ceibwr Bay to Moylgrove. The rocky shore can be explored at Ceibwr Bay, where monstrous rock stacks protrude from the sea.

There are plenty of ascents and descents during the day, and the sea laps on both sides of the path where it passes the curious crater of Pwll y

Wrach, or Witches Cauldron. After turning round a distant headland the path drops down to a beach café. Cross the Iron Bridge, over a creek frequented by wildfowl, then either walk straight into the village of Newport, or continue further along the coast path before heading inland. Mynydd Carningli, a much-revered 'holy mountain', rises behind the village. It is part of the rolling Preseli Hills, from where 'bluestones' were taken to Stonehenge on far-distant Salisbury Plain over 4000 years ago.

Day 2 Newport to Goodwick
22.5km (14 miles)

An easy path leaves Newport, but soon twists and turns, rising and falling on the way to Cwm-yr-Eglwys. The gable-end of St Brynach's Church stands by a sea wall, buttressed against final collapse. Ahead lies Dinas Island, which is actually a headland joined to the mainland. Some walkers short cut behind it, but the walk around the headland is rugged, scenic and worth the extra effort. The highest point is Pen y Fan at 142m (466ft), offering fine views inland to the Preseli Hills. Pass a pub at Pwllgwaelod, where cliffs flank a sandy beach. Continue over headlands and around little coves and bays, then after passing a cliff-top campsite at Penrhyn, the coast path reaches Fishguard Fort.

Follow a road through Lower Town, which was formerly a fishing village. Pass the Ship Inn and either walk up

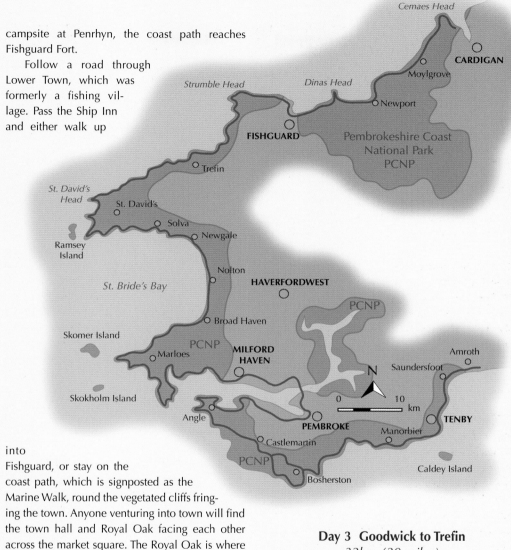

into Fishguard, or stay on the coast path, which is signposted as the Marine Walk, round the vegetated cliffs fringing the town. Anyone venturing into town will find the town hall and Royal Oak facing each other across the market square. The Royal Oak is where an invading French force signed their surrender after the last invasion of Britain in 1797. Nearby Goodwick is approached by road, and long breakwaters can be seen enclosing Fishguard harbour. In the early 20th century this was a thriving transatlantic port, but ferries now sail only to Rosslare in southeast Ireland.

Day 3 Goodwick to Trefin
32km (20 miles)

Follow roads above Goodwick to reach a fine viewpoint and cannon overlooking the harbour. A path threads its way between gorse bushes as it turns a headland, then becomes more difficult as it wriggles along the rugged coast to Carregwastad Point. A memorial stone at Carreg Goffa records the landing of a French invasion force in 1797. They met with little resistance at first in this bleak

A stone on Carreg Goffa records the last invasion of Britain, by a French force in 1797

rocky islets are pounded by the waves. The rugged hill of Garn Fawr rises behind Pwll Deri youth hostel, while the coast path wanders along a rocky ridge at 140m (460ft) on Carn Ogof. After turning round a cliff-girt bay at Pwllcrochan, the path later crosses white cobbly beaches at Aber Bach and Aber Mawr. The sea is full of spiky islets and rocky fangs, then a stout wall, aptly inscribed as the 'Great Wall of China', leads most of the way to Abercastle. There is direct road access to Trefin, or walkers can continue along a wonderfully rugged and convoluted cliff path to reach the village. A small range of services is on offer, but if lodgings cannot be secured, there are bus services elsewhere.

and rugged area, but their campaign became a farce when they got drunk, mistook local women for an army, and finally surrendered in Fishguard.

The coast path passes a solitary cottage at Penrhyn and is delightfully rugged as it approaches Strumble Head. A prominent lighthouse sits on an island and there are other little islands alongside. Colourful slopes of gorse and heather lie beside a remote stretch of cliff path, and far below, a host of

Day 4 Trefin to St Justinian
22.5km (14 miles)

Walkers with a passion for industrial archaeology will find the morning's walk very interesting. The white towers that flank Porthgain's harbour mouth were put there to help ships locate the narrow

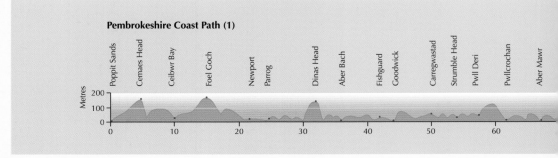

inlet. The towering brick-built hoppers rising from the little harbour once fed crushed stone onto ships. The coast path climbs a flight of steps, then passes a number of headlands and coves. A complex old quarry site is crisscrossed with paths and tracks, and a pool known as the Blue Lagoon is seen on the way down to the beach at Abereiddy.

Looking ahead, the coast path has a rugged range of little hills alongside, and the scenery becomes quite dramatic in places – very much a Celtic landscape. The coast path touches 100m (330ft) as it crosses the slopes of Carn Penberry. Watch for Coetan Arthur, a Neolithic burial chamber formed simply by propping a heavy capstone on a single upright stone. The extreme end of St David's Head features an ancient promontory fort, and you can enter it through the same gateway in its stone ramparts as did its Iron Age inhabitants. Walk above a tiny sandy beach at Porthmelgan on the slopes of Carn Llidi to reach the broad expanse of Whitesands Bay, which is popular with surfers. A path runs easily round to St Justinian, where there is a lifeboat station, and ferries to the nature reserve of

Looking along the length of Whitesands Bay to the hill of Carn Llidi

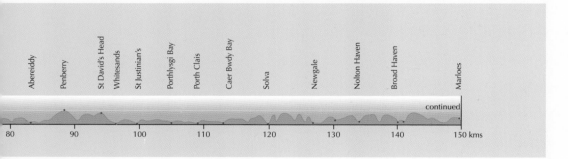

Abereiddy · Penberry · St David's Head · Whitesands · St Justinian's · Porthlysgi Bay · Porth Clais · Caer Bwdy Bay · Solva · Newgale · Nolton Haven · Broad Haven · Marloes

continued

80   90   100   110   120   130   140   150 kms

St David's Cathedral sits in a grassy hollow next to the 'city' of St David's

Ramsey Island. Minibuses allow a rapid link with the cathedral city of St David's, and a visit is highly recommended.

St David, patron saint of Wales, was born and reared in this corner of Pembrokeshire. He travelled the Celtic Christian world and returned here in his old age, dying in 588AD. Vikings destroyed an early monastic site and at least three cathedrals. The current building, in its pleasant grassy hollow, dates from the 12th century. The adjacent Bishop's Palace, now in ruins, was founded in the 14th century. (By some curious reckoning, two pilgrimages to St David's were deemed of equal merit to a pilgrimage to Rome; so visit twice while you have the chance!)

Day 5 St Justinian to Newgale
27.5km (17 miles)

Soon after leaving St Justinian, a sweeping view extends all the way round St Bride's Bay from Ramsey Island to Skomer Island. It takes walkers at least two days to cover that distance. Looking inland, the prominent hump of Carn Llidi is often in view, though confusingly so, since it appears to bob about the landscape every time a circuit is made around a headland or cove. Teas may be available at the head of the narrow inlet of Porth Clais. Further along the coast, the ruins of St Non's Chapel and Holy Well can be inspected. Around 462AD St Non gave birth to St David here during a storm.

Walk round Caerfai Bay and Caer Bwdy Bay and along the cliff tops of Morfa Common. The slabby cliff coast is suddenly broken by a long and crooked inlet at Solva. Yachts lie at anchor and the calm, silver-sheened water is flanked by steep, wooded slopes. The village is split, with the upper part set back from the coast, and the lower part at the head of the harbour. Take a break for food and drink, maybe consider staying for the night, or keep walking. There are some steep little ascents and descents on leaving Solva and approaching Newgale. Cliffs touching 80m

(260ft) in height quickly give way to a long, cobbly storm beach at Newgale, where surfing is popular. If accommodation is a problem, there are buses off-route.

Newgale is something of a frontier in Pembrokeshire, bisected by a rather vague line referred to as the Landsker. To the north is the resoundingly Welsh half of Pembrokeshire, while to the south is 'Little England beyond Wales' – maps reveal a greater number of 'English' place-names here, resulting from the area being half-settled by the Normans, and the division has endured ever since.

Day 6 Newgale to Marloes
24km (15 miles)

Walk along or beside the beach to leave Newgale, passing a chimney at a former small colliery site. Refreshments are available from a pub at Nolton Haven, which has a fine sandy beach flanked by cliffs, and at a hotel at Druidston, where there is a detour away from the cliffs. Later, Broad Haven and Little Haven have shops and pubs. The villages are linked by road, but at low water it's possible to get from one to the other along the beach.

A path crosses the well-wooded slopes of Borough Head, where it runs around 80m (260ft) above the sea. The path hugs the cliffs no matter how indented they are, rising and falling as it crosses valleys. A low point is reached at Mill Haven, where the cliffs take on a pleasant rosy hue. Low-lying St Bride's Haven has a church and a few cottages. A gradual climb leads around St Bride's Estate, where the towers of Kensington, a Victorian edifice, are seen poking above trees, but the eye is more likely to be attracted to the red-glowing cliffs. By the time the route overlooks Musselwick Sands from Black Cliff, a path can be used to head inland to the village of Marloes. This is the only place offering refreshments and lodgings on this remote peninsula, though in case of difficulty, there are buses to other places.

Day 7 Marloes to Sandy Haven
28km (17½ miles)

The golden Marloes Sands, seen from the cliffs of Hooper's Point

Rosy red cliffs remain a feature of the coast path on the way to Martin's Haven. Ferries sail from here to the nature reserve islands of Skomer and Skokholm. The Deer Park is a cliff-girt headland explored by a circular walk, but first have a look at the small wildlife exhibition. Seals are often seen below the cliffs, birds wheel on the thermals, and the cliff views are remarkable, enlivened with islets. This is a significant turning point on the coast path, and long after leaving Marloes, the route actually passes close to the village again.

Gateholm Island is very close to the mainland, and golden Marloes Sands may be busy with visitors. The cliff path passes an old airfield and swings around the top of Westdale Bay. At this point, weary walkers will spot an obvious short cut to the village of Dale, but purists will hug the cliffs all the way round St Ann's Head, passing a lighthouse at the mouth of one of Britain's most notable natural harbours – Milford Haven. The day's walk seldom exceeds 50m (165ft), but does so a couple of times while making its way round to Dale. Note the stout stone forts, built in the 19th century, that guard the harbour mouth.

Looking ahead from Dale, there is a choice of routes depending on the state of the tides. However, it has to be admitted that some walkers skip the next couple of days of the route, omitting the industrial parts of Milford Haven and the ever-present scent of petro-chemicals, in order to get straight back onto the 'real' coastal path beyond Angle.

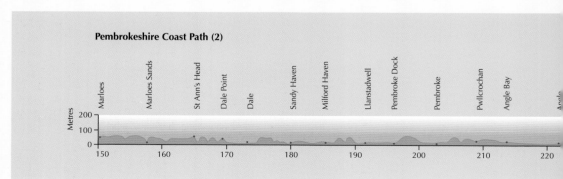

Pembrokeshire Coast Path (2)

Metres: 200, 100, 0

Marloes · Marloes Sands · St Ann's Head · Dale Point · Dale · Sandy Haven · Milford Haven · Llanstadwell · Pembroke Dock · Pembroke · Pwllcrochan · Angle Bay · Angle

150   160   170   180   190   200   210   220

then continue inland by road until signposted back to the coast along farm tracks and field paths. The route follows a low cliff line, passing quite close to the village of St Ishmael's. After passing the Watch Tower and walking around Great Castle Head and Little Castle Head, the tidal inlet of Sandyhaven Pill needs to be crossed. If there is any difficulty at this point, there is farmhouse bed and breakfast available nearby at Skerryback.

Day 8 Sandy Haven to Pembroke
24km (15 miles)

Cross Sandyhaven Pill at low water and pick up the coastal path at a small caravan site. Views round the mouth of Milford Haven are a contrasting mix of low cliffs and concrete, with the natural world jostling alongside industrial complexes. The coast path leaves the national park to pass oil refineries and jetties. It even abandons the coast at Gelliswick Bay, but there are good views while passing through the town of Milford Haven. Watch for 'acorn' markers on lampposts in built-up areas. A road is followed out of town, though there are paths that could be used to make this more pleasant. Pass another oil refinery to reach the straggly village of Llanstadwell, which has a fine old church.

At Neyland the tidal inlet of Westfield Pill, which contains a marina, pushes walkers inland to cross a busy road bridge high above the water.

Leave Dale by road, and if the tide is out, there is no problem crossing the Gann. If the tide is in,

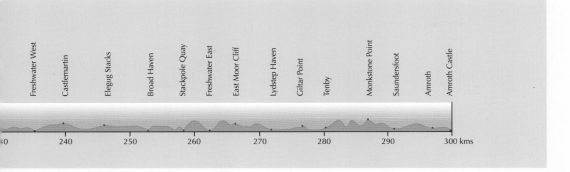

Pembroke Castle reflected in the natural moat formed by the Pembroke river

Continue along the road to cross Cleddau Bridge, high above the tidal Daugleddau. Watch carefully for the route through Llanion and Pembroke Dock. The 19th-century Royal Naval Dockyard has much to commend it, and there are interesting information panels along the way, but it is hard on the feet walking through town by road. Towards the end of the day Pembroke Castle is an imposing structure dating from the 12th century, and the Great Keep rises high above its curtain wall and stout drum towers. As the route enters Pembroke it makes an almost complete circuit, affording the best views of the castle.

Day 9 Pembroke to West Angle Bay
24km (15 miles)

Pembroke seems a long way from the rugged coast, and the whole of today's walk is devoted to getting back onto 'classic' cliff coastline. Roads and field paths only seldom reveal glimpses of the coast, and the most notable early landmark is an enormous power station. Pwllcrochan church is a little gem, sandwiched between the power station and an oil refinery, with nearby marshland threaded by a winding boardwalk. Coast path walkers can use the boardwalk instead of the road if they wish, then continue past the oil refinery to return to the coast. Back inside the national park, a road, path and track lead around Angle Bay to the village of Angle. A muddy coastal track leads to the Old Point Inn, which may date from the 16th century. Field paths and tracks lead around North Hill to West Angle Bay and its café. There is at last a feeling, while enjoying views across the mouth of Milford Haven, that great cliff walking is once again available after the lengthy industrial interlude.

Day 10 West Angle Bay to Broad Haven
26km (16 miles)

A low-level cliff walk, while seldom climbing as high as 50m (165ft), is quite rugged underfoot and includes some short, steep slopes. At length the route drops onto a broad sandy beach at Freshwater West. There is a detour inland along a road to the village of Castlemartin, avoiding a military firing range. Very occasionally, there is a guided walk through Range West, and walkers who can time their arrival to take part in one of these will be able to enjoy a seldom-seen stretch of cliff coast that will prove most memorable. Even if Range West is unavailable, be sure to time your arrival to be able to walk through Range East, which is open most weekends and evenings. (Phone 01646 662367 for a recorded announcement of open and closed periods.)

The Range East walk runs along the tops of limestone cliffs that have been beaten by the sea into impressive formations. Be sure to make the short detour to see the amazing arch of the Green Bridge. The Elegug Stacks are imposing towers of rock, and rugged Bullslaughter Bay is a wild place when heavy seas are hammering the cliffs. Peer into sheer-sided coves and look out for arches punched into headlands. There is something to see at every turn, and don't miss the flight of steps leading down to St Govan's Chapel, wedged into a cleft. Broad Haven is far enough for one day, and safely outside the firing range. The nearest accommodation and refreshments are inland at the village of Bosherston, and there is a pleasant approach via the charming Lily Ponds for anyone staying overnight.

Day 11 Broad Haven to Tenby
28km (17½ miles)

The limestone cliffs continue to produce stunning sights. Sheer in most places, they are perforated with arches or dark caves, split into stacks, always a different scene around every corner. Some walkers might be tempted to short cut behind Stackpole Head, but they would miss many dramatic views. Walk round Barafundle Bay and drop down to Stackpole Quay, where there is a

The dramatic limestone cliffs of Stackpole Head, looking back towards Broad Haven

tearoom among buildings restored by the National Trust. Splendid cliff walking leads past Greenala Point and Trewent Point, followed by sandy paths around Freshwater East.

Back on the cliffs, Swanlake Bay and Manorbier Bay delight the eye, but there is no access to Old Castle Head, which is a military firing range. Walk from Shrinkle Haven to Lydstep Haven, then take care with route finding through a mobile home park. Another fine cliff walk leads to Giltar Point, followed by a descent to a golden strand. Either walk along the broad sands to Tenby, or pick a way along paths a little further inland. The town is essentially a holiday resort, but there is an ancient centre surrounded by a stout defensive wall. Offshore, Caldey Island is home to a monastic community.

Day 12   Tenby to Amroth
18km (11 miles)

Acorn markers on lampposts show the way out of Tenby, and for a time there is hardly a glimpse of the coast. Trees flank the coast path as it climbs over little hills, crossing valleys in between. Roads have to be followed through the village of Saundersfoot, then the route goes through tunnels while following the course of an old railway. (Sometimes, after rockfalls, a higher path is used.) Cross Wiseman's Bridge and follow a clear track set well away from the coast. Later, a path drops down to Amroth, and a coastal road is followed onwards to pass Amroth Castle. Commemorative stones mark the end of the Pembrokeshire Coast Path just before the New Inn. Buses return to Tenby for onward connections, though on Sundays there is a direct bus to Carmarthen.

INFORMATION

Access to Start	Occasional buses run from Cardigan to Poppit Sands. Cardigan itself is served by regular buses, some linking with rail services at Carmarthen.
Getting Home	Occasional buses run from Amroth Castle to Tenby, or on Sundays there is a direct service inland to Carmarthen.
Other Public Transport	Arriva trains serve Goodwick, Milford Haven, Pemroke and Tenby, but the most useful links for walkers are provided by Pembrokeshire Coastal Bus Services. Several buses cover points along almost the entire coastal path, with seasonal variations. Details are listed in a dedicated booklet available from TICs, or see www.pembrokeshire greenways.com.
Maps	OS 1:50,000 Landrangers 145, 147 and 148
	OS 1:25,000 Explorers OL35 and OL36
Cicerone Guide	*The Pembrokeshire Coastal Path*, by Dennis Kelsall
Other Guidebooks	*Pembrokshire Coast Path*, by Brian John, Aurum Press
Tourist Information Centres	Cardigan tel 01239 613230, Newport tel 01239 820912, Fishguard tel 01348 873484, Fishguard harbour tel 01348 872037, St David's tel 01437 720392, Milford Haven tel 01646 690866, Pembroke tel 01646 622388, Tenby tel 01834 842402, Saundersfoot tel 01834 813672.
Accommodation List	There is no dedicated list for the coast path, but the *Pembrokeshire Holiday Guide* lists places along the trail.
Websites	www.pcnpa.org.uk and www.visitpembrokeshire.com

A path drops down to a gap, with Moel Arthur rising steeply on the other side (Day 10)

14 Offa's Dyke Path

Start and Finish	Sedbury Cliff to Prestatyn
Distance and Time	285km (177 miles) taking 1½ weeks
Character	Varying from lowland to upland terrain, from low-level field paths to high-level walks over open and exposed hills. Some parts feature several steep ascents and descents, while other parts are virtually level and easy.
Highlights	The Wye Valley, White Castle, Black Mountains, Hay-on-Wye, Hergest Ridge, Offa's Dyke itself from Kington to Knighton and Long Mountain. Llanymynech Rocks, Chirk Castle, Pontcysyllte Aqueduct, Eglwyseg Mountain and the whole of the Clwydian Hills.

The line of Offa's Dyke is preserved as a rough strip through crops at Forden (Day 7)

Offa, King of Anglo-Saxon Mercia, reigned from the year 757 to 796AD, and was a contemporary of the legendary Charlemagne. While there is no direct evidence to link Offa with the earth embankment that bears his name, no one else's name has been linked with it either. The purpose of the dyke, which is estimated to contain nine billion tons of earth, is not entirely clear. It may have been a defensive structure, or a boundary marker, or both. There are three distinct lengths of the dyke – a short stretch in the south, a longer stretch between Knighton and Buttington, and another stretch further north that ends by the River Dee. The dyke may never have been continuous, and for long stretches there are no traces of it

SCHEDULE

Day	Start/Finish	Km	Miles
Day 1	Sedbury Cliff to Monmouth	29	18
Day 2	Monmouth to Pandy	26	16
Day 3	Pandy to Hay-on-Wye	26	16
Day 4	Hay-on-Wye to Kington	24	15
Day 5	Kington to Knighton	22	14
Day 6	Knighton to Montgomery	29	18
Day 7	Montgomery to Four Crosses	29	18
Day 8	Four Crosses to Pentre	32	20
Day 9	Pentre to Llandegla	21	13
Day 10	Llandegla to Bodfari	26	16
Day 11	Bodfari to Prestatyn	21	13

whatsoever. Maybe the crest of the Black Mountains, or the rivers Severn and Dee formed natural boundaries. Anyone who wants to know more about the structure should visit the Offa's Dyke Centre, roughly halfway along the trail at Knighton. There is a smaller centre, open in the summer months, on the seafront at Prestatyn.

The Offa's Dyke Path was officially opened in 1971, by Lord Hunt, of Everest fame. A commemorative stone bears a plaque declaring the dyke to be 'the most impressive work of the old English kings'. Although the route is often promoted as an archaeological trail, it should be remembered that less than a third of the route actually follows the dyke. A popular misconception is that the dyke marks the border between England and Wales, when in fact this only happens for a couple of short stretches. Bilingual signs read 'Llwybr Clawdd Offa / Offa's Dyke Path', and there are reckoned to be over 700 stiles to cross! The route passes through the Brecon Beacons National Park, as well as three areas of outstanding natural beauty, as it switches continually between England and Wales on its long journey northwards (many walkers haven't a clue which country they are in from day to day!).

The Offa's Dyke Path is a popular choice among long-distance walkers and it can be completed comfortably in less than a fortnight. The route can be regarded as a coast-to-coast trail running south to north through the Marches. Each day's walk seems to present a different theme – wooded riverside, fields, high-level moorland, gentle hills, and of course the serpentine course of Offa's Dyke itself, as it wriggles and writhes over breezy hills and crosses green valleys. The heathery humps of the Clwydian Hills allow walkers to enjoy a final high-level romp with extensive views before the end of the trail. Some stretches may be remote, but overall there are excellent services, and with careful planning, food, drink and overnight accommodation are easily located.

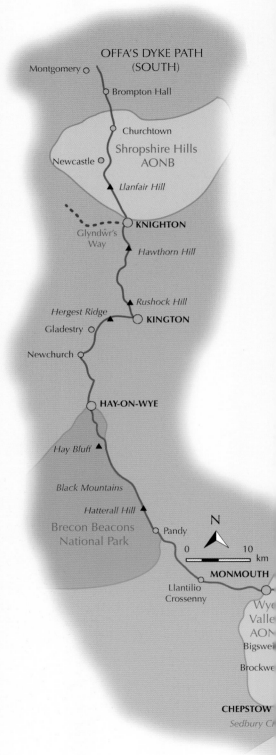

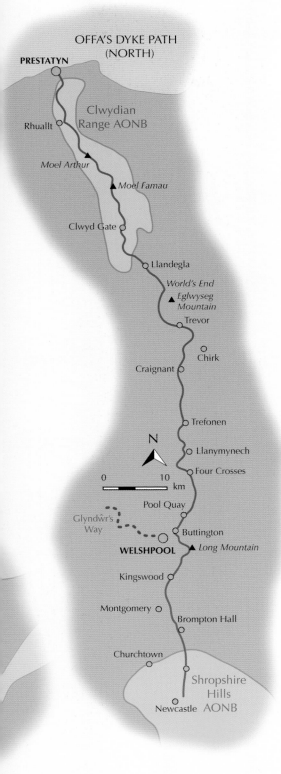

OFFA'S DYKE PATH
(NORTH)

PRESTATYN

Rhuallt

Clwydian
Range AONB

Moel Arthur

Moel Famau

Clwyd Gate

Llandegla

World's End
Eglwyseg
Mountain

Trevor

Chirk

Craignant

Trefonen

Llanymynech

N

Four Crosses

0   10
km

Pool Quay

Glyndŵr's
Way

Buttington

WELSHPOOL   Long Mountain

Kingswood

Montgomery

Brompton Hall

Churchtown

Shropshire
Hills

Newcastle   AONB

Day 1 Sedbury Cliff to Monmouth
29km (18 miles)

Sedbury Cliff rises from the Severn Estuary on the opposite side of the River Wye from Chepstow. A lump of rock bears a plaque announcing the start of the Offa's Dyke Path, which remains just inside England almost all day. A clear stretch of the dyke – a linear, grassy mound of earth, flanked by bracken and brambles – heads northwards, but is soon lost in the suburbs of Sedbury and Tutshill. The route runs parallel to the tidal River Wye, which is seldom in sight, though there is a glimpse across to Chepstow Castle, which dates from the 11th century. Later, there is a fine view of a deeply incised meander from Wintour's Leap. Field paths give way to woodland paths, and another stretch of the dyke is followed past the Devil's Pulpit. This rocky stance, at 198m (650ft), was supposedly the place from which the devil hurled abuse at the monks labouring to build Tintern Abbey in the 12th century!

There is a choice of routes near Brockweir. Either climb as high as 250m (820ft) through fields on St Briavels Common, then descend through woods to Bigsweir, or follow the lazy meanders of the River Wye from Brockweir to Bigsweir, although this latter choice can be very muddy when wet. Continue by climbing through woods, then walk along a wooded brow high above the river before dropping to Lower Redbrook. There are views through the wooded valley to Monmouth. Another climb through fields and woods, now in Wales, reaches the curious Naval Temple, erected in 1800 on the Kymin – it was later visited by Admiral Lord Nelson, who expressed surprise at finding it so far inland. Wonderful views from the whitewashed Round House, at 257m (843ft), extend beyond Monmouth and rumpled patchwork fields and woods to the distant sprawling profile of the Brecon Beacons. All this will be seen at closer quarters over the next couple of days, but for the time being a steep and rugged descent leads to

The well-wooded Wye Valley and the little village of Lower Redbrook

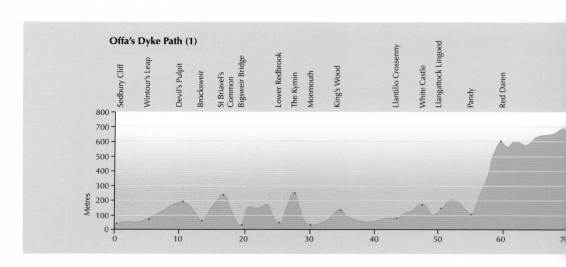

Offa's Dyke Path (1)

Monmouth, birthplace in 1387 of Henry V, and where several fine old buildings may be the subject of evening explorations.

Day 2 Monmouth to Pandy
26km (16 miles)

This whole day's walk is in Wales. Monmouth is left behind after crossing the Monnow Bridge. This stout stone structure is part bridge and part defensive gateway, dating from the 13th century. Throughout this day's walk, the route runs at a low level and there is no sign of Offa's Dyke. Watery Lane leads to Kings Wood, which gives way to farm tracks and field paths at Hendre. The trail plays hide-and-seek with the River Trothy through a gentle countryside of pasture and cultivated fields, and there are several stiles and gates to negotiate. After passing through an apple orchard to reach the village of Llantilio Crosenny, the route passes the unexpected Hogs Head pub at Tre-Adam. A track leads to 12th-century White Castle, which can be explored free of charge. Moats, curtain walls and drum towers enclose the outer and inner ward, and steps climbing a high tower reveal extensive views.

Walk down through fields to cross the River Trothy, and head upstream roughly parallel to its tributary, Full Brook. Climb to the little village of Llangattock Lingoed, passing the whitewashed church of St Cadoc. After crossing Full Brook again the trail climbs through fields and crosses a road at 219m (719ft) before heading down to Pandy. The hill of Ysgyryd Fawr is prominent – its summit said to have been cleft by the keel of Noah's Ark, or ripped asunder by a lightning strike! The Lancaster Arms Inn stands beside a busy road, and there are other pubs and lodgings nearby.

Day 3 Pandy to Hay-on-Wye
26km (16 miles)

The whole of this day's walk runs along the eastern fringe of the Brecon Beacons National Park, climbing gradually along a broad moorland crest that is also the boundary between Wales and England. Farmland near Pandy gives way to a slope of bracken threaded by a green velvet ribbon of a path. Climb higher through gorse scrub, passing a trig point at 464m (1522ft), then continue through grass, heather and bilberry onto Hatterrall Hill, skirting the summit around 525m (1722ft). Keep to the ridge, which bears a clear path crossing a broad saddle, and enjoy views east across the rolling fields of Herefordshire, and west across the

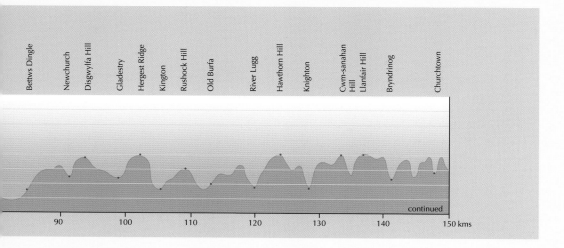

continued

Cloud scuds across the broad moorland crest of the Black Mountains

Vale of Ewyas to the heart of the Brecon Beacons. Tombstone-like markers remind walkers they are following the Offa's Dyke Path. No trace of the dyke has been found in this region, and one assumes that the mountain mass itself provided an effective natural barrier. Some days you will see more ponies than people on the mountains.

Climb past another trig point, this one standing at 552m (1811ft). In mist, little features such as these help walkers to keep track of progress, while on a fine day they can simply enjoy the views. After following the crest above Black Daren and Red Daren, another trig point stands at 610m (2001ft). Another broad hump is crossed, then a long and gradual ascent leads up a rugged moorland slope,

where the path is largely made of stone slabs. The highest point gained is also the highest point on the whole of the Offa's Dyke Path, at 706m (2316ft) on a (curiously) unnamed moorland top. Only the Pennine Way and Southern Upland Way, of all the national trails, climb higher than this.

Follow the stone-built path downhill, cutting across the steep slopes of Hay Bluff. Watch out for marker posts on the lower slopes, as there is a network of grassy paths through swathes of bracken. Cross a road and walk over a hill covered in short grass, taking time to look back at the proud northern escarpment of the Brecon Beacons. Descend through woods and fields to reach the bustling little market town of Hay-on-Wye. In 1962, Richard

Booth opened a second-hand bookshop in Hay, and such bookshops now dominate the whole town. An old castle dating from the 12th century is full of books, as is the former cinema, and anyone who wants to browse the bookshops had better enquire about weekly rates at one of the guest-houses!

Day 4 Hay-on-Wye to Kington
24km (15 miles)

The trail is mostly confined to Wales during the day, but finishes in England. The River Wye leads away from Hay, then the route climbs up through the well-wooded valley of Bettws Dingle to emerge among gently rolling hills. Minor roads and field paths lead to the village of Newchurch, where refreshments are provided on a help-yourself basis in the church. Note the 15th-century Great House nearby. The route climbs over Disgwylfa Hill, following a path of short green grass through the bracken, and climbing as high as 383m (1257ft) before dropping down to Hill House. Field paths give way to a road walk down into the village of Gladestry. The Royal Oak offers food and drink, while help-yourself refreshments are again available in the church.

The steep slopes of Hergest Ridge loom over Gladestry and there is an initial steep climb. A broad green grassy path runs at a gentler gradient through bracken and gorse, and there may be ponies grazing here and there. Enjoy all-round views, especially into the hilly heart of Wales. The trail narrowly misses the 426m (1398ft) summit, which is just inside England. A curious small plantation of monkey-puzzle trees is passed before a long descent to the little town of Kington. A sign on the way into town proclaims it to be 'The Centre for Walking'. Fine old buildings, narrow streets, small shops, a cluttered appearance and a central clock tower are themes that are repeated at other little towns passed on the way through the Marches.

Day 5 Kington to Knighton
22km (14 miles)

Offa's Dyke hasn't been seen for three days, but it suddenly appears again shortly after leaving Kington. The grassy mound can be followed across Rushock Hill, but not across neighbouring Herrock Hill. Cross a valley and pass from England back into Wales for the rest of the day. The course of the dyke is followed past Old Burfa, a restored timbered house dating from the 15th century. Follow the dyke faithfully through Granner Wood, high above the village of Evenjobb, over another hill and down to the River Lugg.

The dyke is lost for a while, but reappears on Hawthorn Hill at 407m (1335ft). A slender monument off to the right commemorates Sir Richard Green Price, who lobbied for railways to be built in Radnorshire. Offa's Dyke has a less imposing monument, simply stating 'Made in the Year 757AD'. Walk downhill to Rhos-y-meirch, then follow another stretch of the dyke over a hill at Frŷdd, dropping down alongside a golf course and into woods. Emerge at the top end of Knighton, which has everything a walker could desire, and make a beeline for the Offa's Dyke Centre, so that you can learn more about the dyke and its trail. Also note that Glyndŵr's Way National Trail starts in the centre of Knighton and wanders through the unfrequented hills of mid-Wales to reach Welshpool.

Day 6 Knighton to Montgomery
29km (18 miles)

The finest remaining stretch of Offa's Dyke is the serpentine High Dyke that runs north through the Shropshire Hills Area of Outstanding Natural Beauty. At the start of the day's walk, search for the commemorative stone where the trail was declared open by Lord Hunt in 1971. A steep climb gradually eases, then the dyke is followed on a splendid roller-coaster romp over the hills, enjoying fine views from Cwm-sanahan Hill at

407m (1335ft). A broad track runs parallel to the dyke as it crosses Llanfair Hill around 430m (1411ft). Teas are offered at Spring Hill Farm, then on the descent to the River Clun and the timbered house of Bryndrinog, a detour could be made into the little village of Newcastle, where the Crown Inn has a little shop alongside.

The dyke is a clear feature as it crosses Graig Hill, then while negotiating a wooded slope it climbs more than 120 steps, installed to protect the ancient earthwork from erosion. After crossing a road at Hergan, note how two lengths of the dyke meet awkwardly at a junction, something that puzzles archaeologists. An undulating stretch passes Middle Knuck, followed by some very steep slopes that are likely to prove arduous. Drop steeply down a forested slope and pass a church in a valley. Climb steeply and cross a gentle rise at 420m (1378ft), then drop downhill into another valley. Climb up a wooded slope, crossing into Wales, then drop down towards Cwm, with a view of the plains and easier walking ahead.

Follow the dyke through woods near Mellington Hall, where snacks are offered, and pass through a gatehouse at the end of a drive. Go through a crossroads that, although in England, is curious because all four roads lead into Wales! This is a long day's walk and walkers could finish

The attractive timbered house of Bryndrinog is passed near Newcastle (Day 6)

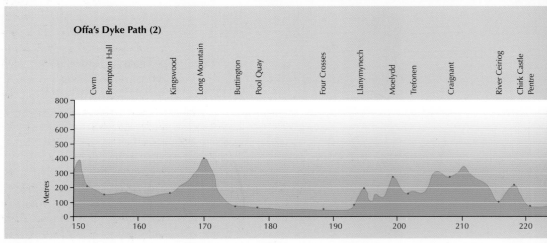

Offa's Dyke Path (2)

early at Little Brompton Farm, rather than continuing all the way to Montgomery. Offa's Dyke runs straight through flat fields, and for once the dyke, the trail and the Welsh/English border all run concurrently. Montgomery is a little off-route, but is well worth the detour.

Day 7 Montgomery to Four Crosses
29km (18 miles)

The dyke is clear and obvious as it runs through low-lying fields, and once the trail crosses the River Camlad it remains in Wales throughout the day. A short climb follows the dyke past Forden and Kingswood, the latter having a pub. The last remnants of the dyke are lost on the sprawling forested slopes of Long Mountain. Field paths lead towards the 408m (1339ft) summit, enclosed by Beacon Ring, the ramparts of an ancient hill fort, then watch carefully for markers on the way downhill through fields to Buttington. A pub lies just off-route, and a busy, narrow road has to be crossed over the River Severn.

A riverside path is used, followed by the towpath of the narrow 18th-century Montgomery Canal, which is often green with pondweed and has rampantly vegetated banks. The towpath is left at a diminutive lock at Pool Quay, in favour of the River Severn again. Snaking earth levées contain the flow in times of flood, as the fields alongside are very low-lying. Looking across the river, a large quarry bites into the Breidden Hills. Pass a sluice gate and watch carefully for the continuation of the trail. The dyke makes another appearance and is followed through flat fields, but the trail degenerates into a mudbath before it reaches Four Crosses. Shops, the Golden Lion pub and lodgings are available. The dyke

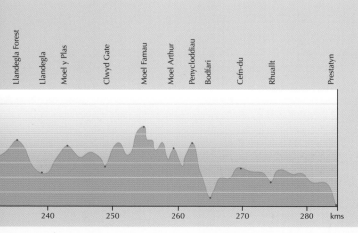

has been buried beneath a busy main road leading to Llanymynech, which is unsuitable for walkers to follow.

Day 8 Four Crosses to Pentre
32km (20 miles)

Follow the Montgomery Canal in a loop from Four Crosses to Llanymynech, delighting at its diminutive architecture and single-leaf lock gates. Leave the towpath at Llanymynech and climb towards the Llanymynech Rocks, where an old limestone quarry is quietly reverting to nature. The trail leaves Wales and descends into England, wandering among low hills on the way to Trefonen. Leaving the village, good stretches of the dyke are followed once again through fields and woods, crossing the old Oswestry Racecourse above 300m (985ft) on Summer Hill. Offa's Dyke crosses Baker's Hill and passes farm buildings at Carreg-y-Big, where refreshments are provided on a help-yourself basis.

A fine length of the dyke leads through rolling fields, crossing Selattyn Hill to reach Craignant. Again, the dyke, trail and Welsh/English border run concurrently, passing Mount Wood before descending to the River Ceirog. The route splits here, with the main route passing Crogen Wladys Farm, and a summer alternative allowing a visit to Chirk Castle. Both routes join to continue along roads and down through fields towards the village of Pentre. Chirk Castle dates from 1310, but has been altered considerably over the years. Its stout red drum towers and curtain wall enclose a courtyard.

Day 9 Pentre to Llandegla
21km (13 miles)

This short day's walk is also very interesting and scenic, but from now until the end of the trail there is nothing more to see of Offa's Dyke, and the last few days are entirely within Wales. First, follow the Shropshire Union Canal, which passes Froncysyllte

and crosses the narrow cast-iron Pontcysyllte Aqueduct. Walkers who suffer from vertigo will find this unnerving, so the trail actually follows a road across the River Dee instead, but those with a good head for heights will enjoy crossing the high aqueduct. Leave the canal at Trefor and climb gradually up a wooded slope to emerge on a scenic road on the slopes of Eglwyseg Mountain. Massive tiers of limestone can be observed as the road passes Trefor Rocks, Castell Dinas Bran and Creigiau Eglwyseg. Leave the road to follow a narrow path contouring a steep slope to reach a forested valley at World's End.

A road climbs onto a bleak moor, then the trail often follows boardwalks across heather and bilberry. Enter Llandegla Forest around 485m (1600ft), where a clear path cuts across other forest paths and tracks. The descent is gradual at first, then steepens and emerges among farm buildings at Hafod Bilston. Walk through fields to reach Pen-y-stryt and Llandegla, pretty little places where there is a little accommodation, shops, pubs and a restaurant.

Day 10 Llandegla to Bodfari
26km (16 miles)

Field paths lead away from Llandegla into the Clwydian Hills Area of Outstanding Natural Beauty. There is a gradual climb into the hills, and the trail is often reluctant to make summit bids, avoiding the 440m (1444ft) top of Moel y Plas and skirting the slopes of Moel Llanfair and Moel Gyw. The hillsides are covered in coarse grass and bracken, giving way to heather and gorse, and there are extensive views. The only place offering food and drink occurs early in the day, where a road crosses a gap in the hills at Clwyd Gate.

Tracks and paths lead back into the hills via Moel Fenlli, whose summit area bears the ramparts of an Iron Age hill fort. Walk round the heathery flanks of the hill and drop down to a gap at Bwlch Penbarra. A fine track climbs steadily towards

The ruins of the Jubilee Tower, a notable viewpoint on top of Moel Famau

Moel Famau and is often busy with walkers. The heathery hilltop is crowned with the early 19th-century ruins of the Jubilee Tower at 558m (1831ft). A viewing platform is equipped with panels allowing identification of distant features from Liverpool to Snowdonia. Keep to the heathery crest of the range over Moel Dywyli and Moel Llys-y-coed, following an obvious green grassy track. Drop steeply to a prominent gap, then climb round the slopes of Moel Arthur, whose top is encircled by the ramparts of another Iron Age fort.

The trail leads down to another gap, then a climb alongside a forest is followed by grassy tracks running up a heathery crest onto Penycloddiau. The multiple rumpled ramparts of yet another Iron Age hill fort enclose the 440m (1444ft) summit. Leave the heather moor to walk down grassy slopes to a gap at Nant, then follow tracks down into a farming hollow at Fron-haul.

Paths lead down to the village of Bodfari, which has a shop, a little nearby accommodation and the Downing Arms.

Day 11 Bodfari to Prestatyn
21km (13 miles)

The final day on the trail remains within the Clwydian Hills Area of Outstanding Natural Beauty, but is much gentler than the previous day. The route climbs into grassy little hills, crossing Cefn-du at 268m (879ft). Roads and field paths lead onwards, with a descent to cross the busy A55 to reach the little village of Ruthin and the Smithy Arms. Climb steeply up a wooded slope, then follow gentler tracks, roads and field paths to pass Marian Cwm on the way to Tan-yr-allt. A narrow, undulating path runs along the top of a limestone

The heathery crest of the Clwydian Range, with Moel Arthur and its hill fort in view (Day 10)

cliff, with a wooded slope leading down to a coastal plain. Eventually, the path slithers down a narrow path and roads lead straight through the seaside resort of Prestatyn to the promenade. The Offa's Dyke Path ends at a large lump of rock bearing a plaque. A seasonal tourist information centre alongside has an exhibition about the trail, which is worth looking at before travelling home.

INFORMATION

Access to Start	Arriva trains serve Chepstow, from where local buses run to Sedbury, though it is necessary to walk to the start at Sedbury Cliff.
Getting Home	Arriva trains serve Prestatyn, as well as occasional long-distance Virgin Trains, and there are National Express buses too.
Other Public Transport	Trains and buses cross the trail at intervals and full details are contained in the *Offa's Dyke Where to Stay* guide, available from TICs.
Maps	OS 1:50,000 Landrangers 116, 117, 126, 137, 148, 161 and 162
	OS 1:25,000 Explorers 201, 216, 240, 256, 265, OL13 and OL14
	Harveys 1:40,000 Offa's Dyke Path South and Offa's Dyke Path North
Cicerone Guide	*Walking Offa's Dyke Path*, by David Hunter
Other Guidebooks	*Offa's Dyke Path South & Offa's Dyke Path North*, by Ernie & Kathy Kay and Mark Richards, Aurum Press
Tourist Information Centres	Chepstow tel 01291 623772, Monmouth tel 01600 713899, Abergavenny tel 01873 857588, Hay-on-Wye tel 01497 820144, Kington tel 01544 230778, Knighton tel 01547 529424, Welshpool tel 01938 552043, Oswestry tel 01691 662488, Llangollen tel 01978 860828, Ruthin tel 01824 703992, Prestatyn tel 01745 889092.
Accommodation List	*Offa's Dyke Path and Glyndŵr's Way Where to Stay*, from Offa's Dyke Association or TICs
Path Association	www.offasdyke.demon.co.uk
Website	www.nationaltrail.co.uk/OffasDyke

A walker follows the course of Glyndŵr's Way along a track above Cemmaes Road (Day 6)

15 Glyndŵr's Way

Start and Finish	Knighton to Welshpool
Distance and Time	213km (132 miles) taking 1½ weeks
Character	Plenty of hills and plenty of ascents and descents, in a quiet and unfrequented part of the country where field paths are not particularly well trodden, although many clear tracks are also followed.
Highlights	Knighton, Llangunllo to Felindre and Llanbadarn Fynydd, Abbeycwmhir, Llanidloes, Bryntail Lead Mine, Staylittle to Foel Fadian, Machynlleth and Parliament House, Abercegir to Commins Gwalia, Llanwddyn and Llyn Efyrnwy, Meifod, Y Golfa and Welshpool.

Powis Castle, near Welshpool, was originally the seat of the Princes of Powys (Day 9)

Owain Glyndŵr was related to the House of Tudor, but was also descended from the Princes of Powys. Until the year 1400 he seemed to be loyal to the Crown, then he suddenly launched an attack at Ruthin to reclaim some land from Lord Grey. With Welsh support, he attacked other border towns before Henry IV moved in with an army. In 1402 a comet was taken as a favourable omen and torrential rain put paid to Henry's counter-assault. Owain Glyndŵr was credited with supernatural powers, and prestigious bardic poets rose to the cause and prophesied against the English. Glyndŵr forged allegiances with the Scots and French, who were already troubling the English, established a parliament at Machynlleth, and severed the Church in Wales from Canterbury's control. Glyndŵr was crowned Prince of Wales in 1404.

Guerilla warfare held the English at bay through 1405, but border fortifications were besieged one after another. Aberystwyth and

SCHEDULE			
Day	**Start/Finish**	**Km**	**Miles**
Day 1	Knighton to Felindre	25.5	16
Day 2	Felindre to Abbeycwmhir	25	15½
Day 3	Abbeycwmhir to Llanidloes	24.5	15
Day 4	Llanidloes to Staylittle	19	12
Day 5	Staylittle to Machynlleth	25.5	16
Day 6	Machynlleth to Llanbrynmair	25	15½
Day 7	Llanbrynmair to Llanwddyn	27	17
Day 8	Llanwddyn to Meifod	24.5	15
Day 9	Meifod to Welshpool	17	10½

Harlech held out until the bitter end, and English control was more or less resumed by 1408. Glyndŵr's last great battle was fought, and lost, at Shrewsbury in 1410. Henry V later offered a pardon, but this was refused, and like most great soldiers, Owain Glyndŵr seemed to fade away. Some say he joined a monastery, and many believe he was dead by 1417. Stirring stuff indeed, explaining why this newly established national trail bears his name and wanders through Powys in mid-Wales.

Glyndŵr's Way was established by Powys County Council and marked with 'dragon' symbols. It was improved and realigned before being

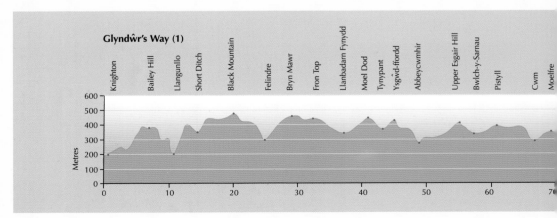

designated a national trail in the year 2000, though some stretches are still being negotiated. You will need a guidebook, or leaflets produced by Powys County Council, since Ordnance Survey maps do not yet show the correct route. This is a quiet trail that has yet to catch the attention of long-distance walkers, and facilities along the way are often very limited. Those who want to explore the empty, rolling, lush green hills of mid-Wales, however, will find this a delightful route, and easily the most 'Welsh' of all the trails in Wales. Bilingual signposts reading 'Llwybr Glyndŵr / Glyndŵr's Way' point the way from Knighton across country to Machynlleth, then back across country to Welshpool. Keen walkers could add another couple of days and follow a fine stretch of the Offa's Dyke Path from Welshpool to Knighton to close the loop.

Day 1 Knighton to Felindre
25.5km (16 miles)

Information about Glyndŵr's Way can be obtained from the Offa's Dyke Centre before leaving Knighton. Climb uphill from the central clock tower, through the Narrows, following fiddly paths between the houses before passing round the wooded slopes of Garth Hill. The Offa's Dyke Path climbs high on the other side of the valley. Roads,

tracks and field paths take Glyndŵr's Way above 400m (1310ft) on Bailey Hill before a descent to the village of Llangunllo. Here there is a pub and a shop run by the local community.

A series of tracks leads back up into the hills and a curious grassy embankment is reached, called the Short Ditch. Its origins are uncertain – some say it pre-dates Offa's Dyke, and others say it was thrown up against Owain Glyndŵr's advance against Knighton. Good tracks wander across the moorland slopes of Pool Hill, Stanky Hill and Black Mountain, sometimes running as high as 470m (1540ft). After crossing a gap at Bwlch the trail crosses one last rise and descends to the little village of Felindre, which has a shop, a couple of bed and breakfasts and the Wharf Inn.

Day 2 Felindre to Abbeycwmhir
25km (15½ miles)

Climb through pastures grazed by cows and sheep, following tracks past Rhuvid Bank to Hope's Castle Farm. Watch for waymarks, as there are several tracks intersecting on the hills. Climb as high as 450m (1475ft) on Bryngydfa and Fron Top, passing a once-fortified hillock at Castell-y-blaidd. Follow a road steeply down to Llanbadarn Fynydd, where there is a shop, the New Inn and a little accommodation. Look out for a plaque commemorating

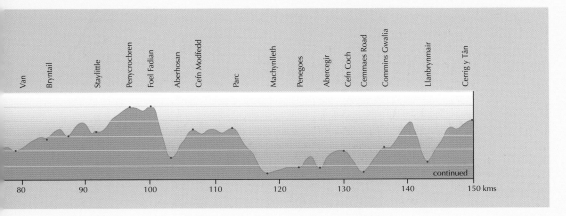

Sheep graze the grassy hills around Rhuvid, high above Felindre

the erection of a weighing machine by William Pugh in 1823, and its removal by another William Pugh in 1885. Another plaque, from 1930, records the repositioning of the first plaque – another momentous occasion for Llanbadarn Fynydd!

Cross the River Ithon and follow a track up towards Castle Bank. The trail stays high, but manages to miss the summits of the hills, climbing as high as 450m (1475ft), but cutting across the upper slopes of Moel Dod, Yr Allt and Ysgŵd-ffordd. Looking in all directions, most walkers would find it difficult to name any of the hills in view, since they lack distinguishing features, yet the overall aspect is quite pleasing. A steep descent on a wooded slope is followed by a road running parallel to Batchell Brook, and at length the trail reaches the tiny village of Abbeycwmhir. There is a ruined

abbey here, a Cistercian foundation of the 12th century whose masonry can be found in a number of other buildings in the area, even as far away as Llanidloes. The pub is called the Happy Union Inn, and there is a little accommodation nearby. Owain Glyndŵr's standard might be seen flying in the grounds of the hall.

Day 3 Abbeycwmhir to Llanidloes
24.5km (15 miles)

Climb over the forested slopes of the Sugar Loaf on the way out of Abbeycwmhir. Cross Clywedog Brook and gradually ascend over Upper Esgair Hill, touching 460m (1510ft) before following a muddy track down to Bwlch-y-sarnau. This tiny village sits on a gap and has no facilities for way-farers. The route drops onto a level boggy area and continues straight through a forest. Follow a road past the farm of Waun and continue round the lower, forested slopes of Pistyll. A fiddly series of tracks and paths requires careful route finding as the trail wanders at around 400m (1310ft) across the steep slopes of Rhydd Hywel, which is crowned by a whirling windfarm.

After crossing steep-sided Nant Feinion, the trail moves mainly through fields and eventually reaches a crossroads at Newchapel. The Baptist chapel was actually founded in 1740, but has been rebuilt twice, so the current structure largely dates only from 1954. Cross wooded, steep-sided Nant y

Bradnant, then follow a minor road straight to Llanidloes. This is a fine little town, with all facili-ties, centred on a 15th-century timber-framed mar-ket hall. After walking all the way from Abbeycwmhir, note that St Idloes Church contains masonry from the ruined abbey seen at the start of the day.

Day 4 Llanidloes to Dylife
19km (12 miles)

This is a short day's walk, as the route enters an 'empty quarter' where overnight accommodation is particularly sparse, though strong walkers

High in the hills between Llanbadarn Fynydd and Abbeycwmhir

might consider a long day's walk to Machynlleth. First, leave Llanidloes and cross the River Severn, then climb up a forested slope and walk past a golf course and down through fields to the tiny lead-mining village of Fan. Wander among low hills, then drop down through the ruins of Bryntail Lead Mine. Lead was produced here in the 19th century, then the 'waste' barytes was processed afterwards. There are helpful and informative panels located around the site.

The dam of the Clywedog Reservoir dominates the old mining site and was completed in 1967. There is a café beside the road, and Glyndŵr's Way runs along part of the rugged reservoir shore, which is remarkably convoluted. After climbing through forest on Banc y Groes, the trail runs through more forest at the head of the reservoir, emerging to cross the Afon Llwyd. Walk along the foot of a slope, within sight of the village of Staylittle. Owain

Glyndŵr fought a decisive battle nearby in 1401. Cross the Afon Clywedog and climb steeply uphill, then at a gentler gradient walk up a track on a broad moorland slope over 430m (1410ft). The Star Inn, a little off-route down at Dylife, offers the only accommodation on this stretch of the trail.

Day 5 Dylife to Machynlleth
25.5km (16 miles)

Penycrocbren stands at 469m (1539ft) above Dylife and was the site of a Roman fortlet. After passing Y Grug the route crosses a steep-sided valley drained by the Afon Clywedog, then a track climbs across a moor and there is suddenly a view of the shining lake of Glaslyn at 480m (1575ft). The highest part of Glyndŵr's Way is where the trail cuts across the steep slopes of Foel

Foel Fadian is the highest point reached on Glyndŵr's Way

Fadian around 510m (1675ft). Looking south, broad and bleak moorlands lead the eye to the sprawling summit of Pumlumon Fawr. All the height gained since leaving Llanidloes is lost quite suddenly on the descent to Nantyfyda and Dyffryn Dulas.

A winding track climbs across the slopes of Cefn Medfedd. The trail passes an isolated guest-house at Talbontdrain, then climbs steeply onto forested Rhiw Goch, around 350m (1150ft). Staying high in the hills, cross a gap at Bwlch, then follow a forested crest. Emerging from the trees on a hummocky hill, descend to a road and walk down the Roman Steps to reach the bustling and attractive little town of Machynlleth, where there is a monumental clock tower in the centre of town. Visit the Parliament House, where Owain Glyndŵr established his parliament and was crowned Prince of Wales. There is an excellent exhibition devoted to the man and his cause, and the vivid colours of his standard are often displayed around town.

Day 6 Machynlleth to Llanbrynmair
25km (15½ miles)

Roads have to be followed most of the way from Machynlleth to Forge and Penegoes. A break can be taken at a working watermill before the route climbs into the hills, crossing Bryn Wg. Walk through the pretty little village of Abercegir, formerly a centre for

wool, weaving and knitting, then walk over 260m (850ft) on the grassy crest of Cefn Coch. There are fine views north towards Cader Idris in southern Snowdonia. Descend to Cemmaes Road, which has a pub, then the route wriggles around low hills, almost touching 250m (820ft) on Commins Gwalia. A wet and muddy lane gives way to a gradual climb across the steep slopes of Moel Eiddew, taking the trail into forest around 390m (1280ft). After a moorland walk there is a steep descent, followed by a road walk to the village of Llanbrynmair, where there is a shop and a hotel.

Day 7 Llanbrynmair to Llanwddyn
27km (17 miles)

Glyndŵr's Way originally stayed fairly low beyond Llanbrynmair, but now climbs high on the crest of Cerrig y Tân and passes through a forest on the slopes of Panylau Gwynion, around 420m (1375ft). Walk down a broad moorland slope to reach a minor road in the Nant yr Eira valley. The road passes a couple of isolated farms, then a rugged track leads across the slopes of Pen Coed. Take care over route finding on the way down to the Llangadfan. A pub in the village has the curious name of the Cann Office, derived from the Welsh 'cae'n y ffos', meaning a fortified field.

Leaving Llangadfan, Glyndŵr's Way climbs past farms and fields to reach the sprawling Dyfnant

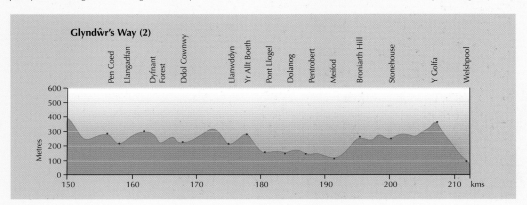

Forest. A series of forest paths, tracks and roads are negotiated, with a descent through farmland to cross the Afon Cownwy at Ddol Cownwy. Climb over a forested gap at 350m (1150ft) to reach the village of Llanwddyn, which is dominated by the reservoir dam of Llyn Efyrnwy. Water was impounded here in the 1880s to slake the thirst of distant Liverpool, and many people were resettled in new houses in Llanwddyn. After heavy rain, water spills over the full width of the dam in a milk-white cascade. Most of mid-Wales is good birdwatching country, but this area is particularly fine, featuring the red kite, buzzard, curlew, grouse, skylark and lapwing. The RSPB operate a centre here and can supply more details.

Day 8 Llanwddyn to Meifod
24.5km (15 miles)

Walk down from Llanwddyn to Abertridwr, then follow a road up to a forest. The trail runs through,

or alongside, the forest to the village of Llwydiarth, where there is a shop. On the way from Llwydiarth to Dolanog and Pontrobert, Glyndŵr's Way sometimes coincides with the Ann Griffiths Walk, which celebrates a local 18th-century composer of hymns. Imaginative information plaques highlight places associated with her. Both trails run alongside the Afon Efyrnwy, but Glyndŵr's Way climbs through rolling farmland, reaching 280m (920ft) before dropping down to Dolanog and the Ann Griffiths Chapel.

Continue parallel to the Afon Efyrnwy through a wooded valley, following a farm road to Pontrobert. Cross the river and climb past a pub, the Royal Oak, and continue through rolling farmland. Pass a Quaker meeting house, built in 1700 and associated with nearby Dolobran Hall. The trail eventually leads down to Pentre and Meifod, where there is a shop, pub and limited lodgings.

The last high viewpoint of Y Golfa before the descent into Welshpool

Day 9 Meifod to Welshpool
17km (10½ miles)

The last day's walk is short enough to be completed in a morning, although it is remarkably convoluted as it makes its way over wooded hills and rolling farmland. An early highlight is the little Llyn Du on Broniarth Hill, which often attracts waterfowl. The highest point gained during the day is the broad bracken crest of Y Golfa at 341m (1119ft), which is a splendid viewpoint on a clear day. All that remains is to descend to the busy little town of Welshpool, which is a typical Marches town. Walk straight through the town centre and cross the narrow Montgomery Canal at the Powysland Museum. A slender stone in a grassy space marks the end of Glyndŵr's Way.

The afternoon could be spent wandering through lovely parkland to explore Powis Castle and its gardens. The castle dates from around 1275 and was once the seat of the Princes of Powys. Welshpool has plenty of fine buildings, and some of its churches and old inns are noteworthy. As Welshpool was a major transport centre, some buildings were formerly coaching houses, the canal was once flanked by 30 warehouses, and the old railway station is now a visitor centre. The livestock market hosts the largest one-day sheep market in Europe!

Keen long-distance walkers could continue for a couple more days by linking with nearby Offa's Dyke Path, following it southwards to finish back at Knighton, thereby completing an enormous circular walk.

INFORMATION

Access to Start	Arriva trains serve Knighton, as well as buses.
Getting Home	Arriva trains serve Welshpool, as well as buses.
Other Public Transport	Most towns, but few villages, along the trail have bus services, while Machynlleth has good bus and rail services.
Maps	OS 1:50,000 Landrangers 125, 126, 135, 136, 137 and 148
	OS 1:25,000 Explorers 200, 201, 214, 215, 216 and 239
Cicerone Guide	*Glyndŵr's Way*, by Ronnie and Chris Catling
Other Guidebooks	*Glyndŵr's Way*, by David Perrott, Aurum Press
Tourist Information Centres	Knighton tel 01547 529424, Llanidloes tel 01686 412605, Machynlleth tel 01654 702401, Lake Vyrnwy tel 01691 870346, Welshpool tel 01938 552043.
Accommodation List	*Offa's Dyke Path and Glyndŵr's Way Where to Stay*, from Offa's Dyke Association or TICs
Website	www.nationaltrail.co.uk/GlyndwrsWay

A walker approaches Over Phawhope bothy at the head of the Ettrick valley (Day 7)

SCOTLAND

16 Southern Upland Way

Start and Finish	Portpatrick to Cockburnspath
Distance and Time	341km (212 miles) taking up to 2 weeks
Character	A long and often rugged trail that crosses remote and unfrequented moorlands, as well as passing through forest and fields, crossing high hills and occasionally running through towns and villages.
Highlights	Castle Kennedy, New Luce, Craigairie Fell, Glen Trool and Galloway Forest Park, St John's Town of Dalry, Culmark Hill to Sanquhar and Wanlockhead, Lowther Hills, Ettrick Head, Scabcleuch to St Mary's Loch, Blackhouse to Traquair and Minch Moor, Melrose and Roman road to Lauder, Lammermuir Hills, Abbey St Bathans – and collecting 'merks' along the way!

Tiny Cove Harbour is seen before the end of the trail at Cockburnspath (Day 12)

The Southern Upland Way is a challenging coast-to-coast trail across Scotland – from Portpatrick on the Irish Sea near Stranraer, to Cockburnspath on the North Sea near Dunbar. The route traverses remote terrain through the Galloway Forest Park as well as over the hills beyond Dalry. The highest part of the trail crosses the grassy giants of the Lowther Hills. There are heathery hills and broad moors along the way, separated by gentle green valleys. Belted Galloway cattle might be noticed early on the trail, while later, red grouse might start alarmingly from underfoot on extensive heather moors. The Southern Upland Way is a wild and wonderful route, with a surprising sense of space and solitude, but is also a rather quiet and under-used trail.

Some walkers believe that the route spends far too much time in coniferous forests or along roads, but this is far from true. There are indeed plenty of forests, but in recent years the route has been shifted away from some of them, while other forests have been clear-felled and replanted with a mixture of species, including broadleaf trees along the margins.

Michael Ancram, of the Scottish Office, opened the trail back in 1979, but since that time it has remained fairly quiet. Relatively few people walk it, and this may be because few are even aware of it, or perhaps because people just can't figure out a workable schedule to tie in with the sparse facilities along the way. This is a great pity, since all the information needed to complete it is readily available. At intervals along the trail, leaflet dispensers are stocked with information about facilities and features of interest, such as geology, archaeology, history and wildlife, enabling wayfarers to enhance their appreciation of their surroundings as they travel across country.

Towns are few, and some villages have very little in the way of food, drink and accommodation. Careful planning is the key to a successful conclusion, and careful planning ensures that you will be

SCHEDULE			
Day	Start/Finish	Km	Miles
Day 1	Stranraer to New Luce	36	22
Day 2	New Luce to Bargrennan	27	17
Day 3	Bargrennan to Dalry	39	24
Day 4	Dalry to Polskeoch	29	18
Day 5	Polskeoch to Wanlockhead	29	18
Day 6	Wanlockhead to Beattock	32	20
Day 7	Beattock to St Mary's Loch	34	21
Day 8	St Mary's Loch to Traquair	19	12
Day 9	Traquair to Melrose	29	18
Day 10	Melrose to Lauder	16	10
Day 11	Lauder to Longformacus	24	15
Day 12	Longformacus to Cockburnspath	27	17

able to enjoy the rigours of the trail in the knowledge that your needs will be taken care of at the end of each day. Backpackers with all their camping gear can often pitch in the wilds and easily cover manageable distances each day. On some remote stretches, there are bothies available – basic shelters that help to break a long and difficult stage. Those who want the luxury of bed and breakfast, inns and hotels should ensure that they have an up-to-date accommodation list, and make advance bookings to ensure a bed each night. Similarly with food and drink – you need to know where the shops and pubs are, or carry provisions along any particularly remote stages. Some parts of the Southern Upland Way run at a high level, but even some of the lower stretches can be remarkably rugged.

Waymarking is on the whole good, but in mist it can be difficult to spot marker posts on open moors if they are far apart. Good map-reading skills are required at times. Quite apart from waymarks, there are also 'waymerks' along the course of the Southern Upland Way.

'Waymerks' are specially minted coins of various designs, hidden in 'kists', or special containers, on remote parts of the trail. The kists were made by local artists and are usually visible from the trail, so there is no need to dig. There are 13 kists to find, and the idea is that walkers should take one 'merk' from each, to keep as a memento of their journey. If you collect all 13, then you'll be doing very well. The scheme was inaugurated for the 21st anniversary of the trail in 2005, and it is planned to restock the 'kists' for the foreseeable future.

Day 1 Stranraer to New Luce
36km (22 miles)

Portpatrick is named after St Patrick, who is reputed to have leapt

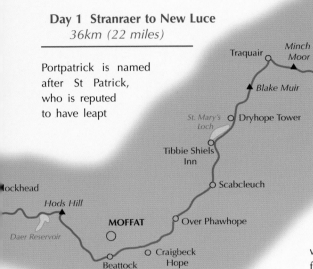

soon descends to a sandy beach, followed by a rocky beach, then chains assist on a rocky climb. Head inland along a lighthouse access road, then cross a moorland around 150m (490ft) at Knock and Maize, taking care to locate a hidden kist of merks. Roads and tracks pass close to Stranraer, which has a full range of services and is a bustling ferryport. A woodland walk leads to Castle Kennedy, where there is a shop and the Plantings Inn. If this day's walk seems too long, then this is the only place it can be conveniently broken.

Follow a road alongside White Loch, which gives access to the castle and its gardens, but the Southern Upland Way leaves it to follow roads and tracks onto Airyolland Moss. The trail used to follow a track through an extensive forest on Glenwhan Moor, but has been rerouted alongside to offer better views. Look for another kist of merks on the slopes of Craig Fell, then cross two footbridges – one over a railway and the other spanning the Water of Luce. The lovely little settlement of New Luce has the Kenmuir Arms Hotel and shop, but is a little off-route. Either walk there, or arrange for a pick up, or catch one of the rather infrequent buses serving the village.

from Ireland to Scotland and left the imprint of his feet by the rocky harbour. He then walked around Loch Ryan to convert the heathen, but was beheaded by the natives in Glen App. Nonchalantly tucking his severed head under his arm, he then swam back to Ireland! Today's visitors to the pretty little harbour village will get a better reception, but given the nature of the Southern Upland Way, it is wise to obtain the annually produced booklet detailing services and accommodation along the route before starting the walk.

Leave the rocky harbour in Portpatrick, climbing up steps inscribed with a geological commentary on the way to the cliff top. The coastal path

Looking towards the Galloway Hills from the summit of Craigairie Fell

Day 2 New Luce to Bargrennan
27km (17 miles)

Kilhern Moss, above New Luce, was settled thousands of years ago, and the burial chambers known as the Caves of Kilhern can be visited by a short detour. Walk down to the Water of Luce, then follow a narrow road uphill, passing a couple of farms. Before reaching Kilmacfadzean, follow a vague path across a boggy moor, within sight of wind turbines on Artfield Fell. Enter a forest and follow a broad ride and track, then another ride to a grassy clearing at Laggangarn. A wooden beehive bothy has been planted in this

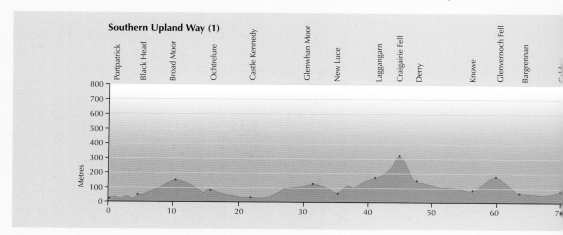

remote spot especially for Southern Upland Wayfarers. There are tumbled stone dwellings and a couple of ancient standing stones nearby.

The trail has been rerouted over the 320m (1050ft) summit of Craigairie Fell, where wide-ranging views reveal vast areas of moorland and forest, along with the rugged outlines of the Galloway Hills ahead. A track passes Derry Loch and the isolated farmstead of Derry. The farm access road runs through extensive forest, passing a couple more habitations along the way, to reach the tiny little settlement of Knowe. A forest path climbs up to another narrow road, which is followed past a couple of houses. Leave the road to wander over the rugged slopes of Glenvernoch Fell, dropping down to a road at Garchew before another rugged slope drops down to Bargrennan. The House o' Hill Hotel provides food, drink and accommodation in this tiny village.

Day 3 Bargrennan to Dalry
39km (24 miles)

The Southern Upland Way used to head straight for Glen Trool, but has been pleasantly rerouted alongside the River Cree and Water of Trool into the Galloway Forest Park. There is access to the Glen Trool Visitor Centre, just off-route. Another

kist of merks is hidden beside the trail, and a Covenanter memorial is passed at Caldons. As the route passes high above Loch Trool, walkers should bear in mind that they tread in the footsteps of English soldiers who in 1307 were ambushed in this remote place by Robert the Bruce. Imagine boulders crashing down on you, and being picked off by arrows as you flee in confusion. The dead lie buried at the head of the loch in boggy ground known as the Soldier's Holm. A rugged path climbs from Glenhead, though if flooding is likely at Trostan Burn, use a forest track instead. The track leads close to White Laggan bothy near Loch Dee. This is the only place offering shelter on this very long day's walk.

Hard-surfaced forest tracks cross the Black Water of Dee and pass close to Clatteringshaws Loch. The loch is a reservoir, and was previously a bog, where in 1307 Robert the Bruce successfully ambushed another large English force. He achieved this by using a few men and a herd of cattle, making noise all through the night to convince the English that they were surrounded and outnumbered. At first light, as the English soldiers were confused and mired in the bog, Scottish archers picked them off with ease. Forest paths lead onwards, and there is a particularly well-hidden kist of merks to find along the way, a clue to its location being provided by an osier arch.

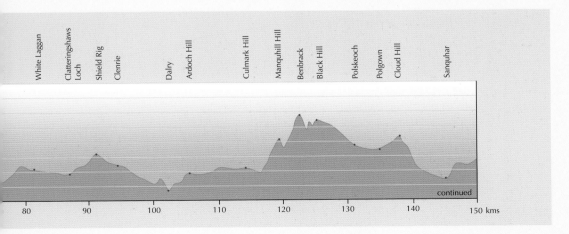

Cross rugged moorland on Shield Rigg, over 305m (1000ft), and head for an isolated house at Clenrie. The stony access track gives way to a narrow road running alongside Garroch Burn, passing a few houses. A path later leaves the road and climbs over the low slopes of Waterside Hill. St John's Town of Dalry is seen from here, and is approached by walking alongside the Water of Ken. There are shops, a hotel and other lodgings. Note that some accommodation providers in Dalry will pick up and drop off walkers, enabling this long day's walk and the next long day to be covered in three easier days.

Day 4 Dalry to Polskeoch
29km (18 miles)

Walk up the main street to leave Dalry and continue through fields to pass Ardoch Hill and cross Earlstaun Burn. Paths become vague, but there are fine views of the hills ahead. The route is remarkably direct, following a road to Butterhole Bridge, climbing gently over Culmark Hill, then climbing again beyond Stroanpatrick. Watch carefully for marker posts on the long moorland approach to Manquhill Hill. The trail narrowly misses the 421m (1381ft) summit. Cross a forested gap then climb up a steep and grassy slope to reach a trig point on

top of Benbrack at 580m (1903ft). Enjoy the views, which on a clear day even extend to the fells of the Lake District in England, and enjoy the experience of being among such remote uplands.

Follow a fence onwards along the moorland crest to reach the neighbouring summit of Black Hill, then walk beside a forest until the trail is directed into the forest from High Countam. Pause at the Covenanter memorial called Allan's Cairn, where there is a view towards the higher Lowther Hills. Walk along forest rides, then continue down a track to reach the Chalk Memorial bothy at Polskeoch. Basic shelter is provided here on this remote stretch, but anyone willing to walk to the nearest farmhouse bed and breakfast for the night can strike southwest off-route to Holm of Dalquhairn, returning in the morning.

Day 5 Polskeoch to Wanlockhead
29km (18 miles)

A track leads out of the trees to pass Polskeoch Farm, then a road runs down through the valley, passing a couple more farms. Waymarks lead   uphill from Polgown and there is a kist of merks beside the trail. A gap on a high crest is crossed around 400m (1310ft), and Sanquhar can be seen in the distance sitting low in Nithsdale. Make a beeline towards the

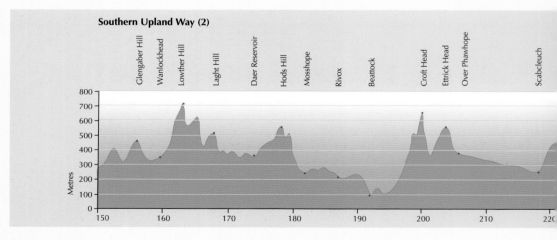

Southern Upland Way (2)

town, which is easy on the moorland slopes, but the final approach is rather fiddly, passing close to the tottering ruins of Sanquhar Castle, dating from the 14th century. Sanquhar has the widest range of services so far along the Southern Upland Way. Among its many fine old buildings is the oldest post office in the world, dating from 1712, and the Tolbooth Museum is well worth a visit. The tall obelisk on the high street stands on the site of an older monument, where the Covenanter Reverend Richard Cameron posted the Sanquar Declaration of 1660, renouncing allegiance to Charles II. The 'killing times' saw

the wholesale persecution of Covenanters, and the hills are littered with stone monuments recalling the names of many now regarded as martyrs.

The delightfully named Coo Wynd is the way out of Sanquhar – a long, broad, grassy track climbing onto the moors. Cows were led up and down it, from grassy pastures to milking parlours. The trail crosses a valley at Bog, then climbs higher on the moors to reach a gap around 410m (1345ft) between the hills. Drop steeply down into a forested valley and look out for a cunningly hidden kist of merks. There is a choice of routes – one is a direct path high on the slopes of Glengaber Hill, touching 475m (1560ft), whereas the other stays low for a little longer, and is to be used when the grouse are breeding, or when grouse shooting is taking place. Both routes meet outside Wanlockhead.

Walk as directed through the village, which is the highest in Scotland at around 425m (1395ft). Lead was once mined here, along with a little silver and gold, and the remains of the industry form a vast outdoor museum that is well worth exploring. Those with a particular

Forest and moorland at Dalgonar, after leaving the Polskeoch bothy

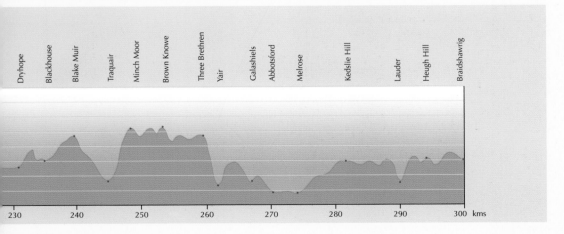

interest in industrial archaeology should spend an extra day here, first visiting the museum. The Wanlockhead Inn offers food and drink, but lodgings are quite limited in the village.

Day 6 Wanlockhead to Beattock
32km (20 miles)

The Southern Upland Way climbs high above Wanlockhead to pass close to the prominent 'radome' on top of Lowther Hill at 725m (2379ft). This is the highest point on the trail and views are remarkably extensive, except where blocked by the monstrous dome. The route is a roller coaster as it drops down into dips and climbs over humped hills while heading for Laght Hill. Dip into a kist of merks and drop down to a road at Over Fingland. This was formerly a Roman road, but it is soon left behind as the trail crosses Potrail Water, then links forest paths and tracks to weave around the hillsides to the Daer Reservoir. Cross the reservoir dam, a massive earthen structure which since 1956 has impounded water destined for Lanarkshire.

A steep climb up Sweetshaw Brae is followed by another climb onto Hods Hill at 567m (1860ft). The trail follows the edge of a forest, then enters the forest and drops into a valley. The line of the route is curious – a trench was cut through the forest and a gas pipeline buried there, but rather than planting trees on top, the land was left clear to be used by the Southern Upland Way. Brattleburn bothy is signposted a little off-route, offering a chance to break this long stage. After climbing over Craig Hill the route crosses Garpol Water in a broad

clearing, then crosses another forested rise to reach a charming pool near a road. The road leads down to the straggly village of Beattock, which has the Old Stables pub and a little accommodation. Anyone needing food supplies would have to walk off-route to the small town of Moffat, a busy place often frequented by tourists, but removed from the roar of the main road and main line railway that run past Beattock.

Day 7 Beattock to St Mary's Loch
34km (21 miles)

Leaving Beattock, the Southern Upland Way goes beneath the busy A74, then quickly heads through quiet, low-lying countryside close to Moffat Water. A forest track is followed uphill, almost to Craigbeck Hope, which offers accommodation. The route climbs from the forest, over Gateshaw Rig and Croft Head, zigzagging down to a dramatic gap in the hills, facing Craigmichan Scar. Watch carefully to spot a kist of merks on the way to the broad gap of Ettrick Head at 530m (1740ft). Another forest track leads down to Over Phawhope bothy, which is remarkably well equipped, helping to break this long day's walk if required.

The Southern Upland Way crosses Croft Head, at 637m (2090ft), between two forests near Ettrick Head

A long road walk chases Ettrick Water downstream, passing a handful of farms and houses. The surrounding hills are attractive, but the tarmac is hard underfoot and the road rolls onwards, seemingly without end. At Scabcleuch, a signpost points straight uphill and a rugged path heads upstream beside Scabcleuch Burn. Cross a broad moorland gap around 450m (1475ft), and on a hot day look out for a refreshingly cold spring bursting from a rock. The trail reaches a fine crest, then drops down into old fields around the ruin of Riskinhope Hope. After climbing round Earl's Hill and briefly entering forest, walkers follow a clear track downhill to reach the Tibbie Shiels Inn, sitting between the Loch of the Lowes and St Mary's Loch. This is a wonderfully scenic end to the day, and it is worth taking an evening stroll to the striking white statue of James Hogg, the Ettrick Shepherd, a renowned poet and friend of Sir Walter Scott. An inscription says, 'He taught the wandering winds to sing' and his faithful dog Hector lies at his feet.

Day 8 St Mary's Loch to Traquair
19km (12 miles)

This is a fairly short and easy day, beginning with a walk along the shore of St Mary's Loch to Bowerhope, then continuing along a woodland track. A short stretch of the River Yarrow is followed before the trail heads close to Dryhope Tower, a 16th-century peel. Mary Scott, the 'Flower of Yarrow', was born here. She married Auld Wat of Harden, a notorious Border reiver, and is reputed to have served him his spurs on a plate, thus dropping a heavy hint that it was time for him to go and raid someone's cattle, if he wanted food on the table! A track and path are followed across a hillside to nearby Blackhouse, where the ruins of Blackhope Tower can be seen, which was a Douglas property. James Hogg was a shepherd at Blackhouse, composing poetry in his spare time.

A grassy forest track climbs onto moorlands, crossing 464m (1522ft) Blake Muir, which offers good views of the surrounding hills. Look out for a kist of merks cleverly disguised as a boundary stone. The moorland track runs downhill and fields are passed on the way to a road. The road leads to a stout stone cross in the little village of Traquair. There is limited accommodation here, and anyone needing a greater range of services can walk to the nearby 18th-century mill town of Innerleithen. Traquair House claims to be the oldest continually inhabited house in Scotland, with a history stretching back to 1107. The famous Steekit Yetts, or 'closed gates', were apparently locked following the departure of Bonnie Prince Charlie in 1745, and a vow was made that they would never be opened again until a Stuart was restored to kingship.

Day 9 Traquair to Melrose
29km (18 miles)

A forest track climbs from Traquair, passing a small log hut, the Minch Moor bothy. Further uphill is the Resolution Point, a curious sculpture relying on an optical illusion to view shapes cut into the heather moorland. A fine track passes the Cheese Well and climbs to 512m (1680ft) before entering a forest. There is a hidden kist of merks on the way down to a forested gap, then the trail climbs over Hare Law and broad Brown Knowe at 524m (1719ft). The moorland crest eventually leads to the Three Brethren, which are three big pepperpot cairns at 464m (1522ft). Walk down beside a forest, then down through the forest to pass a hotel at Yair and cross a bridge over the River Tweed. A old stone bridge spans this fine salmon-fishing river.

The Southern Upland Way climbs over a gap around 275m (900ft) on Hog Hill, then descends towards Galashiels. The route doesn't really enter the town, but skirts the suburbs and crosses the shoulder of another hill. There is a view of Abbotsford, a fine house standing on a site bought in 1811 by the poet and novelist Sir Walter Scott. The house was still being developed in 1826 when Scott's publishing firm, Ballantyne, suffered bankruptcy. Scott wrote furiously to earn money to pay off his debts right up to his death in 1832. A footpath and cycleway run parallel to the River Tweed from Galashiels to Melrose. Spend the evening admiring the fine buildings around Melrose. The Romans had a fort here, called Trimontium, after the three prominent peaks of the nearby Eildon Hills. St Cuthbert lived here in the 7th century, and the rose-coloured abbey ruins date from the 12th century. A waymarked trail called St Cuthbert's Way runs from Melrose to Lindisfarne, from Scotland to England, linking the Southern Upland Way with the Pennine Way, as well as visiting many more places associated with the hermit saint.

Day 10 Melrose to Lauder
16km (10 miles)

This is a short and easy day's walk. A splendid suspension footbridge spans the River Tweed and a notice informs 'passengers' how they should conduct themselves. After a short riverside walk the route roughly follows the course of a Roman road northwards. Look back from time to time to see the three big humps of the Eildon Hills, and follow a fine track over the broad top of Kedslie Hill. Keep

an eye peeled for a kist of merks before crossing the broad top of Woodheads Hill at 303m (994ft). There are fine views of Lauder huddled in a broad valley, with the moorlands of the Lammermuir Hills beyond. The town has a spacious main street, many fine buildings and services, and access to Thirlestane Castle, a Disneyesque edifice dating from the 16th century, but flamboyantly altered and extended over the years.

Day 11 Lauder to Longformacus
24km (15 miles)

Use the access road for Thirlestane Castle to leave Lauder, then head uphill past Wanton Walls. The trail often runs above 300m (985ft) as it crosses the first few grassy humps of the Lammermuir Hills, and in poor visibility careful route finding is required. A clear track climbs from the remote farm of Braidshawrig to the high crest of the moors, then a clear path leads onwards, passing yet another kist of merks. The summit of Twin Law rises to 447m (1467ft) and is crowned with two ancient sprawling burial cairns, surmounted by huge, well-built cairns (one of which has a niche containing a visitor book!). A verse on a plaque refers to the Battle of Twinlaw, in which twin brothers, who weren't aware of their kinship, died at each other's hands while engaged in single combat in an effort to resolve an impending conflict between the native Scots and invading Saxons.

A long and winding path descends from Twin Law, crossing Watch Water, then heading for the dam of Watch Water Reservoir. There is a small café here, which is the only place in the area offering food and drink. The rest of the route simply involves following a

Southern Upland Way (3)

road to the village of Longformacus. Bear in mind that lodgings are very limited here, and there is no shop or pub.

Day 12 Longformacus to Cockburnspath
27km (17 miles)

Follow a road out of Longformacus, then climb through fields and continue across moorland, with fine views back to the Lammermuir Hills. Walk alongside forest and woodland, keeping an eye on marker posts, reaching 315m (1035ft) before dropping down a forest track to a road. The route runs round the slopes of Abbey Hill, pathless at first, then using a forest track. This leads down through a pleasant valley to the charming little village of Abbey St Bathans. Cross a footbridge over Whiteadder Water and walk downstream to another part of the village – an old mill complex with a small restaurant.

Walk up through a valley, passing one final kist of merks, and cross Blakestone Moor. Farm tracks and field paths take the trail across country and down to cross the busy A1 and a railway. Woodland tracks give way to flights of steps in Pease Dean, emerging at a mobile-home park at Pease Bay. The long coast-to-coast walk is almost over, but not until a fine cliff-top walk has been completed. There are wonderful views of rustic Cove Harbour, with the eye being led to the far distant coast of Fife. A path runs inland to reach the end of the Southern Upland Way in the village of Cockburnspath. There is a shop, very limited accommodation, and an old weather-beaten church that is worth visiting. There are regular buses linking with onward transport connections via Edinburgh or Berwick-upon-Tweed.

INFORMATION	
Access to Start	Scot Rail trains and Scottish Citylink buses serve Stranraer, from where Stagecoach buses run to Portpatrick.
Getting Home	Regular Perrymans buses from Cockburnspath run to Edinburgh and Berwick-upon-Tweed for onward rail and bus travel.
Other Public Transport	Places such as Sanquhar, Moffat, Innerleithen, Melrose and Lauder have good transport links, but in other places services can be sparse or completely absent.
Maps	OS 1:50,000 Landrangers 67, 73, 76, 77, 78, 79 and 82
	OS 1:25,000 Explorers 309, 310, 319, 320, 322, 328, 329, 330, 337, 338, 345 and 346
Cicerone Guide	*Southern Upland Way*, by Alan Castle
Other Guidebooks	*Southern Upland Way*, by Roger Smith, Mercat Press
Tourist Information Centres	Stranraer tel 01776 702595, Newton Stewart tel 01671 402431, Dalry tel 01644 430015, Sanquhar tel 01659 50185, Moffat tel 01683 220620, Melrose tel 01896 822555, Lauder tel 01578 722808, Dunbar tel 01368 863353.
Accommodation List	*Southern Upland Way Accommodation Guide*, from TICs
Websites	www.dumgal.gov.uk/southernuplandway and www.southernuplandway.com

The River Spey, flanked by banks of bleached cobbles, passes below Ordiquish (Day 2)

17 Speyside Way

Start and Finish	Buckie to Aviemore
Distance and Time	135km (84 miles) taking up to 1 week
Character	A varied trail that includes some easy, low-level walking, often along disused railway trackbeds, as well as moderate hillwalking. The terrain varies from coast to fields and woodlands to moorlands, along with riversides.
Highlights	Tugnet, Fochabers, Dufftown, Craigellachie to Ballindalloch along an old railway trackbed parallel to the River Spey, Glenlivet to Tomintoul, Cromdale to Grantown-on-Spey, Boat of Garten to Aviemore.

The Speyside Way runs through fields and woods on its way through the Cromdale Hills

The River Spey has long been famous as a salmon-fishing river, and the rich earth alongside has earned Speyside the soubriquet 'larder of Scotland'. The area is also world-famous for its distinctive single malt whiskies, and there are distilleries throughout the length and breadth of Speyside. Some of them will invite you in to sample a 'wee dram', so this could be regarded as a whisky trail. The area has become popular with walkers following the establishment of an easy and generally low-lying long-distance trail. The middle part of the Speyside Way runs along a charming old railway trackbed, complete with old stations, bridges and tunnels. As the route stretches from the coast, through a river valley to the fringes of the Cairngorms National Park, there is a wide range of scenery and habitats along the way. Villages surrounded by distilleries are visited one day, then bustling little towns another day, while some stretches of the trail seem far removed from habitation.

Unlike most of the other trails described in this book, the Speyside Way was opened piecemeal over a period of nearly 20 years. First, in 1981, the main backbone of the route was opened, from Spey Bay to Ballindalloch, with a short side-spur to Dufftown. Next, a hilly extension to Tomintoul was opened in 1990, which is now regarded as another side-spur. A coastal path was added in 1999 from Buckpool Harbour to Spey Bay, then in the year 2000 a lengthy stretch was opened between Ballindalloch and Aviemore.

SCHEDULE			
Day	**Start/Finish**	**Km**	**Miles**
Day 1	Buckpool Harbour to Fochabers	16	10
Day 2	Fochabers to Craigellachie	21	13
Day 3	Dufftown to Ballindalloch	26	16
Day 4	Ballindalloch to Tomintoul	24	15
Day 5	Ballindalloch to Grantown-on-Spey	21	13
Day 6	Grantown-on-Spey to Aviemore	27	17

There is a plan to extend the route even further from Aviemore to Newtownmore.

The Speyside Way is an ideal introduction to long-distance walking, and it has a good range of services along the way, though accommodation in some places is a bit sparse and it would be well to book ahead at busy times of the year. Some thought needs to be

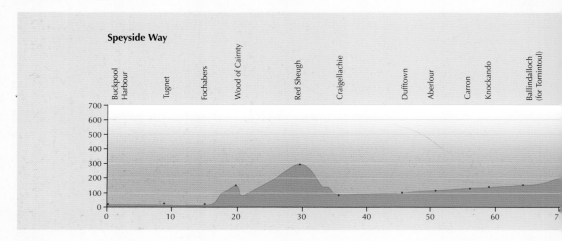

given to the side-spurs to Dufftown and Tomintoul, since anyone walking along them will either have to walk back again to continue along the main trail, or catch a bus back, in which case up-to-date timetables need to be obtained in advance. There is also a useful summer bus service that operates to most places along the route.

Day 1 Buckpool Harbour to Fochabers
16km (10 miles)

Buckpool Harbour is near Buckie and easily reached by bus from nearby towns. Follow a road along the coast to nearby Portgordon, then walk along an old railway trackbed that drifts inland. Paths lead through a forest to return to the coast at Tugnet, where the River Spey debouches into the North Sea among chaotic drifts of gravel. There is an interesting visitor centre here, covering the fishing industry and local wildlife, and old grass-covered icehouses can be inspected, where fish were once stored after being landed.

Follow a track inland, drifting away from the wild and wooded banks of the River Spey. A short detour onto the Garmouth Viaduct allows fine views of the river; otherwise continue onwards and the track runs alongside the river later. There is barely a glimpse of the river while walking through Warren Wood and Bellie Wood, then the trail runs into the delightful little town of Fochabers. There is a neat central green, sporting an ornate stone fountain and surrounded by fine stone buildings. Take a look at the shops, which sell wholesome local produce. Baxters of Fochabers, the quality foodstuffs manufacturer, has a visitor centre attached to their industrial kitchens, and it is surprising what can be put in a tin, such as a whole pheasant in a Burgundy wine sauce (not for nothing does Speyside have the reputation of being the 'larder of Scotland'!).

Day 2 Fochabers to Craigellachie
21km (13 miles)

Walk through fields to leave Fochabers and join a minor road at Ordiquish. Later, a short diversion to the Earth Pillars is recommended, where thick drifts of gravelly earth have been weathered into fluted forms, and there is a good view along the meanders and gravelly banks of the River Spey. The road is followed a long distance across a hillside, with farms along the way, forest above, and views of agricultural acres stretching into the distance. The highest point reached is almost 150m (490ft), then there is a descent to the Boat o' Brig. There was once a ferry, or boat, here, until it was replaced by a bridge.

A farm track gives way to forest tracks on the slopes of Knock More. Another forest track climbs gradually higher on the slopes of Ben Aigan, reaching 285m (935ft) before a good viewpoint at Red Sheugh. Pause to see the River Spey snaking to the distant sea, then continue down the track. Another long road walk leads at length to the distillery village of Craigellachie. A decision needs to be made about a spur route at this point. You could walk from here to Dufftown, and either stay there, get a bus back, or walk back. Alternatively, you could simply get a bus to Dufftown and walk back in the morning.

Day 3 Dufftown to Ballindalloch
26km (16 miles)

Dufftown, whose square is dominated by a huge stone clock tower, has an annual whisky festival that draws aficionados from around the world, and claims to be the 'whisky capital' of Scotland. The

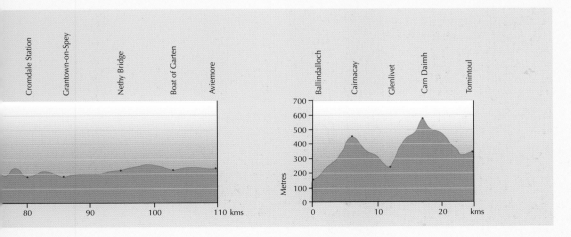

A fine old railway trackbed is followed from Craigellachie to Ballindalloch

Glenfiddich Distillery is equipped for visitor tours. The trackbed of an old railway can be followed in gentle loops parallel to the River Fiddich. The river flows through a steep-sided wooded gorge as it approaches Craigellachie, where a left turn leads back onto the main part of the Speyside Way. The route skirts the village, which largely grew around the junction of two railways in the middle of the 19th century. Of the nearby distilleries, only the Macallan offers tours, but is inconveniently on the 'wrong' side of the Spey. The old railway trackbed runs parallel to a road and passes through a tunnel to reach Charlestown of Aberlour. The old station site has been partly restored and partly extended and houses the Speyside Way Visitor Centre.

Obviously, any information about the trail can be found here. The little town has shops, pubs and other services, and is the home of Walkers Shortbread.

For the rest of the day, simply keep following the old railway trackbed, which is often very popular with walkers. It runs roughly parallel to the River Spey, passing the Dailuaine Distillery, then crossing the Bridge of Carron. Pass the old station at Carron and continue to Knockando. The old clapboard station at Tamdhu is delightful, and if it still had rails you could well imagine waiting for an old steam train here. The next station along the line is a stone-built one at Blacksboat. Later, the old line crosses the River Spey to reach another old station at

Ballindalloch. This is far enough for today, but bear in mind that accommodation is sparse in this area, and a decision needs to be made about a lengthy spur route leading to Tomintoul.

Day 4 Ballindalloch to Tomintoul
24km (15 miles)

This is a fine day's walk, and one that heads for the hills via the Glenlivet Crown Estate. Unfortunately, as this is a spur from the main route, some walkers might be tempted to omit it, which would be a great pity. If following this route, be sure to carry up-to-date bus timetables so that you can easily get back to Ballindalloch to continue the following day. First, follow roads to the Brig o' A'an, Delnashaugh Hotel and Bridge of Tommore, then follow a road, track and path high onto the heathery slopes of Cairnacay. The route touches 470m (1540ft) before heading for the hump of the Hill of Deskie and a descent to the River Livet. Walk uphill a short way

to reach the Glenlivet Distillery, which has a restaurant, offers guided tours and can be very busy.

Climb into the hills again, traversing the rugged slopes of Carn Liath, then walk alongside a forest and climb to the stone-peppered summit of Carn Daimh at 570m (1870ft). This is the highest point reached on the trail and a splendid viewpoint. Look northwards along the Avon, which feeds into the Spey, then south to the wild, remote Cairngorm plateau, which may be flecked with snow early and late in the year. There is a long and gradual descent, partly through forest, then down a moorland slope, crossing Conglass Water before entering Tomintoul, which is situated over 305m (1000ft). Small houses, regular in layout and dating from the 18th century, flank the long main street. Larger and more ornate buildings stand around a green in the town centre. Anyone staying overnight can enjoy a full range of facilities, but it is also possible, with careful timing, to get a bus back down to Ballindalloch in the evening, rather than the following morning.

A view of Ben Rinnes, from the slopes of Carn Liath above the Glenlivet Distillery

Day 5 Ballindalloch to Grantown-on-Spey
21km (13 miles)

Back at Ballindalloch, the Speyside Way continues a little further along the old railway trackbed, then suddenly climbs away from it and passes within sight of the Tormore Distillery before following a stretch of the A95. The route is often confined to forest as it runs through the Garvault Plantation, Woods of Knockfrink, Meikle Park Wood and Tom an Uird Wood, though there are field paths between them, one of which is surfaced with chunky stone slabs. All of a sudden, the trail again makes use of a stretch of the old railway trackbed, as far as Cromdale station. The little village of Cromdale is just off-route and offers food, drink and accommodation.

Cross the River Spey at Boat of Cromdale, where another ferry was eventually replaced by a bridge. A meandering trail leads through wonderful woodlands of Scots pine and birch, growing from hummocky ground enlivened by bilberry scrub where enough light is available. Watch carefully for markers, as there is a veritable network of paths here. The appropriately named Forest Road offers the easiest access to Grantown-on-Spey, where the high street and the square feature fine buildings and the greatest range of facilities so far on the trail.

Looking towards the deep cleft of the Lairig Ghru from the end of the trail at Aviemore

Day 6 Grantown-on-Spey to Aviemore
27km (17 miles)

The Speyside Way crosses the Old Spey Bridge after leaving Grantown-on-Spey, and the Spey Valley Smokehouse is passed as the old railway trackbed is joined once more for the first half of the day's walk. This offers quick and easy walking, often within sight of the River Spey at first, then pulling away from the river to pass low-lying meadows. At length the village of Nethy Bridge is reached and there are places offering a comfortable lunch break. Follow a road out of the village, then switch to a forest track, and finally a path along a forest ride left unplanted to carry a pylon line. Nearby, but out of sight, is Loch Garten, which is visited every summer by ospreys, so

expect the approach road to be busy. The Speyside Way is routed alongside the road for safety.

The last stage of the route from Boat of Garten to Aviemore runs through pine forests and hummocky heaths, and runs parallel to the Strathspey railway throughout. Enjoy views across the pine-clad heath towards the Cairngorms. Sometimes there are splendid single Scots pines among the heathery wastes, and the sight of the spectacular cleft of the Lairig Ghru cutting through the Cairngorms adds a dramatic touch to distant views. The Speyside Way currently ends by following the main A9 into Aviemore, passing shops and restaurants on the way to the mainline station. There is a plan to extend the route further to Newtonmore, but it would be wise to check whether this has happened before embarking on the trail.

INFORMATION	
Access to Start	Elgin has good Scot Rail and Scottish Citylink bus services and local buses run to Buckie.
Getting Home	Aviemore has good Scot Rail and Scottish Citylink bus services.
Other Public Transport	Buses serve all the towns and villages along the trail, and in the summer months a service links most places along the trail.
Maps	OS 1:50,000 Landrangers 28 and 36
	OS 1:25,000 Explorers 403, 419 and 424
	Harveys 1:40,000 Speyside Way
Cicerone Guide	The Speyside Way, by Sandy Anton
Other Guidebooks	The Speyside Way, by Jacquetta Megarry and Jim Strachan, Rucksack Readers
Tourist Information Centres	Elgin tel 01343 543388, Dufftown tel 01340 820501, Aberlour tel 01340 881266, Tomintoul tel 01807 580285, Grantown-on-Spey tel 01479 872773, Aviemore tel 01479 810363.
Accommodation List	The Speyside Way Accommodation and General Information, from TICs
Website	www.speysideway.org

The view upstream from Victoria Bridge near the Inveroran Hotel (Day 5)

18 West Highland Way

Start and Finish	Milngavie to Fort William
Distance and Time	153km (95 miles) taking up to 1 week
Character	Easy, low-level walking at the start, followed by a hill climb and rugged lakeside paths. A long and often stony old military road leads across exposed moors, climbs a high pass and runs through remote glens.
Highlights	Conic Hill and Loch Lomond, Falls of Falloch, General Caulfeild's military road, Màm Carraigh, Rannoch Moor, Devil's Staircase, Tigh-na-sleubhaich, Glen Nevis.

Looking back along the trail from Màm Carraigh above Bridge of Orchy (Day 4)

A trail that has a 'captive audience' on its doorstep is bound to be popular, and the West Highland Way is one of the most popular trails in Britain, starting at Milngavie near the city of Glasgow. Since opening in 1980 the trail has enticed Glaswegians from the city, as well as attracting other walkers from all around the world. They come to admire the sheer size and splendour of Loch Lomond, the majesty of the high mountains, the wilderness qualities of open moorlands, and the proud remnants of ancient Caledonian forests. Domestic Highland cattle, with their long horns, and large herds of stocky red deer are likely to be seen along the way. Walkers tread day after day along an 18th-century military road, and visit wayside inns once frequented by cattle and sheep drovers. The history of the Highlands unfolds before those with enquiring minds, while others simply enjoy charming nooks and dramatic vistas, taking sunshine and storm in their stride on their journey north.

The West Highland Way is essentially a low-level route, passing between the mountains rather than climbing over them. Those who wish to head for the heights will find plenty of Munros, or mountains above 915m (3000ft), rising conveniently close to the route – at Rowardennan, Crianlarich,

SCHEDULE			
Day	**Start/Finish**	**Km**	**Miles**
Day 1	Milngavie to Drymen	20	12½
Day 2	Drymen to Rowardennan	24	15
Day 3	Rowardennan to Crianlarich	30	18½
Day 4	Crianlarich to Inveroran	25	15½
Day 5	Inveroran to Kinlochleven	30	18½
Day 6	Kinlochleven to Fort William	24	15

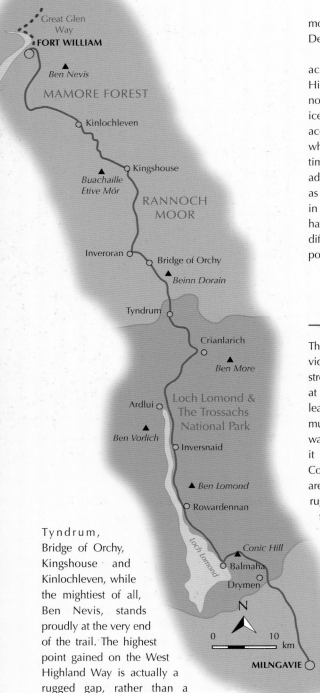

Great Glen
Way
FORT WILLIAM

Ben Nevis

MAMORE FOREST

Kinlochleven

Kingshouse

Buachaille
Etive Mór

RANNOCH
MOOR

Inveroran

Bridge of Orchy

Beinn Dorain

Tyndrum

Crianlarich

Ben More

Ardlui

Loch Lomond &
The Trossachs
National Park

Ben Vorlich

Inversnaid

Ben Lomond

Rowardennan

Loch Lomond

Conic Hill

Balmaha

Drymen

N

0   10   km

MILNGAVIE

Tyndrum,
Bridge of Orchy,
Kingshouse and
Kinlochleven, while
the mightiest of all,
Ben Nevis, stands
proudly at the very end
of the trail. The highest
point gained on the West
Highland Way is actually a
rugged gap, rather than a

mountain, around 550m (1800ft) at the top of the Devil's Staircase.

Walkers will find plenty of food, drink and accommodation at intervals along the West Highland Way, but there are long stretches with nothing, and some places have only minimal services. When planning to walk the trail, which can be accomplished within a week, be sure to know where shops and pubs are located, and at busy times it is wise to book indoor accommodation in advance. Some would-be trekkers choose this route as their first experience of a long-distance trail, and in many ways it is a good choice. However, if you have overestimated your abilities, and find it very difficult, it is also easy to leave the trail at many points and catch a bus or train back home.

Day 1 Milngavie to Drymen
20km (12½ miles)

The first day on the trail is low level and easy, providing an opportunity to limber up for the more strenuous days ahead. The West Highland Way starts at a stone obelisk in the centre of Milngavie and leaves town alongside Allander Water. This is very much a suburban stretch, used by joggers and dog walkers more than long-distance backpackers, and it passes through the woodlands of Mugdock Country Park. Craigallian Loch and Carbeth Loch are small, pleasant pools, while looking ahead the rugged hump of Dumgoyne can be seen. The route follows the trackbed of an old railway, and there is access to the Glengoyne Distillery and its visitor centre if required. The railway trackbed continues to Gartness, then a road is followed onwards, passing a campsite at Easter Drumquhassle. The lovely little village of Drymen is off-route, but offers food, drink and lodgings. It has recently become a gateway to Loch Lomond and the Trossachs National Park. The West Highland Way runs through the national park until beyond Tyndrum.

Day 2 Drymen to Rowardennan
24km (15 miles)

The trail climbs gradually from Drymen and wanders through Garadhban Forest, leaving by way of an enormous ladder stile over a deer fence. Follow a path across the Burn of Mar and climb high on the steep and rugged slopes of Conic Hill, though missing the 360m (1181ft) summit. An amazing view of Loch Lomond opens up – a vast expanse of water studded with islands like enormous stepping stones to the far shore. The loch narrows as it extends northwards into the Highlands, where it is flanked by toweringly high mountains, most notably Ben Lomond. Walkers who start early in the year will probably see serried ranks of snow-capped peaks, but in poor weather it is likely that dull grey cloud will be clamped low and firm on the summits. Walk down across the rugged gap of Bealach Ard and drop down through forest to reach the little village of Balmaha, which has food, drink and accommodation.

The afternoon, and indeed most of the following day, is spent following the shore of Loch Lomond. No other trail in Britain spends so much time beside a lake, but as the shores are often well wooded, there may not even be a glimpse of the water for long periods. Although there is a shoreline path round Arrochymore Point, the trail is set back from the water on the way to Cashel. Ross Point is also omitted, in favour of a climb over a wooded hill. The Rowardennan Hotel is passed on the way to Rowardennan youth hostel, and there is also a ferry available, crossing Loch Lomond to Inverbeg on the far shore. Some walkers like to spend two nights at Rowardennan so that they can climb Ben Lomond, and this is to be encouraged in clear weather – both for the extra challenge, and the chance to enjoy splendid Highland views.

The prominent hump of Dumgoyne dominates the early stages of the West Highland Way (Day 1)

Day 3 Rowardennan to Crianlarich
30km (18½ miles)

What looks like an easy lakeshore walk on the map is rather more difficult in practice, and this is a long day's walk too. Walkers can break early at Inversnaid or Inverarnan if the going proves too rough or the weather is bad. Bear in mind that much of the way is forested, and when it rains, it seems to drip incessantly in the woods, where mud and tree roots are slippery. A clear track leads from Rowardennan to Ptarmigan Lodge, then there is a choice – you can either continue along the track, or take a more rugged path, closer to the shore of Loch Lomond, but which takes longer to complete. Both routes meet just beyond the Rowchoish bothy to continue past Cailness. The path is quite tortuous in places, then suddenly reaches the Inversnaid Hotel, providing well for wet and muddy walkers when the occasion demands. For those who are struggling, there are ferries across the loch.

Another difficult stretch of wooded lakeshore path leads onwards. Pass Rob Roy's Cave and pick a way carefully across the steep slopes, noting how narrow the head of Loch Lomond is becoming. At one point the trail climbs and passes the Doune bothy, returning briefly to the shore before climbing again from Ardleish. A descent leads to a campsite at Beinglas Farm, well beyond the head of the loch, and there is a path leading to the Drover's Inn at Inverarnan if anyone wants more comfortable lodgings for the night.

Those who have the stamina to continue can follow a good track and path onwards through Glen Falloch, passing the powerful Falls of Falloch. Later, the West Highland Way crosses the river and passes beneath the main A82. Follow a track to Keilator and continue to a forest, then drop down to the right to reach Crianlarich. This little village has shops, pubs and a range of accommodation options.

Day 4 Crianlarich to Inveroran
25km (15½ miles)

The West Highland Way climbs to 330m (1080ft) on a forested slope above Crianlarich, then drops down to cross the broad green floor of Glen Fillan, passing an old monastic site associated with St Fillan. The trail stays low in the glen as it makes its way alongside the River Fillan and through woods to Tyndrum. This little village can be quite busy, with the Green Welly Stop managing to attract almost every visitor. Heading north from Tyndrum, the West Highland Way is squeezed beside the main road and railway on the floor of the glen, flanked by Beinn Odhar and Beinn Bheag. When a broad strath is reached, they all fan apart around the isolated farmstead of Auch. The trail runs parallel to the railway most of the way to Bridge of Orchy, following the course of an 18th-century military road built by General Caulfeild.

Most services at Bridge of Orchy revolve around a large hotel, and anyone staying here will doubtless head for Kingshouse the following day. Those who are able to press on further today to Inveroran could reach Kinlochleven the following day, but whatever option is chosen, bear in mind that lodgings are particularly sparse on the way to Kinlochleven and it is wise to book ahead. The trail climbs a forested slope beyond Bridge of Orchy, reaching a wonderfully wild viewpoint around 320m (1050ft) on Màm

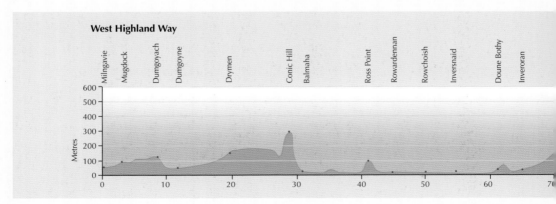

Blackrock Cottage and Buachaille Etive Mór on the approach to Kingshouse (Day 5)

Carraigh. A moorland path leads down to the Inveroran Hotel, splendidly situated at the head of Loch Tulla. Stalwart literary Lakeland walkers William and Dorothy Wordsworth stayed here on their tour of the Highlands in 1803, though the hotel has since been demolished and rebuilt.

Day 5 Inveroran to Kinlochleven
30km (18½ miles)

The whole of today's walk is spent following General Caulfeild's military road, which was built in the mid-18th century following the brutal suppression of Bonnie Prince Charlie's rising of 1745.

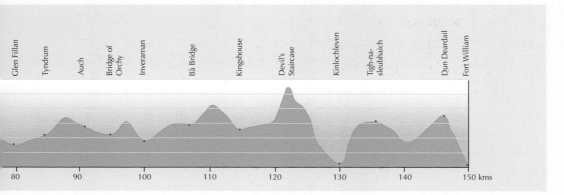

Looking back along the trail, through the glen in the direction of Kinlochleven

On a clear day, the traverse of Rannoch Moor is a delight, but in foul weather there is no shelter from the elements, and without even a decent view the trail can become a treadmill. A fine track climbs from Victoria Bridge, passing occasional small forests while enjoying more and more wide-open views. Interconnected lochans are strewn across the broad, bleak and hummocky moor, and without the stony track offering a sure guide and firm footing, progress would grind to a halt. The middle of the moorland track is reached around Bà Bridge, and the highest part lies just beyond, around 450m (1475ft). A gradual descent leads to Blackrock Cottage and the Kingshouse Hotel, while the frowning face of Buachaille Etive Mór

completely dominates the final parts of Rannoch Moor.

Almost everyone takes a break at the Kingshouse, and many stay for the night. The West Highland Way avoids the busy A82 as much as possible on the way to Alltnafeadh, then shuns popular and dramatic Glen Coe altogether. Instead, it climbs the Devil's Staircase, a stony zigzag track that climbs to a gap around 550m (1800ft), which is the highest point gained on the trail. In clear weather, Ben Nevis can be seen near the journey's end. A long and winding descent begins, and at each turn walkers who expect to see Kinlochleven are surprised to find yet another rugged spur or valley to cross. A broader track winds down through a wooded valley and finally lands on flat ground, practically at sea level. Massive water pipelines descending to the town from distant Blackwater Reservoir were laid to provide hydroelectric power for an aluminium smelter. Kinlochleven is a busy place offering a splendid range of facilities for the weary wayfarer at the end of a long day.

Day 6 Kinlochleven to Fort William
24km (15 miles)

The last day's walk starts with a steep climb up a rugged wooded slope. A fine track is joined – the military road again. This climbs at a gentler gradient through a wild and scenic glen flanked by the lofty Mamores. The highest part of the track is reached around 330m (1080ft) near the ruined farmstead of Tigh-na-sleubhaich, then the ruins of Lairigmor are passed on the descent. The track turns a rocky corner and heads straight towards a forest. Walk downhill, almost to a road, then climb again to leave the forest, cutting across an open slope to reach another forest. Roughly contour through the forest, then follow a path up to a gap where there is a fine view of Ben Nevis, towering high above Glen Nevis. Follow a track down through Nevis Forest and then a road to the outskirts of Fort William, where a large 'thistle' sign marks the end of the West Highland Way at a busy road junction.

Some walkers leave Fort William as soon as they arrive, while others spend the night here before travelling home. Others keep a day in reserve so that they can climb Ben Nevis, the highest mountain in Britain, as a thrilling finale to the trail. Keen long-distance walkers, however, are happy to continue straight from the West Highland Way onto the Great Glen Way, to finish at Inverness.

INFORMATION	
Access to Start	Glasgow is a major transport hub served by Virgin Trains, and there are regular Scot Rail services to Milngavie.
Getting Home	Scot Rail trains and Scottish Citylink buses leave Fort William.
Other Public Transport	Ferries can be used to cross Loch Lomond in the early stages to link with bus services. The middle part of the trail is often within easy reach of buses and trains. Buses also serve Kingshouse and Kinlochleven.
Maps	OS 1:50,000 Landrangers 41, 50, 56, 57 and 64
	OS 1:25,000 Explorers 347, 348, 364, 377, 384 and 392
	Harveys West Highland Way
Cicerone Guide	*The West Highland Way*, by Terry Marsh
Other Guidebooks	*The West Highland Way*, by Bob Aitken and Roger Smith, Mercat Press
	The West Highland Way, by Jacquetta Megarry, Rucksack Readers
Tourist Information Centres	Glasgow tel 0141 2044400, Drymen tel 01360 660068, Tyndrum tel 01838 400246, Fort William tel 01397 701801.
Accommodation List	*The West Highland Way Pocket Companion*, from TICs
Website	www.west-highland-way.co.uk

The route follows a broad track beside the Caledonian Canal near Fort Augustus (Day 3)

19 Great Glen Way

Start and Finish	Fort William to Inverness
Distance and Time	117km (73 miles) taking up to 1 week
Character	Mostly an easy, low-level trail with gentle uplands towards the end. Clear, firm tracks link with quiet roads and paths, often close to the Caledonian Canal, or beside huge lochs, or through forests and fields.
Highlights	Inverlochy Castle, the Caledonian Canal, Gairlochy, Achnacarry, South Laggan to North Laggan, Leiterfearn Forest, Bridge of Oich to Fort Augustus, Telford's Bridge at Invermoriston, Urquhart Castle, Loch Ness, Abriachan Forest, Inverness.

A whitewashed lighthouse overlooks Loch Lochy near Gairlochy

The Great Glen is the most remarkable valley in the whole of Britain. Ruler-straight from coast to coast through Scotland, it owes its formation to the ancient Great Glen Fault, which literally rips straight through the Highlands. As a low-lying glen, it was tailor-made as a through route, attracting the attention of road makers in the 18th century, canal builders in the 19th century, and railway engineers early in the 20th century, though they only got halfway through. The Caledonian Canal was a remarkable enterprise – the first government-funded transport project in Britain. Although the canal is said to measure 96.5km (60 miles), only 35.5km (22 miles) is actually man-made, with the rest of the navigation being through long, straight lochs, including mighty Loch Ness.

Prince Andrew opened the Great Glen Way in 2002. It is essentially a low-level trail, mostly quite easy, and would serve as an ideal introduction to

SCHEDULE			
Day	**Start/Finish**	**Km**	**Miles**
Day 1	Fort William to Gairlochy	17	10½
Day 2	Gairlochy to North Laggan	22	13½
Day 3	North Laggan to Fort Augustus	14	9
Day 4	Fort Augustus to Invermoriston	13	8
Day 5	Invermoriston to Drumnadrochit	23	14
Day 6	Drumnadrochit to Inverness	29	18

long-distance walking. Alternatively, it could be used to extend the distance of the West Highland Way, to which it links at Fort William. The trail from Fort William to Inverness often runs concurrent with the Great Glen Cycleway, but there are stretches that are only for walkers. While there are plenty of facilities along the trail, these are unevenly spread, so at times accommodation, food and drink may be rather limited. Those with an interest in history can immerse themselves in the turbulent strife associated with Highland clan rivalry, while those with an interest in wildlife will find that many seabirds and waterfowl make their passage from coast to coast through the Great Glen (those of a more imaginative disposition can keep an eye peeled for the Loch Ness Monster!).

INVERNESS

Abriachan

Loch Ness

Drumnadrochit

Foyers

Invermoriston

Fort Augustus

Aberchalder

Invergarry

Laggan

N

Achnacarry

Loch Lochy

0   10   km

Gairlochy

Spean Bridge

Corpach

FORT WILLIAM

▲ Ben Nevis

West Highland Way

Day 1 Fort William to Gairlochy
17km (10½ miles)

The Great Glen Way starts at the Old Fort at Fort William, built in 1690 to replace a wooden structure of 1654. The civilian settlement of Maryburgh, which grew alongside, is now the bustling town of Fort William, proclaiming itself 'The Outdoor Capital of the UK'. The trail passes through the suburbs to follow the River Lochy to the 13th-century ruins of Inverlochy Castle. Cross the Soldier's Bridge over the River Lochy and walk through the coastal village of Caol to reach nearby Corpach and the Caledonian Canal.

Inspect the sea lock, basin and double lock before leaving Corpach, marvelling at the design of the canal. A broad track runs alongside the waterway to reach Banavie Swing Bridge. Eight locks rise in close succession at Neptune's Staircase, and it takes cruisers about 90 minutes to pass from top to bottom. As the canalside track continues through quiet countryside, there are features barely noticed, such as the Sheangain Aqueduct, ruins of Tor Castle and the Loy Aqueduct. The charming Moy Swing Bridge is the only manually operated bridge on the waterway. There is a tearoom at Gairlochy, but only a little accommodation in the area. Walkers should carry a local bus timetable so that they can easily move off-route to Spean Bridge or beyond.

Day 2 Gairlochy to North Laggan
22km (13½ miles)

This whole day's walk runs along the northern shore of Loch Lochy. After leaving Gairlochy, the trail hugs the shore and wanders through woods of oak, birch, beech and alder. A road has to be followed to Clunes, but there is also the opportunity to detour to Achnacarry, where the Clan Cameron Museum can be visited. The Camerons settled in this area around 1660 after vacating disputed Tor Castle. The 19th chief, 'Gentle Lochiel', supported Bonnie Prince Charlie in 1745, and because of his support, many other Highland clans rallied to the cause. Achnacarry was used as the Commando basic training centre during the Second World War, and featured one of the most gruelling military training regimes in the world.

A long forest track runs along the shore of Loch Lochy, with views being opened and closed depending on clear-felling and replanting. The farmstead of Kilfinnan sits on a delta at the mouth of Kilfinnan Burn, and a narrow road leads round Ceann Loch, at the head of Loch Lochy. Nearby is the site of the Battle of the Shirts, which took place on a hot day in 1544, when 300 Frasers faced 600 MacDonalds and Camerons to settle the score after a perceived insult. The carnage was great, leaving only four Frasers and eight of their opponents alive at the conclusion of the battle. A short stretch of the Caledonian Canal runs from South Laggan to North Laggan, and facilities are rather limited in the area. Food and drink can be enjoyed on the *Eagle*, a Dutch barge converted into a restaurant and moored on the canal.

Day 3 North Laggan to Fort Augustus
14km (9 miles)

During the morning, the Great Glen Way runs along the well-wooded southern shore of Loch Oich. This long and narrow loch is also the summit level of the Caledonian Canal, only 32m (105ft)

above sea level. Leiterfearn Forest is a lush, green, damp and mossy nature reserve, while views across the water reveal the ruins of Invergarry Castle. Part of the trail follows an old military road, dating from 1725, as well as a railway trackbed, dating from 1903. Both routes fell from favour and the main road through the glen now runs through Invergarry. Food, drink and limited accommodation are available just off-route at Aberchalder, otherwise the trail leads back onto the Caledonian Canal.

Have a look at the graceful span of the Bridge of Oich, then pass Cullochy Lock as the Caledonian Canal begins to step downwards. The canal broadens considerably where little Kytra Loch is incorporated into its course. There are occasional views down to the rapids of the River Oich, as both the canal and the river run concurrently to Fort Augustus. This was a remote spot when St Cumin of Iona founded a monastic settlement in the 6th century. Little else happened here until after the Jacobite Rising of 1715, when a fort was constructed, then later rebuilt to make way for a military road in 1726. The fort was destroyed in the Jacobite Rising of 1745, rebuilt afterwards, then the site given to the Benedictines in 1876, who built an abbey and vacated it as recently as 1997. The little town is often very busy with tourists, straddles a fine flight of five locks on the canal, and has a full range of services.

Day 4 Fort Augustus to Invermoriston
13km (8 miles)

This short day's walk could easily be added to the previous short day's walk, but those who wish to explore around Fort Augustus or take a cruise on Loch Ness can make time for a longer break. Loch Ness isn't seen as much as walkers might expect, since the trail often runs through forestry plantations where views are limited. However, when views are available, the sheer size and scale of the loch is amazing – its length is 37km (23 miles), its

A view of part of Loch Ness on the way from Fort Augustus to Invermoriston

surface level is only 16m (52ft) above sea level, yet its depth is as great as 230m (755ft). Even on a dull day, the surface of the loch reflects enough light to brighten the surroundings more than neighbouring areas. A long forest track seems to overshoot Invermoriston, but the trail doubles back to follow a road into the village, passing semi-ruinous Telford's Bridge spanning a fine waterfall. The Glenmoriston Arms was originally a drovers' inn dating from 1740, and Johnston and Boswell stayed here in 1773 en route to the Hebrides.

Day 5 Invermoriston to Drumnadrochit
23km (14 miles)

The whole of this day's walk runs along the forested northern slopes flanking Loch Ness, and

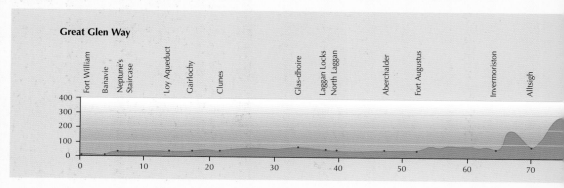

Great Glen Way

there are views from time to time when the trees allow. The first stage climbs above Invermoriston, then descends gradually to run close to the youth hostel at Alltsigh on the shore of Loch Ness. Forest tracks zigzag uphill, and there is an amazing long-distance view both ways through the Great Glen from around 300m (985ft). The trail later pulls away from the loch and follows a minor road past farmland, moorland and forest. A descent through the Clunebeg Estate leads to Lewiston and Drumnadrochit, where a full range of services is available. On the way there, a detour might be contemplated to the romantic ruins of 13th-century Urquhart Castle.

As the whole world knows, Loch Ness is home to the legendary Loch Ness Monster. At Drumnadrochit there are two hotel-based centres vying with each other to attract as many tourists as possible. The 'original' Loch Ness Monster Visitor Centre and the 'official' Loch Ness 2000 Exhibition can supply as much background information to visitors as is demanded, but at the end of the day, everyone must make up their own minds about the 'monster'. It all started when St Columba visited in the year 565AD. One of his followers swam across the loch to fetch a boat when suddenly, 'with a great roar and open mouth', a monster bore down on him. Columba commanded the monster, 'Think not to go further, nor touch thou that man', and the monster sank into the deep. Its next appearance was in 1934, when it was captured in a grainy photograph that is known all over the world, and from

that point the area gained its biggest and most enduring tourist attraction.

Day 6 Drumnadrochit to Inverness
29km (18 miles)

Loch Ness fills the Great Glen almost as far as Inverness, but the Great Glen Way gradually pulls away from its shore after leaving Drumnadrochit, and this is the longest and highest part of the route. A gradual ascent on a forested slope gives way to a track across rugged moorland, passing an isolated farm at Corryfoyness. The highest point on the trail is reached on a track running through Abriachan Forest around 380m (1245ft). The forest

A statue of Flora MacDonald looks back through the Great Glen from Inverness

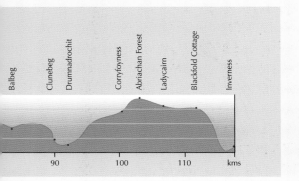

is owned and managed by the local community and is proving popular with visitors. There are several trails in addition to the Great Glen Way. Soon after leaving the forest there is a long road walk across heather moorland, with distant views of Ben Wyvis to the north.

An old drove road leads from Blackfold into a remnant Scots pine forest, where rare black grouse might be spotted. The trail emerges on a brow overlooking castle-like Creag Dunain Hospital, and later passes through its grounds to reach the suburbs of Inverness. The route into the city includes a short stretch of the Caledonian Canal, before island hopping on suspension footbridges across the powerful flow of the River Ness. The river leads through the heart of the city, where the Great Glen Way climbs to a conclusion in front of Inverness Castle. A statue of Flora MacDonald, who helped Bonnie Prince Charlie to escape from Scotland, gazes longingly back through the Great Glen, and most walkers finishing the trail do the same.

INFORMATION

Access to Start	Scot Rail trains and Scottish Citylink buses serve Fort William.
Getting Home	Scot Rail trains and Scottish Citylink buses leave Inverness.
Other Public Transport	Scottish Citylink buses run through the Great Glen between Fort William and Inverness and are never far from the trail.
Maps	OS 1:50,000 Landrangers 26, 34 and 41
	OS 1:25,000 Explorers 392, 400 and 416
	Harveys 1:40,000 Great Glen Way
Cicerone Guide	*The Great Glen Way*, by Paddy Dillon
Other Guidebooks	*The Great Glen Way*, by Jacquetta Megarry and Sandra Bardwell, Rucksack Readers
Tourist Information Centres	Fort William tel 01397 703781, Spean Bridge tel 01397 712999, Glengarry tel 01809 501424, Fort Augustus tel 01320 366367, Drumnadrochit tel 01456 459050, Inverness tel 01463 234353.
Accommodation List	*Great Glen Way Accommodation and Services Guide*, from TICs
Website	www.greatglenway.com

APPENDIX 1
Useful Contacts

National Countryside Organisations
Natural England
Northminster House
Peterborough
PE1 1UA
Tel 0845 6003078
Website **www.naturalengland.org.uk**

Countryside Council for Wales
Maes-y-Ffynnon
Penrhosgarnedd
Bangor
Gwynedd
LL57 2DW
Tel 0845 1306229
Website **www.ccw.gov.uk**

Scottish Natural Heritage
Great Glen House
Leachkin Road
Inverness
IV3 8NW
Tel 01463 725000
Website **www.snh.org.uk**

National Walking Organisations
Ramblers' Association
2nd Floor Camelford House
87–90 Albert Embankment
London
SE1 7TW
Tel 020 7339 8500
Website **www.ramblers.org.uk**

Ramblers' Association Wales
3 Coopers Yard
Curran Road
Cardiff
CF10 5NB
Tel 029 2064 4308
Website **www.ramblers.org.uk/wales**

Ramblers' Association Scotland
Kingfisher House
Auld Mart Business Park
Milnathort
Kinross
KY1 9DA
Tel 01577 861222
Website
www.ramblers.org.ukscotland

The Backpackers Club
Website
www.backpackersclub.co.uk

Long Distance Walkers Association
Website **www.ldwa.org.uk**

Hostelling Organisations
Youth Hostels Association (England &
Wales)
Trevelyan House
Dimple Road
Matlock
Derbyshire
DE4 3YH
Tel 0870 7708868
Website **www.yha.org.uk**

Scottish Youth Hostels Association
7 Glebe Crescent
Stirling
FK8 2JA
Tel 01786 891400
Website **www.syha.org.uk**

Independent Hostels
Website
**www.independenthostelguide.
co.uk**

National Transport Information
Traveline
Tel 0870 6082608
Website **www.traveline.org.uk**

Transport Direct
Website **www.transportdirect.info**

National Trusts
The National Trust
PO Box 39
Warrington
WA5 7WD
Tel 0870 4584000
Website **www.nationaltrust.org.uk**

National Trust for Scotland
Wemyss House
28 Charlotte Square
Edinburgh
EH2 4ET
Tel 0131 2439300
Website **www.nts.org.uk**

Mapping Organisations
Ordnance Survey
Romsey Road
Southampton
SO16 4GU
Tel 0845 6050505
Website **www.ordnancesurvey.co.uk**

Harvey Maps
12–22 Main Street
Doune
Perthshire
FK16 6BJ
Tel 01786 841202
Website **www.harveymaps.co.uk**

APPENDIX 2
Route Summaries

Route	Start/Finish	Distance	Time
1 South West Coast Path	Minehead to South Haven Point	1016km (631 miles)	45 days
2 South Downs Way	Winchester to Eastbourne	163km (101 miles)	6 days
3 North Downs Way	Farnham to Dover	193–245km (120–152 miles)	9–11 days
4 The Ridgeway	Overton Hill to Ivinghoe Beacon	139km (87 miles)	6 days
5 Thames Path	Thames Barrier to Thames Head	294km (183 miles)	11 days
6 Cotswold Way	Chipping Campden to Bath Abbey	164km (102 miles)	7 days
7 Peddars Way and Norfolk Coast Path	Knettishall Heath to Cromer Pier	149km (93 miles)	7 days
8 Yorkshire Wolds Way	Hessle to Filey Brigg	127km (79 miles)	6 days
9 Cleveland Way	Helmsley to Filey Brigg	176km (109 miles)	9 days
10 Pennine Bridleway (South)	Middleton Top to Summit	195km (121 miles)	7 days
11 Pennine Way	Edale to Kirk Yetholm	435km (270 miles)	18 days
12 Hadrian's Wall Path	Wallsend to Bowness-on-Solway	135km (84 miles)	6 days
13 Pembrokeshire Coast Path	Poppit Sands to Amroth Castle	299km (186 miles)	12 days
14 Offa's Dyke Path	Sedbury Cliff to Prestatyn	285km (177 miles)	11 days
15 Glyndŵr's Way	Knighton to Welshpool	213km (132 miles)	9 days
16 Southern Upland Way	Portpatrick to Cockburnspath	341km (212 miles)	12 days
17 Speyside Way	Buckie to Aviemore	135km (84 miles)	6 days
18 West Highland Way	Milngavie to Fort William	153km (95 miles)	6 days
19 Great Glen Way	Fort William to Inverness	117km (73 miles)	6 days

CICERONE NATIONAL TRAILS

South West Coast Path
ISBN 9781852843793

The South Downs Way
ISBN 9781852844295

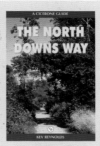

The North Downs Way
ISBN 9781852843168

The Greater Ridgeway
ISBN 9781852843465

The Thames Path
ISBN 9781852844363

The Cotswold Way
ISBN 9781852845520

The Cleveland Way and the Yorkshire Wolds Way
ISBN 9781852844479

The Pennine Way
ISBN 9781852843861

Hadrian's Wall Path
ISBN 9781852843922

The Pembrokeshire Coastal Path
ISBN 9781852843786

Offa's Dyke Path
ISBN 9781852845490

Glyndŵr's Way
ISBN 9781852842994

Southern Upland Way
ISBN 9781852844097

The Speyside Way
ISBN 9781852843311

The West Highland Way
ISBN 9781852843694

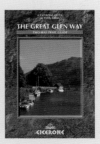

Great Glen Way
ISBN 9781852845032

LISTING OF CICERONE GUIDES

Cicerone's mission is to inform and inspire by providing the best guides to exploring the world

Since its foundation over 30 years ago, Cicerone has specialised in publishing guidebooks and has built a reputation for quality and reliability. It now publishes nearly 300 guides to the major destinations for outdoor enthusiasts, including Europe, UK and the rest of the world.

Written by leading and committed specialists, Cicerone guides are recognised as the most authoritative. They are full of information, maps and illustrations so that the user can plan and complete a successful and safe trip or expedition – be it a long face climb, a walk over Lakeland fells, an alpine traverse, a Himalayan trek or a ramble in the countryside.

With a thorough introduction to assist planning, clear diagrams, maps and colour photographs to illustrate the terrain and route, and accurate and detailed text, Cicerone guides are designed for ease of use and access to the information.

If the facts on the ground change, or there is any aspect of a guide that you think we can improve, we are always delighted to hear from you.

Cicerone Press
2 Police Square Milnthorpe Cumbria LA7 7PY
Tel:01539 562 069   Fax:01539 563 417
e-mail:info@cicerone.co.uk   web:www.cicerone.co.uk

CICERONE